D1600861

Democracies and Tyrannies of the Caribbean

DEMOCRACIES AND TYRANNIES OF THE CARIBBEAN

William Krehm

With an Introduction and Notes by Gregorio Selser

LAWRENCE HILL & COMPANY
Westport, Connecticut

Published in the United States of America
by Lawrence Hill & Company, Publishers, Inc.
520 Riverside Avenue, Westport, Connecticut 06880

Library of Congress Cataloging in Publication Data

Krehm, William.
  Democracies and tyrannies of the Caribbean.

  Includes index.
  1. Central America—Politics and government—1821–1951.
2. Dominican Republic—Politics and government—1930–1961.
3. Venezuela—Politics and government—1935–1958.
I. Title.
F1438.K7413   1984   972.8   84-15726
ISBN 0-88208-168-3
ISBN 0-88208-169-1 (pbk.)

HB   9   8   7   6   5   4   3   2   1
PB   9   8   7   6   5   4   3   2   1

Printed in the United States of America

Contents

Latin America: The Period of the Beribboned Panthers

Christ walks the streets gaunt and sickly, Barabas has slaves and epaulets, and the lands of Chibcha, Cuzco and Palenque have seen panthers decked with ribbons.

RUBÉN DARÍO

EARLY IN THE TWENTIETH CENTURY the custom arose of borrowing from the animal kingdom to designate the autocrats of Central America. In the Isthmus people talked about "pantherism," the authoritarian regime of the panther, that feline which stalks its prey on deliberate, velvety paws but at the moment of attack hurls itself on its victim with the speed of lightning, claws sharpened, poised and ready. Other sobriquets associated the unrestricted use of power with the lion, the tiger, the snake; even the ass was introduced where it was a case of brutes beyond redemption. Nicaraguan poet Darío broadened the "pantherist" geography, twinning the lands of Chibcha and Cuzco in the South American Andes with those of the Palenque Mayas in the framework of the invariable military dictator—the panther with ribbons and epaulets, glittering emblems of command which hung from uniforms barely dissimulating the human lumps of lard they embraced.

Later on, at about the time when the Spaniard Ramón del Valle Inclán was exalting the idea of "the Tyranny of the Flag," José Vasconcelos, Mexican writer, teacher, and politician, made another raid on the zoo in connection with Venezuelan autocrat Juan Vicente Gómez: his name grotesquely transformed, he would be known to the end of his days as "Bison Gómez."

Perhaps the poets' and writers' vengeful nomenclature was some compensation for the pain of peoples without any possibility of removing the autocrats from power. It was no longer easy, as in the nineteenth century, to commit expeditious tyrannicide in the ancient Greek manner. Gabriel García Moreno, the lugubrious Ecuadoran theologian slain by a now-forgotten executioner, inspired in the poet-writer who had most fiercely fought him, Juan Montalvo, an anthological discovery: "My pen killed him." Not many pens—or typewriters—could have put forward such a claim, given the protective vigilance that surrounded the despots, which to a great extent explains their privileged durability. *El Señor Presidente* Manuel Estrada Cabrera of Guatemala enjoyed power from 1898 until 1920, when guns blew him off his throne. In view of the frequent failures of attempts to kill him, he genuinely believed that some sort of divinity presided over his precious life.

Many years later the "panther" epithet fell out of use for diatribes, and writers borrowed inexhaustibly from zoology. In the Dominican Republic, for example, dictator Rafael Leonidas Trujillo was in turn a vulture, a hyena, a "jackal of the Caribbean," and even a vampire, in view of his famous Draculesque thirst for blood.

The exercise of power may not necessarily be linked with criminal activities. The ambition for power itself can explain not a few of the beribboned panthers' aberrations, but certainly Trujillo took personal pleasure from torturing and murdering his adversaries. In most cases terror is a function of politics, an efficient mechanism of compulsion and dissuasion for any dictator jealous of his power. Here there is no great difference between military and civilian autocrats.

Certain North American historians, political experts, and sociologists make the exercise of power by state terror appear endemic to a region so exceptionally rich in authoritarian governments—as endemic as were mosquitos, malaria, and yellow fever until their eradication early in our century. It is suggested, for example, that the Conquistadorial tradition of violence was perpetuated as a definite Spanish heritage, and that this purported predisposition was "enriched" by indigenous biological contributions or transplants and injections from Africa. The Trujillos, Estradas, and Gómezes thus become as inevitable as hurricanes and earthquakes; but lacking from this description and analysis are the origin and nature of the phenomenon and the context in which it is generated, reproduced, and maintained. All of this predestination and ineluctability theory is the product of pseudo-academic prejudice. The "banana republics" and "banana presidents" are a product of pre-existing objective conditions, not an incurable evil peculiar to wayward Latin Americans. And these conditions exist in a much broader framework of power and neighbor relations, where the presence of the world's greatest power, the United States, imposes the rules of the game—at least since it won its "splendid little war" against Spain in 1898. Nor does it seem too accidental that in Central America and the Caribbean junior powers began to install themselves, emanating from the major power and expressing themselves in the economy, in politics, and in society, with permanent effects. For example—to cite one classic case—the banana corporation United Fruit.

Without the concessions granted throughout the decades to the fruit company, Estrada Cabrera would be as incomprehensible as, ten years after Estrada's fall, Gen. Jorge Ubico would be, nor would the U.S. government's actions to dislodge President Jacobo Arbenz's regime by threat and violence have any plausible explanation. The pejorative epithet "banana republic" applied to Central American and some Caribbean nations is above all linked to the power United Fruit exercised over a large number of them, especially over the unhappy republics of Guatemala and Honduras, the axis of its neocolonial hegemony.

O. Henry's jocular description of Honduras in "Cabbages and Kings" conceals a reality less picturesque and literary, that of a nation and people submitted to the discretion of tinpot generals and doctors who opt from the outset for loyalty to the foreign company rather than to a national identity and an autonomous destiny of the country's own, that is, free and independent of foreign tutelage and paternalism. Alienation is induced from outside. Although it is initially produced by the weight of easy bribery, it is soon affirmed by use of the armed forces. The picture changes when one makes a political or social analysis of it rather than literature.

And in the case of Latin America, especially in the first half of the twentieth century, it is important to recognize the service lent by Anglo-Saxon analysts in broadcasting its problems to the world, as Latin Americans were perhaps still in no position to do.

Thus one appreciates the value, each in its time, of John Kenneth Turner's *Barbarous Mexico;* John Reed's *Insurgent Mexico;* Carleton Beals's *House in Mexico, Mexico: An Interpretation, Mexican Maze,* and *Porfirio Díaz;* Melvin M. Knight's *The Americans in Santo Domingo; The Banana Empire* by Charles D. Kepner and Henry J. Soothill; Margaret M. Marsh's *Bankers in Bolivia;* Leland H. Jenks's *Our Cuban Colony;* Thomas Rourke's *Tyrant of the Andes;* and *Dollar Diplomacy* by Scott Nearing and Joseph Freeman; to cite only a few of the works most consulted by students north and south of the Rio Grande.

They were important contributions not only for readers in English but especially for Latin Americans themselves, for the most part without means and opportunities to make such descriptions and studies of their own reality, and above all lacking the necessary knowledge and scientific discipline to tackle them. These books illustrated and taught much up to the decade of the thirties. Rare as they were

and as hard to come by for those who were not specialists in the
material, translations made by enterprises that pioneered in Latin
American and Spanish affairs minimized the difficulty. Then World
War II and its special interests created a virtual vaccum. The flow of
books in English and in translations was renewed in the fifties, but
that left the ten previous years bibliographically orphaned, apart
from books connected with the war.

Among the exceptions is the text compiled by journalist William
Krehm, based on his own dispatches to *Time* magazine at the end of
the first half of the forties when he was covering the Central American isthmus, Venezuela, and the Dominican Republic. Among the
odd circumstances of its publication was that it appeared in Spanish—
first in Mexico, then in Buenos Aires in 1959—when only the type-
script existed in its original English. Now the original version of *Democracies and Tyrannies of the Caribbean* appears in print for the first
time.

This book by Krehm has the essential characteristic of journalistic
writing, with an equal share of virtues and defects. The fame achieved
by its initial editions in Spanish heaped troubles upon the head of the
author, whose career as *Time* correspondent finally had to stop. One
could see then that his lineage was in the tradition of North American
journalists concerned about Latin American problems; that, unlike
the Carleton Bealses—and, why not? the John Reeds—he was not
persistent in his incursions into such indispensable fields as economics
and sociology, so that in his descriptions anecdote superimposed itself
on deep analysis; but that he succeeded completely in communicating
to the reader the *climate* of the tragicomedy of the dictatorships he
studied, along with a feeling of pity and impotent fury, without penetrating into the entrails of the problem. I appreciated that writing for
Time was not the same as writing for a United States or Canadian
university, and stressed that it was merit enough to have captured
substantive aspects of the drama and to have been prepared to write
about it in a spirit of committed sympathy and solidarity with the
chastised and the humiliated. I emphasized the honesty, frankness
and courage of the author and attributed highest importance to his
book, given the notable lack of information then available on those
countries. At more than twenty years' distance a rereading brings out
more than ever the freshness of description and successful evocation
of the atmosphere of the place and time: and of the context of what
he relates.

Most important is the first-hand view by a keen journalist. The
events transpire before one's eyes and ears, and Krehm lets them
capture him entirely while living enjoyably with the people he describes and their surroundings. The true journalist has no less en-

thusiasm to know what is happening than to share it with the readers to whom he surrenders himself.

At times Krehm seems infected from afar by O. Henry, and to be amusing himself in this multiple Macondo of generals who hold power for a few years and think themselves immortal. Immortal, that is, as dictators, durable and resistant to the years and to the assaults of rivals and opponents. And because they think or wish it so, fierce as panthers or jackals or lions or vultures when their hold on power needs defending.

But this is only one aspect of the drama. Along with it goes another not so often treated by historians and chroniclers of the Latin American scene. Krehm is in fact a privileged spectator of a key period, the Good Neighbor Policy undertaken a decade earlier by President Franklin D. Roosevelt. According to the mythology, the policy Roosevelt initiated in 1933 was an honest and intelligent turn of the rudder in what had been a permanent course, an unvarying model in the conduct of Latin American affairs since 1898: the use of open or dissimulated violence, known as "Gunboat Diplomacy," as an executive function of U.S. intervention in its so-called backyard. For those exercises gunboats were an invariable instrument of pressure since the first Roosevelt, the famous Theodore of the "Big Stick Policy," inaugurated it under the no less famous corollary that amended—not for the first time—the "doctrine" of Monroe. This Big Stick Policy had been complemented since the presidency of William H. Taft by Dollar Diplomacy. The Big Stick and the Dollar formed together a unique hegemonic instrument in the region known as the North American Mediterranean, since a considerable time before the Bolshevik revolution of 1917. And in those waters Gunboat Diplomacy was performed by the naval squadron ironically known as the Banana Fleet, since its job was to watch over, tutor, and lead the banana republics.

Few countries of that peculiar Mediterranean escaped the preventive and punitive incursions of Marine bluejackets in the years between the first and the second Roosevelt. Perhaps Costa Rica and El Salvador were the exceptions that proved the rule. All the others, including Mexico from Madero to Calles, had to suffer the outrage of landings or threats of invasion by sea or by land. Early in the twenties, ex-foreign minister Isidro Fabela of Mexico wrote a book with a title defining the protest against these repeated affronts, *United States Against Liberty*. Not long afterward, early in 1928, at the Fifth Panamerican Conference in Havana, the principles of nonintervention and self-determination of Hispanic American peoples and nations agitated the Panamerican Union's habitually calm debates for almost a month, stimulated by the guns of Sandino's men, which

confronted in the mountains and forests of Nicaragua the invasion
ordered by President Calvin Coolidge and Secretary of State Frank B.
Kellogg.

On assuming the presidency Franklin Roosevelt proclaimed the
Good Neighbor Policy and accepted—with little enthusiasm—the
Panamerican recognition of the principles of nonintervention in the
internal affairs of any other state in the hemisphere and of respect for
their peoples' free self-determination. As we have indicated, there is a
startling mythology about that innovation, which was strictly window
dressing and in essence maintained untouchable the spirit and nature
of the hegemonic relationship.

It was in Roosevelt's time that the patriot guerrillero Augusto C.
Sandino was assassinated, at the instigation of U.S. Ambassador Arthur Bliss Lane; in Roosevelt's time that the dictatorship of Sandino's
formal murderer, Anastasio Somoza García, was installed; and in
Roosevelt's time that the barbarous dictatorships of Maximiliano Hernández Martínez (El Salvador), Jorge Ubico (Guatemala), Tiburcio
Carías Andino (Honduras), Fulgencio Batista (Cuba), and Rafael L.
Trujillo (Dominican Republic)—to mention only those in the immediate neighborhood of the United States—were reinforced or initiated.

Also in Roosevelt's time—toward the end of his third term—crisis
overtook all these satrapies and they suffered serious shocks, with
varying timetables and results. This apparent contradiction came
about because the principles of the Four Freedoms and the Atlantic
Charter, thought out and broadcast to stiffen antifascism and anti-
Nazism in the total war against Germany, Italy, and Japan, stirred
libertarian longings in Central America and the Caribbean. They
were just what certain middle-class and popular sectors dreamed
about in their yearning for representative democracy.

Krehm had the rare privilege of witnessing those explosions and,
here and there, the triumph of rebellions. His testimony is excep-
tional for the wealth of material it provides, live action as in cinema or
television. As a foreigner of Anglo-Saxon origin he had special immu-
nity to act as a spectator or active interviewer of official and opposition figures, to mix with "Pantherist" troops or with insurgent irregu-
lars, and to use that material for the purposes of his profession. He is
not a neutral witness. On the contrary, without being a tepid leftist, he
took sides for change and for political, social, and economic progress,
in the style of the warm and well-intentioned Rooseveltian liberals of
his time. He has no further pretensions, nor should we ask of him
more radical attitudes, for even the position he took was to offend his
Time employers.

Krehm's book remains today as valuable as was its first edition in

Spanish, for its precious accounts of situations and events, of personalities and communities of a Latin American region rarely covered
at the time by journalists and scholars. In some ways it continues to be
a classic, indispensable for those who wish to acquaint themselves with
a period like the forties. It was a period that could well merit distinction for its libertarian rebellions, which he describes with a mixture of
good humor, perspicacious observation, professional skill, and, above
all, sympathy and tenderness. Today, facing its supreme ordeal, that
great corner of the Caribbean still looks hopefully toward those who
approach it with his courageous, inquisitive and understanding spirit.

GREGORIO SELSER
Mexico, February 1984

Foreword

Lıke a sleepwalker Washington today seems under a compulsion to reenact some of the least happy episodes of its relations with Central America. It is sinking deeper and deeper into the quagmire of El Salvador's civil war. In Honduras, Americans are training forces for the invasion of Nicaragua. Off Nicaragua's coast an American fleet holds vigil. Such activities were routine enough in the days of Theodore Roosevelt. But a quarter of a century later, under another Roosevelt, a new page was turned in Washington's dealings with Latin America, and such intervention was forsworn. How, then, did we get back to square one? And why does there seem to be so strong an element of circular insanity in America's relations with its southern neighbors?

Forty years ago I blundered into an unusual situation that permitted the answers to such questions. Part of the tale is told in the present book, which now, thirty-six years after it was written, is appearing in its original English for the first time. In 1948, a Spanish translation was brought out in Mexico, and over the following decades there were pirated editions in whole and in part in South and Central America. Now Lawrence Hill has undertaken to publish the original, and he has asked me to write a chapter explaining why it had not turned up in English before now.

That indeed calls for a bit of telling. I am a Canadian, and from my mid-teens I belonged to left socialist groups. Their activities consisted for the most part of addresses to half-empty halls on the menace of fascism, on the promise of the socialist millennium, and on the intricacies of the Chinese Revolution. The defeat of the Spanish Republic and the circumstances that led up to it and the nightmare of the Moscow trials left the members of our group in a state of puzzlement and disarray. Early in 1941, with enough savings to live on frugally for one year, I arrived in Mexico City to rethink matters and, of all things, to practice the violin. I spent a quiet, fruitful year working at my music and doing some freelance writing.

At the time Mexico was a welter of contradictions. Its politics had been restored to something of a second virginity by President Lázaro Cárdenas. Amongst much else, he had thrown open the country's doors to the Spanish Republicans. With every ship from Europe they flocked in from the French and North African concentration camps. In the Café París you could find every faction of the fallen Republic, strategically grouped around cups of coffee, refighting the military and political battles of the civil war. Almost everybody was there— Indalecio Prieto, General Miaje, Julian Gorkin. Most were struggling to start life anew as salesmen, publishers, workers, petty businessmen. Dry Spanish wit crackled amidst the hiss of the *espresso* machines as they took apart the older shop-keeper immigration from Spain, the *gachupines,* the corruption of Mexican politics, and, of course, their opponents.

For me it offered a heartwarming reunion with people I had known in Spain during the civil war. At that point in Mexico, the sources were at hand to reconstruct the last tragic period of the Spanish Republic. I put together a long report on the Spanish gold reserves, which had found their way to Moscow, partly in payment for Russian arms shipments—a heavy political price had already been exacted for these—and partly "for safekeeping." Some years later the subject achieved a certain prominence in the international press. At the time it was completely ignored. That report I sent to *Time* magazine as background material. It was accepted. That began my relationship with *Time* Inc.

Mexico also served as an asylum for a constant stream of refugees from Central America. I got to know the leaders and sent the material I gathered to *Time.* Though much of it was accepted and paid for, little was used. Central America was still not rated newsworthy. But whether used or not, it did not escape the attention of the wartime U.S. censor. What with my political activity in Canada and my experiences in Spain, my dossier at the U.S. embassy in Mexico City got off to a fine start.

When I had traveled to Mexico, by bus, Canadians had not needed American transit visas. By the time I had gone through my savings and was ready to go back home, this had changed. I applied for a transit visa to return home. It was refused.

This was long before the days of nonstop flights from Mexico to Canada, and boat passages were scarce because of the war. I therefore decided to make my way to British Honduras and find a boat to Canada there. First I made my way to Guatemala City by third-class coach, sleeping two nights on wooden benches as the train chugged from the arid central plateau of Mexico to cross swelling tropical rivers. In Guatemala I applied to the British consulate for permission to enter British Honduras. For reasons of wartime security, it was necessary for them to check with Canada.

I settled down in a *pension* in the Guatemalan capital and took to spending my days at the national library. Systematically, I worked my way through a decade of newspaper files, as well as background sources. I was intrigued by the little country where Jorge Ubico played Napoleon amidst coffee bushes and banana groves, while his fellow citizens, clammy with terror, huddled in the shadow of huge fortresses.

At one point in my researches I interviewed the editor of the local newspaper, and was interviewed in turn. In the Guatemala of those days every outsider was news, and the great issue on Ubico's mind was the recovery of Belize or, as it was then known, British Honduras. The British had acquired it in the nineteenth century in return for the promise to build a road, which in fact was never built. Inevitably, as a citizen of a British Commonwealth country, I was asked my views on Belize. And as a doctrinaire socialist, the reply had long since been codified in my mind and was readily forthcoming. The interview appeared in banner headlines with the Belize question twisted out of all proportions. One did not ask or get corrections from newspapers in Ubico's Guatemala.

My money was running out, and wartime exchange controls made it impossible for me to have more sent from Canada. So I made my way to the Atlantic coast by railway to await permission to enter British Honduras from Puerto Barrios. When the answer came, it was a refusal. So there I was, stranded in a sweltering hellhole of mosquitoes and open sewage canals. On top of that, my Guatemalan visa had run out.

One day two Guatemalan detectives called and told me to pack my bags. They took me to the railway tracks and ordered me to start walking to the capital—some two hundred miles away across mountains and valleys. Things were done that way in Ubico's Guatemala. I protested strongly enough for them to send a telegram to the capital and get permission for all of us to travel by train.

In the capital, I was ushered into the offices of the police chief.

"Señor," he said to me, "do you travel with or without money?"

I informed him that I had wired the United States for money. I was released. Shortly afterward, my money arrived.

I remember my visit to the national pawnshop. I had pawned my camera and my violin. Before the transaction was concluded, the friendly pawnbroker asked me to perform on the violin so that he could reach an evaluation. The amount he came up—one quetzal—

could have been taken as unflattering musical criticism. But then the
dictator as a matter of policy kept the economy so demurely deflated
that every one-quetzal bill seemed to its citizens a magic carpet.

Once my money arrived, I redeemed my possessions and went on
to San Salvador by bus. In the modest boardinghouse where I settled,
barefoot servants each morning would burn the soiled toilet paper
from the bathrooms in the patio. At night giant cockroaches rumbled
over the floor like tanks and chewed holes in my manuscripts. Several
times a month the boarders would hastily wrap themselves in their
sheets in the middle of the night and rush out into the streets as minor
earth tremors shook the house. El Salvador was in an active seismic
zone. Attentive observers, too, could not overlook the social fault that
ran through the fundaments of the dictator's regime.

As in Guatemala I took to spending my days in the public library,
inching my way through a decade or more of newspaper files. I listened to the students' conversations at my boardinghouse, wandered
through the marketplaces with my eyes and ears open.

I worked up my Guatemalan material and sent it to *Time*. It was
accepted—and remained unused in their files for the next two years.

When I finally tired of waiting for the visa that never came, I
went back to Mexico. In Mexico at the time the American ambassador
was George S. Messersmith, a schoolteacher turned diplomat who
could not quite resist the temptations that the wartime powers of such
a post had placed in his hands. Predictably, my coverage of the Mexican scene did little to improve the deplorable impression that I was
leaving in those quarters.

Particularly fresh in my mind is a speech given by Eduardo Villaseñor, head of the Mexican central bank. In it he expressed his
country's unhappiness with the severity of American wartime restrictions on exports to Mexico—restrictions that he felt were at times
damaging to the war effort. Mexico was sending enormous amounts
of metals and fibers and other strategic materials north. Dollars
flooded into the country, and since there was little enough to spend
them on, they were exerting inflationary pressures on Mexico's ec-
nomy. So consistent had been Washington's rejection of requests for
equipment vital to Mexico's economy that Villaseñor proposed replacing all the U.S. agencies set up to consider such requests and replacing
them with a single one entitled Agency for the Rejection of All Mexican Requests for Priorities. Whatever the merits of Villaseñor's com-
plaints, the U.S. embassy chose a remarkable way of dealing with so
delicate a situation: it tried to suppress this speech by the head of the
country's central bank by threatening to cut off the newsprint supplies of recalcitrant newspapers. For me the procedure was particu-

larly fascinating because much of the newsprint in question was of Canadian origin.

I interviewed the hulking Texan press attaché at the embassy on the subject. At one point he literally flew out of his chair and roared at me:

"Don't you try upsetting the apple cart!"

For anyone as vulnerable to the embassy's displeasure as I was, that, indeed, was a foolhardy thing to do.

The results were not long in coming. Shortly afterward, *Time* dropped me as a stringer.

My Washington solicitor wrote me that he had the impression that the real hindrance to getting a transit visa lay somewhere in the U.S. embassy in Mexico City. He suggested that I make application at an American consulate in another country. In this way it was determined that I was to delve further into the workings of democracy under some of the favorite regimes of the State Department.

I flew to San Salvador. In those days the Pan-American Airways plane on the Mexico-Panama run stopped in Guatemala overnight and continued to San Salvador the next morning. At my hotel in Guatemala I learned that a revolution had broken out in San Salvador. I found myself headed into the eye of the storm with nowhere to send my story. Swallowing my pride, I wired *Time,* asking whether they wanted coverage.

By the time I got to San Salvador their affirmative reply was awaiting me.

The drama turned out to be a little more bloodcurdling than expected. When the defeated revolutionists sought asylum at the U.S. embassy, they were refused. Some were turned over to the dictator's forces, and were shot. That left the little land in quite a stir.

I wrote my story and booked passage to Tapachula in southern Mexico, counting on the overnight stop in Guatemala City for filing my dispatch. But would the Guatemalan censor pass the cable? One thing I had going for me: there was no love lost between Ubico and the Salvadoran dictator, Hernández Martínez. The tapering isthmus was hardly roomy enough to house two such powerful personalities. To make sure, however, I tacked a final sentence onto my cable: "Contrast unpopularity of Salvadoran dictator with the position of General Ubico, architect of the New Guatemala. For details consult my mailer on Ubico of 1941."

That clinched it: the dispatch went through.

In Tapachula I made plans to return to San Salvador and resume my quest for that American visa. Airspace was severely rationed during the war, and it turned out that no plane seats were available for days. And to cross Guatemala by bus I needed a Guatemalan visa. I made application at the Guatemalan consulate, but word came that it was refused. I cabled the dictator: "For reasons unknown I have been refused a visa to Guatemala. From my cable filed to *Time* at All American Cable office in Guatemala City last Sunday you can convince yourself of my admiration for Your Excellency's regime."

Within three hours, there was a rap at the door of my room. It was the Guatemalan consul, the very soul of obsequiousness, with a cable in hand. It was from Ubico himself: "Informed of your request, I have ordered that visa be issued to you at once."

I went on to Guatemala and spent a week there bringing my earlier material up to date. It was sent to *Time* from San Salvador. Immediately *Time* used it for a full-page story. In a matter of days Ubico was overthrown.

That added a further and most unforgivable item to my dossier at the State Department. In the lore of some U.S. embassy types in Central America, I personally had been responsible for Ubico's downfall.

It is hard now to reproduce the farcical cloak-and-dagger atmosphere of wartime Central America. Anybody slightly out of the ordinary might at once be taken for a foreign agent. I remember entering El Salvador on one occasion by land, and being asked for a few colons in bakshish by the immigration official.

"You know, señor, that in wartime we have all sorts of people coming around with British passports claiming to be British subjects. How do we know that they aren't German spies? So you see," said he, stretching out his palm, "we do have to be careful?"

As I look back upon my adventures of the period I am struck by the contrast between my uninterrupted series of pratfalls in dealing with my visa problem, and the almost somnambulistic surefootedness with which I was able to find myself in the right place at the right time for news coverage when the Central American revolutions started popping. Of course, there was some connection between the two. Not only was I fortunate in being at the scene of momentous events, but my Latin America experiences served me as an invaluable decompression chamber in which I was able to free myself from the dogmatic rigors in which the social concerns of my early youth had been locked.

Once back in Mexico City, I found that not only had *Time* sent me generous payment for my efforts; they asked me also to return to Central America to cover the remaining republics. This time I went back with a substantial retainer and an expense account.

By the time I got to Managua *Time* had become something of a magic word. To the minds of the less sophisticated Central Americans, now that the magazine had begun to print the truth about Central

American democracy, it could only be a matter of weeks before the good fairies would make a clean sweep of the bad fairies in the State Department and the promises of North American war propaganda would be fulfilled in the isthmus. Some while later, a friendly U.S. diplomat with access to my dossier informed me that one of the sins attributed to me was that I had been passing myself off in Honduras as an American agent. Had that been true, it would certainly have been unpardonable, especially in someone who had run up such mileage in open quest of a U.S. visa that would enable him to return to his own country.

Befittingly for the correspondent of a magazine that was perceived as the maker and shaker of Central American destinies, I was not left unattended in Nicaragua. At my hotel I was constantly sought out by a local German who had served the U.S. Marines during their stay and was now notoriously in the pay of dictator Somoza. His name escapes me, so I will call him "Heinke." When I had finished my week's researches and was ready to go on to Costa Rica, I dropped in at the office of the U.S. military attaché to pick up the necessary priority for a plane ticket.

"A priority for passage to Costa Rica?" the attaché sneered. "Not a chance for at least a week. Don't you know that there is a war on?"

Back in my hotel, I found Heinke waiting for me as usual. I was in a mood for some deviltry, so over drinks I explained to him my difficulty in getting passage out of Nicaragua. "However," I added, "if I am stuck here for another week, I won't waste my time. I have begun compiling an alphabetic list of Somoza's rackets and I have reached the letter R. Now, with this extra time, I can complete it right down to Z, and look into his cattle racket in special depth."

Heinke gulped down his drink, and took a hasty leave. I saw him to the door to confirm that he had set out in the direction of the U.S. embassy. Hardly did I have time to recount my experiment to an opposition politician who had dropped in on me when I was called to the phone. It was the attaché's office: my plane priority was waiting for me for passage the very next morning.

The incident illustrated the cozy intimacy between the Somoza regime and the U.S. embassy.

On my return to Mexico, *Time* offered me the post as head of their Mexican bureau, with Central America as part of my territory. Of course I accepted.

The presidential campaign was getting under way in Mexico, and the candidates were staking out their territories. The favorite of the U.S. embassy was Ezequiel Padilla, the handsome foreign minister in Avila Camacho's cabinet. Padilla's great eloquence usually anticipated Washington's merest wish, and that was enough to make him intensely unpopular in a country where pro-American sympathies usually come seasoned with reservations. Of that, Miguel Alemán, minister of the interior and candidate of the official party, was well aware, and he played the situation to the hilt. His supporters lampooned Padilla as a gringo stooge in public, but privately Alemán curried favor with the U.S. embassy. Ambassador Messersmith did his mighty best to see that nothing unfavorable to Padilla crept into the North American press. Indeed, from reading papers in the United States you might well have carried away the impression that Padilla had as good as been elected.

I felt that conscientious reporting required that the North American public ought to be given some inkling of Padilla's unpopularity in Mexico. Some of my best sources on the subject were inevitably in the Alemán camp, but I tried sifting the information that came to me from them. Alemán's private secretary was a Nicaraguan lawyer, Rogelio de la Selva. Rogelio's brother, the poet Salamón, was not only an intimate friend of mine of long standing, but had been closely linked to the Nicaraguan rebel, Sandino, who had held the Marines at bay. Over a glass of wine, Salamón could hold an audience in thrall by the hour with his recollections of life in his homeland under the heel of the United States.

The material that I sent to *Time* on Padilla did not escape the ambassador's ever wakeful eye. From friendly sources around the embassy I gathered that there was not only mounting displeasure with *Time*'s new correspondent, but a determination to do something about it. Just what and when I had no way of knowing.

I was not kept in suspense very long. My visitor's visa required renewal every six months. And in December 1944 when I presented myself at the Ministry of the Interior for this formality, I was ushered into an adjoining room, photographed, and detained.

I penned a note to Rogelio de la Selva, the minister's secretary, and asked an official to deliver it. Within minutes I was released. But I was given three days to leave Mexico. It was made clear to me that nothing could be done, because my expulsion did not originate with the Mexican government. However, I was assured that I could return to Mexico whenever I wished, but not as *Time* correspondent.

I put through a call to *Time* in New York. I recall remarking to the editor at the other end that I felt like a character in a Kafka tale.

"A what sort of tale?" came the puzzled response. Kafka was still relatively unknown in this hemisphere and long-distance communication was not by a long shot what it has since become.

Within a couple of hours instructions reached me from New York. I must issue no public statement on what was happening to me. *Time* would take up the matter in Washington.

Kind friends wise in the ways of Mexico stepped in with advice and practical help. It was decided that I should not sleep in my apartment. Jack Glenn, a *March of Time* producer who happened to be in Mexico on an assignment, threw himself into the fray with such wholeheartedness that an old ulcer came to life again. He looked up Padilla, who assured him that he had nothing to do with my expulsion. I did not doubt that he was speaking the truth: as number two in the embassy's affections, Miguel Alemán simply had to try harder. A note appeared in the Mexican papers stating that I was being expelled for having insulted the President of the Republic. In actual fact, absorbed as I was by Central America, I had not mentioned President Avila Camacho in my dispatches since taking over the bureau.

I saw Eduardo Villaseñor, head of the central bank. He had no difficulty in grasping the situation. Months later a *Time* editor passing through Mexico was told by Ramón Beteta of the Treasury how much he and Villasēnor had regretted not having succeeded in helping me.

Placating messages were coming to me from my contacts in the Ministry of the Interior. I might as well leave quietly since nobody could say no to the U.S. embassy. But I had decided to dig my toes in. The three days of grace given to me to leave the country had run out, and I was still leading a semi-underground existence, avoiding our apartment and the *Time* office as much as possible.

But one night I had a telephone call to make and was missing the coin for a pay telephone. So I dropped into the *Time* office nearby to use the phone there. Three detectives, two Mexicans and one American, were there waiting for me. I was taken to a detention center. Later I learned that my wife and a Canadian friend had roused the first secretary of the Canadian embassy when I failed to turn up, and made the rounds, pounding likely doors in an attempt to locate me. It was two or three days before she heard from me again—and then by a telegram from Guatemala.

Next morning two Mexican plainclothesmen took me to the Guatemalan embassy for a visa. Ambassador Willy Toriello received me with a hug, and ordered the two Mexicans to wait outside: "Señores, here you are on Guatemalan soil."

I had got to know Toriello when he arrived as a refugee some months back. He had driven his brother Jorge around Guatemala City in a wild getaway amidst police bullets after an unsuccessful plot against the new Guatemalan dictator, General Federico Ponce. Then he had gotten out to Mexico, while Jorge stayed behind to overthrow the dictator through his contacts with young army officers. Over cups of coffee, while my visa was being prepared, we exchanged notes on my adventures in wonderland and the state of the isthmus.

When the plane stopped at Tapachula for refueling, an official appeared with a telegram announcing that I was not to be allowed to leave the plane. Ambassador Messersmith was taking no chances. At about that time he was assuring the press corps that my expulsion from Mexico in no way infringed upon the freedom of the press.

For the next three months I was to remain in Guatemala, professionally in a state of suspended animation. My salary ran on, but there was little enough in a small country to justify a fulltime correspondent, even in the blossom-time of revolution. During this time *Time* conducted its pourparlers in Washington.

Finally, having settled matters there to its satisfaction, the magazine assigned me Central America, the West Indies, Venezuela, Columbia, Ecuador, and Peru as my new territory. I set out on a three-month trip around the Caribbean.

Throughout the region the political calendar read high spring. The sweeping propaganda of the Allies had been taken in dead earnest by the local populations, and with the Nazi defeat the millennium seemed at hand. Latin America appeared to be on the verge of sloughing off its grotesque tyrannies.

Of all the political leaders that I came to know in this assignment the most memorable was Rómulo Betancourt, head of the Acción Democrática opposition party in Venezuela. In his blend of idealism and hardheaded practical sense, he stood cubits higher than any other leader on the Latin American scene. A brief period in the Costa Rican Communist party as a young exile made him just a shade suspect in Washington for years to come.

There was immediate empathy between us. At his modest home I came to know Juan Bosch, later elected president of the Dominican Republic until he was overthrown by an American-backed coup, and Rómulo Gallegos, the great novelist who also was chosen president of his country, only to be overthrown in his turn by a military coup that Washington did not frown on.

Learning that I was going on to Peru, Betancourt gave me a letter of introduction to Victor Raúl Haya de la Torre, the perennial crusading prophet of the Peruvian APRA (Association of Revolutionary Parties of America). When at our next meeting I expressed some misgivings about APRA's leader cult, Betancourt had a thoughtful reply: "Oh, that is just the difference between Peru and Venezuela. If we attempted any such thing here, they would laugh in our faces [*nos tomarían en guasa*]."

Time had by now arranged my affairs with Washington so that I could return to Canada for a vacation. On my way back I was able to spend a month in their New York offices. My new territory comprised the Pacific coast countries of South America together with Venezuela and Bolivia.

While in New York I learned how I had come to be hired as a member of the staff in the teeth of State Department's displeasure. Henry Luce, it appears, had been getting a bit bored with the war and had welcomed as a distraction the colorful coverage that I was sending in from Central America. But even as I was in the New York office, chill winds were making themselves felt. Charles Wertenbaker, the senior editor who had spread a protective wing over offbeat characters like myself, was shifted elsewhere. In a couple of years he was out of the organization. His successor seemed concerned above all that *Time* correspondents comport themselves as "ambassadors of *Time* Inc." Whittaker Chambers was wallowing in masochistic penance for his years as Communist agent, and his views in the organization were in the ascendant. Chambers's response to Latin America's problems was simple enough: "Why rock the boat?" It was the classical attitude of the shipwrecked mariner. It did not trouble him that most Latin Americans might feel that they were not aboard.

I remember an editorial luncheon at the *Time* offices with Nelson Rockefeller. Rockefeller, who had served briefly as Coordinator of Inter-American Affairs in the U.S. Department of State, enlarged on the importance of getting along amicably with those southern neighbors.

"Otherwise where would it all lead to?" he asked. "Before long we would find ourselves occupying Mexico City again like Pershing in 1916."

I corrected Rockefeller. "Pershing did not get to Mexico City. Pancho Villa got the better of the encounter, and Pershing withdrew with his mission unaccomplished."

Rockefeller had confused two episodes in their history that Mexicans revere quite as much as Americans do Paul Revere's ride: the *Niños Heroes,* the cadets who resisted to the death the American occupation of Chapultepec Castle in 1847, and Villa's victory over Pershing in 1916.

Rockefeller consulted an aide and accepted the correction. There were people far less sensitive than Nelson Rockefeller involved in the formulation of United States policy in Latin America. Yet it was significant that after years of such involvement, Rockefeller could still not sort out the two great legendary episodes in their relations with the United States on which Mexicans nurture their wounded pride.

I went on to Peru. There the popular leftist party APRA (Association of Revolutionary Parties of America) was generally pro-American. From his student days its leader, Victor Raúl Haya de la Torre had preached the unification of Latin America and the redemption of the highland Indian and the mestizo of the coast. The party's martyrology stretched back over decades. Right until the elections shortly before my arrival, APRA had been outlawed as an international organization because of its stance advocating Latin American unity.

Despite Haya's great charisma, he was hopelessly outmaneuvered by his opponents. From the underground he had mobilized his followers to elect José Luis Bustamante as president of the republic. No sooner was the new government set up than the editor of a rightist paper was assassinated and the anti-APRA parties pointed an accusing finger at APRA. At once the APRA ministers resigned to make possible an impartial investigation, a gesture positively lyrical in its naiveté. For impartial investigation is what they got least of. The campaign unleashed against Haya by the rightist parties of the large landowners and the Communists was incredibly vicious. Urbane socialites who were perfectly at home in the salons of three continents had developed a new version of the Marquis of Queensbury rules: any blow above the belt was ruled out as foul.

I was caught in the cross fire, as was to some extent the American ambassador, Prentice Cooper, a noncareer diplomat from Tennessee. Because he maintained friendly relations with Haya, the rightist and Communist press did not hesitate to hint at a homosexual liaison. That was the sort of hardball that was played in courtly Lima in 1947.

Editorials in the anti-APRA press attacked me as an Aprista agent. *Time* received letters threatening a boycott of the magazine unless they changed their correspondent.

I do not know how the State Department rated Cooper's diplomacy, but my new senior editor at *Time* held mine in low esteem. Though my territory stretched from Venezuela to Chile, I was kept confined to Peru. Little of my political coverage was used, and when it was, it was often twisted beyond recognition. Attempting to stave off the inevitable, I concentrated my efforts on back-of-the-book items and stories for *Life*—art, archeology, science, and such miscellaneous items as the original Kon-Tiki expedition out of Callao. My success was enough to draw a kind remark from the back-of-the-book editor (after my firing) that I had been the best back-of-the-book reporter they had.

Once Bustamante had served his purpose, he was overthrown by a General Odría. APRA was driven into the underground again. When the students of a high school struck in protest, the army surrounded the building with machine guns and killed two students. That story I sent in, and for once *Time* carried it straight.

A letter came from *Time* announcing the abolition of the Lima bureau and the termination of my employment. A few hours later two detectives called to fetch me into the presence of General Odría. The news of my dismissal was not yet out, so that I could still manage some bluffing in the acrimonious encounter that took place in the presidential palace.

"You've got to understand once and for all," Odría growled at me, "that we aren't Anglo-Saxons here."

"Of course, Your Excellency," I shot back, "but you are supposed to be democrats. You did sign a treaty in Rio guaranteeing human liberties."

I went on to the U.S. embassy to give my friends my double tidings—my command interview with the Great Man, and my firing.

To make matters still more awkward, I was not able to leave Peru for another three months. My wife was expecting our first child and was not able to travel. During this time I put my mind to earning a living by freelance writing. I reworked an article of mine on bird guano that *Life* had carried and sold it to *Reader's Digest.* And here we come to the point of this lengthy tale.

Sample chapters of this book on Central America had been going the rounds of New York publishers for some time. Usually they were received with enthusiasm, but interest soon vanished without further comment. Of course, I connected this with the "involuntary censorship" of the war years: books on foreign countries would be submitted to the State Department by publishers. But hard proof up to this moment I had none. But now my agent sent me a letter from *Reader's Digest* after they had carried my bird guano article. They could consider no further manuscripts from me, so please don't send any. We were still some years from the glory days of Joe McCarthy, but blacklisting was already beginning.

That effectively severed my ties with Latin America. It had become out of the question for me to earn my living as a journalist in that part of the world. Though I have since visited and revisited other areas of Latin America, I have not set foot again in Central America. Its further fate I have followed—often in anguish—from afar.

WILLIAM KREHM

Democracies and Tyrannies
of the Caribbean

I

Sharpshooting Theosophist

Early in April 1944, tired and dusty, I entered a Guatemala City hotel. I had been two days coming down from Veracruz, and the most recent paper I had seen was the one my spare shoes were wrapped in. In the hotel dining room, at a neighboring table, a middle-aged woman with a Salvadoran accent was talking of revolution in a jumpy, ecstatic way. A Zionist Congress in Berlin would not have been more sensational than the audible mention of the word "revolution" in dictator Ubico's Guatemala. I approached the brave lady, apologized for overhearing: Please, what revolution was this?

"You don't know? It finally happened in Salvador!"

Yes, there had been a military coup against dictator Martínez there two days before. The Salvadoran radio reported all under control once more, but the people had suffered too long to be subdued that easily.

I was on my way to El Salvador to gather material for a book on Central America. And here the political upheavals long foreseen in the isthmus had already begun.

Leaving the plane at San Salvador the next day, I was aware at once of a grimness in the air. It was apparent in the unsmiling manner of the tough police at the airport, in the forced casualness of the Pan American Airways personnel. On our way to town we were stopped at two sentry posts. There was nothing routine about the inspection; the police scanned our faces as though eyes and noses were the dots and dashes of some revolutionary code. They took a peek under our seats for good measure. In the dirty sprawling suburb we passed through, the National Guard in spatterdashes and steel helmets patrolled in force. Alongside them chickens and hogs and barefooted, haggard women toting baskets of vegetables on their heads—an ungodly number with the bulge of pregnancy before them—were milling about in quest of a livelihood. Life is quick to regain its rut.

San Salvador was not readily recognizable as the capital of one of

3

the wealthiest of Latin America's small countries. Three hundred-odd tremors and quakes a year had taught the Salvadorans a makeshift manner of construction. Even the Cathedral was of wood; corrugated iron sheeting covered the walls of most of the one-story downtown buildings: it was easier to pick up and start anew. But the city's slatternly appearance was due as much to the social setup as to geology. For the coffee-growers who produced its chief export, the country is primarily a plantation for the amassing of fortunes to be squandered in Europe. In Monte Carlo and Biarritz, Salvadorans earned themselves a proud reputation as the most prodigal of Latin Americans, while back home the capital wore the appearance of a colonial outpost. Overcrowded adobe houses with four and five persons sleeping within a few dingy square yards; open-ditch drainage in muddy streets on the outskirts; filthy, swarming markets; dilapidated, barnlike cinemas. Through this, elegant men and women flitted lightly in their roadsters from their residences to their princely casino and countinghouses, without a trace of civic pride to be wounded by the sordidness of it all.

Inured to quakes, San Salvador had this time experienced a novel form of destruction. As the Pan Am station wagon entered the center of town, we skirted a block of smoldering ruins where only the casino still stood erect. A girl in our car burst into sobs; her home had been somewhere amidst the charred timber and warped iron. Fireproof though it was, not even the casino had escaped unscathed. Mistaking the blue-uniformed bowlers lounging on its roof-garden for police, the rebel planes had dropped a bomb that cut through three stories and wrecked the bowling alley beneath, while the bona-fide police, entrenched in the National Palace a block away, had thought the casino a rebel stronghold and directed their fire at it. In the next block a cheap cinema had become a mound of rubble. In it two years ago I had shuddered at newsreels of remote London's blitz, while the urine of customers relieving themselves against the back wall trickled down the aisle. At the Hotel Nuevo Mundo, where I stopped, the walls of the spacious dining room were pocked with shrapnel; a shell intended to silence a rebel radio station across the plaza had come through the window and burst over scores of Easter tourists. Fortunately it had hit an eavestrough on its way in and exploded in midair, scattering its shrapnel over the diners' heads. But for that providential eavestrough there might have been an embarrassing array of corpses with foreign passports.

And how had this come to pass in a land that had been sung far and wide as a model of order?

With an area of but 13,176 square miles El Salvador, after Haiti, is the most densely populated of the American republics. To grasp what its two million inhabitants mean in terms of overcrowding, one must bear in mind that its territory bristles with mountains, and sizable stretches in the east are arid wasteland. Most of the population is crammed into the western section which, with a yield per acre twice that of Guatemala and Costa Rica, is the most productive coffee region in the world. The secret of that efficiency in large part is the presence of a teeming proletariat. They are a diligent folk who don't have to be bludgeoned into working on the plantations. With no land of their own, hunger turns the trick. The permanent laborers live in wretched straw huts, scattered over the coffee fincas; during harvest time seasonal workers flock in from the rosary of villages along the highways.

The concentration of the land into a few hands dates from the sixties of the last century when coffee bcame important. Peasants who refused to sell were pressed into military service, and their farms fell into the usurers' clutches. In time the mountainsides became a fairyland under snowy wisps of coffee blossoms, and the country a kettle of social unrest.

In 1943 earnings on the coffee fincas were about twenty cents a day—a little higher during picking season—with a few fistfuls of corn and beans thrown in. Most of their vitamins the peons got bootleg from sylvan herbs and flowers munched from roadside hedges. Scientists have catalogued at least twenty-five such plants, rich in vitamins, that Nature, anticipating the harsh epoch of coffee, scattered charitably over the Salvadoran countryside. Without these the peons' labor could never have been what it is.

Tight though the land is, the system of ownership interferes with its rational use. In the coastal lowlands there were in the forties at least 300,000 acres that served only to raise cattle and malarial mosquitoes. Drained, irrigated, and entrusted to the tender care of homesteaders, these lands could have been capable of supplying the grain needs of the entire country. In the mountain department of Chalatenango, near Honduras, the peasants raised wheat on steep slopes eroded almost to ruin; when the rains came, the Lempa River was virtually a moving column of mud. By any sensible criterion Chalatenango ought to be turned to pasture and the country's grain grown on the coast. But these are problems that have never robbed El Salvador's coffee barons of a night's sleep.

Long-lived dictatorships had not been the bane of El Salvador as of neighboring Guatemala. Related to Mexico's Aztecs rather than to Guatemala's meek Maya-Quichés, its people are too self-assertive. Moreover, El Salvador's Indians have been entirely assimilated, and there are no differences of language and culture to buttress social hierarchies. Rare, indeed, has been the president who engineered his reelection and saw the end of his second term. Yet democracy could scarcely flourish alongside such rasping social inequalities. A heavy military boot had to be applied to keep the lid of the cauldron from blowing off.

Under President Pío Romero Bosque (1926–30), nepotism reigned shamelessly. The president not only found room for his son in his cabinet of four; he allowed him to carry on a profitable business, buying up at a 40 percent discount the IOUs with which state employees were paid and having them redeemed at par. But the presidential election of 1930 was eminently fair; voters' thumbs were stained with indelible ink to prevent them from repeating their democratic duty. Amongst the eight candidates who presented themselves were Arturo Araujo, a fuzzy-minded landowner known for his humane treatment of his peons, and General Maximiliano Martínez Hernández. At the last moment Martínez threw in the sponge and accepted the vice-presidential place on the Araujo ticket. With the backing of the moderate Labor party, the Araujo-Martínez slate triumphed. Martínez became vice-president and war minister.

The times were trying.* Coffee had toppled from its golden throne. As prices collapsed, the treasury, embarrassed enough during the boom years, was picked quite bare. Araujo raised forced loans from the banks, some of the proceeds of which stuck to his colleagues' fingers. Unemployment spread in the towns; wretched as they had been, wages were slashed on the coffee fincas. Rebellion simmered amongst the peons. The private banks did a fat business of foreclosing mortgages. El Salvador's propertied classes scare easily; the scene was ripening for the advent of a heavy-handed savior. When, on December 2, 1982, War Minister Martínez, hiding behind a directorate of young officers, overthrew the inept Araujo, he had the coffee *finqueros* solidly on his side. The United States minister informed the loyal forces at Santa Tecla that he could not tolerate their resistance.† Araujo fled to Guatemala, and the young officers' directorate stepped down to make place for Hernández Martínez.

Martínez's origins were draped in obscurity. He was born at San Matías in El Salvador in 1881, of humble Indian stock. Much of his

---

*The author refers to the Wall Street Crash of October 1929, whose effects were felt in the following years throughout the world.

†The United States was committed by the "Washington Pacts" of 1923 not to recognize any Central American government arising from a coup d'état or violation of the constitution. When the minister—the term for U.S. diplomats below ambassadorial rank—notified the Araujo loyalists that he did not support them, this decided the issue in favor of Martínez.

childhood was spent as a water-carrier. His use of his maternal sur-
name Martínez rather than the paternal Hernández was explained by
the lack of a legal title to the latter. He was a studious youngster and
somehow managed to attend the military academy in Guatemala. On
returning to El Salvador, he entered the army and sat in at the law
course of the university for a year.

This whiff of learning stirred a deeper hunger in his soul. He
found a short cut to satisfying it in theosophy. Before long he had
learned to bandy about astral planes, cosmic cycles, and other
theosophic hardware with the best of them. He became a vegetarian.
It was during this period that he formulated the principle that was to
guide his career: "It is a greater crime to kill an ant than a man—for a
man on dying becomes reincarnated, while an ant dies dead."

He conducted original experiments in agriculture: to prevent the
ants from eating the seed, he took to planting corn two feet beneath
the surface. Such farming technique was of no great aid in helping
him maintain the natural children that he accumulated as the years
wore on. In 1930, on the eve of his rise to greatness, he was living with
his future wife, Doña Concha, and their children in a battered house
on the outskirts of the capital. She supplemented their income by
taking in sewing. A natural son by another woman worked as a chauffeur. Ploddingly, Martínez had risen to the rank of general with a
salary of something like four dollars a day.

During the 1930 election campaign, at Araujo's suggestion, he
had done the right thing by Doña Concha for the good name of their
joint ticket. His friends chipped in to buy him a presentable uniform
for his inauguration as vice-president.

Humble as were his origins, Martínez in power soon became the
idol of the propertied classes. The economic setup in El Salvador
creates social problems more akin to those of Eastern Europe than
those of any other American country. Led by austere young intellectual Agustín Farabundo Martí, formerly secretary to the Nicaraguan
guerrilla Sandino, the Communists found a most fertile field there. At
first, Martínez actually paid out rope to the Communists to bring
matters to a point where drastic surgery could be applied. During the
third week of January 1932 some nuns in one of the capital's suburbs
reported a group of men meeting furtively in a deserted loft. The
police thus bagged Martí and his comrades of the Communist Central
Committee and had them executed.* Izalco is the name both of an

---

*Martí and the students Mario Zapata and Alfonso Luna were shot "in
cold blood" after the insurrection had failed, in strict pursuance of the martial
law that had been decreed *after* their arrest.

active volcano and of a town near the Guatemalan border, but on January 22, 1932, it was the town that erupted. Bands of peasants butchered the police with machetes, armed themselves and went on to take Sonsonate. Sonzacate, Nahuilzalco, Juayúa, and other centers fell into their hands as their number swelled. Landowners were assassinated, their houses looted, their wives set to making tortillas for the "Red Army." It was a cross between an old-fashioned Indian uprising and a *jacquerie* of starving peasants, daubed here and there with a sophisticated veneer of communism. For three days the peons sipped their triumph. They got royally drunk, listened to the thrilling oratory of their leaders, and occasionally raped their masters' womenfolk.

Then the government planes flew overhead; truckloads of soldiers with modern equipment closed in from the capital. The Indians fought like lions, charged machine guns with machetes, but it was futile. The army went about its work thoroughly; slaughter begun to recapture towns was continued for the crimson joy of it. By the time the U.S.S. *Rochester* and the Canadian warships *Skeena* and *Vancouver* dropped anchor at Acajutla, General José Tomás Calderón was able to assure them that their aid was unnecessary and boasted of already having liquidated 4,800 "Bolsheviks": "Bolsheviks" who had never heard of Marx, but who knew a lot about gnawing hunger. Before the episode was closed the toll of their dead ran to at least 10,000.* In the capital, where no uprising had occurred, the police, the army, and a hastily organized Civil Guard of rich young men rounded up suspects, carted them to the outskirts of the city, finished them off, and dumped their bodies into shallow graves. Public health was endangered by the stench of rotting corpses, but the bulk of the planters felt that the body politic had been fortified by a salutary bloodletting.†

---

*Krehm uses statistics still generally accepted in the 1940s, which echo the official version. The bibliography of recent years has put them where they belong. Miguel Mármol, a contemporary witness who participated in the frustrated rising, maintains government casualties totaled "twenty-two dead, nearly all in open combat and the rest in circumstances yet not determined, and four wounded." On the other hand, among the peasants there were "thirty thousand dead" in the following weeks, in purported vengeance for "the real damage we did them, because in fact we did none." See Roque Dalton, *Miguel Mármol: Los sucesos de 1932 en El Salvador* (San José, Costa Rica: Editorial Centroamericana, EDUCA, 1972), p. 355. A United States researcher, however, reduces the number of victims considerably below Miguel Mármol's figure. See Thomas P. Anderson, *Mantanza: El Salvador's Communist Revolt of 1932* (Lincoln, Neb.: University of Nebraska Press, 1971).

†The massacre of peasants continued in the ensuing weeks and months, with the special participation of "white guards" set up for the purpose as "paramilitary" commandos are in our time.

And on the strength of that, Martínez had their loyalty for many years. Power offered him ample opportunity for indulging his philosophic whims. He preferred being addressed as "maestro" rather than President. In soporific undulating tones, he broadcast weekly at forums of the only legal party, his Partido ProPatria. In a single lecture he was known to answer questions as varied as the following: "Where will the Allies invade Europe?" "Have snakes, spiders, and horses a sense of beauty?" "Why does a man smile to himself as he walks down the street?" The answer to the last, in case the reader should not know it, is: "Mind dominates matter. If you heat water you get steam. What, then, will supersteam be like? Though we know it, in reality it exists." In another lecture he shook the pillars of science as hitherto known: "Biologists have only discovered five senses. But ten really exist. Hunger, thirst, procreation, urination, and bowel movement have not been included." The school texts were seasoned with pinches of Buddhism and theosophy.

He effected cures by giving his patients water previously exposed to the sun in blue, red, and green bottles on the terrace of the presidential palace. When an epidemic broke out in the capital, he had the street lamps covered with colored cellophane. His young son died of peritonitis because he refused to permit an operation until he had tried his colored waters. The day after the lad's death, the shattering of glass could be heard for blocks around the presidential palace. Doña Concha was venting her feelings on the Maestro's store of magic waters. Henchmen found it wise to simulate theosophic convictions, and turn to the president as to a confessor. They swallowed his pills, powders, and liquids submissively; those surviving might even be compensated with a promotion. He let the word get around that "invisible legions" watched over him, and he could even be present unseen to eavesdrop on conspirators. With such signal advantages, it was but natural that his regime should be a lengthy one.

The Maestro's only serious philosophic setback was after the Communist revolt of 1932, when the local theosophic lodge expelled him for his part in the carnage.

Though the food at the presidential palace was cooked by his mother-in-law, he tested each dish for poison and vitamins by holding a little pendulum over it. If the pendulum swung one way, the dish could be eaten to advantage; if it moved otherwise, the victuals were left untouched. The same all-purpose pendulum suspended over a topographic map would indicate where water was to be found and where lost treasures lurked. When a local North American resident offered to distribute rope-soled shoes to school children, Martínez forbade it because shoes would keep beneficial radiations given off by the earth from the children's bodies. At the drop of a hat, in tolerant tones, he was ready to advise chemists on chemistry, engineers on engineering, and agronomists on agriculture. There is something in the balmy isthmus air that makes dictators omniscient.

Poor when he came to power, Martínez accumulated a sizable fortune, through miserliness and an eye for opportunities. Doña Concha's fingers, calloused from needles, sprouted diamonds. He had interests in a gold mine, textile factories, a newspaper, a radio station. Wherever he acquired a farm, a paved road sprang up as though by magic. His intimacy with the cattle interests warped the country's economic policy: he tried making of tight little Salvador a cattle export country, and wrecked free-trade agreements with Guatemala and Nicaragua to protect the domestic livestock industry. Yet overpopulated El Salvador stood most to gain from a unified Central American market that would have permitted a certain industrialization. Though prosperous, Martínez, of all Central American dictators, did least to feather his own nest.

His foreign policy was no less original than the man himself. During his first two years in the presidency, the United States State Department refused to recognize him: the 1923 Central American treaties, which it had begotten, midwived, and godfathered, barred recognition of regimes come to power by violent revolutions. When United States recognition was not forthcoming, Martínez won a certain inexpensive popularity throughout the isthmus by posing as knight crusader against "Yankee imperialism." He went further and wooed Japan. El Salvador became the first country to recognize Manchukuo, the "country" formed by the Japanese occupiers in North China. The laws were amended to permit Japanese immigration. For a time he even harbored high hopes of weaning the Japanese away from their tea-drinking to coffee. His sentiments toward European totalitarianism were equally warm. He beat Germany and Italy to first place in recognizing Franco's regime in Spain.* A German officer was brought in to head the military college. The German consul, Baron von Hundelshausen, was at the same time manager of the official Mortgage Bank and even transacted his consular business in the bank's offices.

The earlier years of Martínez's rule had their progressive facet: he permitted others to undertake pressing financial reforms. A British expert was brought in to help establish a central bank. The planters, who had been losing their farms under the auctioneer's hammer, received relief through a moratorium. The Mortgage Bank, founded

---

*An impressive feat, since Hitler's Germany and Mussolini's Italy were Francisco Franco's military allies from the outset in overthrowing the Spanish republic, beginning in July 1936.

in 1934, reduced the interest rate from as much as 18 percent to 6 percent, and during the subsequent nine years did not foreclose a single mortgage. Rural credit banks, financed in part by the Mortgage Bank, were organized by Dr. Alfonso Rochac, an able young economist, to provide credit to small farmers on a cooperative basis. The purpose was to make it unnecessary for them to sell their crops to the first bidder. Since the coffee-planters bought corn for their peons from just these small farmers, the Coffee Association was less enthusiastic about the rural credit banks than about the Mortgage Bank that helped its members save their own hides.

Shortly after the 1932 Communist uprising, Martínez set up a Council of Social Defense to distribute land amongst poor peasants on a thirty-year installment basis. No provision, however, was made to provide credit for these settlers, and the project failed dismally. When in 1943 it was reorganized as *Mejoramiento Social S.A.,* ninety percent of the settlers were in arrears and half of these had lost their plots. Further land distribution was suspended; large estates bought from Martínez's henchmen at fancy sums for subdivision were now resold to other Martínez intimates for a small fraction of the purchase prices. These sundry financial institutions were linked by interlocking directorates. Around them bustled a group of bright young lawyers, who battened on the legal fees connected with their operations; their privately held stock was owned to an unhealthy extent by a few families. Because it yielded so much foaming milk to those at the dugs, the Mortgage Bank was dubbed *La Vaca* (The Cow) by its critics. Yet this cluster of semiofficial banks gave Salvador a mechanism for mild social reform that no other Central American republic could boast.

In public Martínez made a practice of claiming credit for these organizations. But they featured on the lengthy list of subjects forbidden to the press without special police permission. For he sensed that economic institutions of democratic intent would in the long run be incompatible with political despotism. Events proved him right. The April 1944 revolt was hatched amidst the Mortgage Bank's ledgers.

On coming to power, Martínez had sworn to respect the constitution that barred a second term. But he reelected himself in 1935 by the simple device of handing over the presidential sash to his war minister for six months before the "elections." Four years later he hit on something politically epoch-making—not the secret ballot but secret elections. He suddenly announced that open town-hall meetings had been held and had unanimously voted him President again. Nobody had seen these meetings, for which the constitution, moreover, made no provision. Early in 1944, when he again felt the tease of spring in his bones, residents of the capital were amazed to read in their papers one morning that the provinces had voted to amend the constitution to allow Martínez to remain at the helm until December 1949. Very visible in contrast were Martínez's police and spies, who respected neither persons nor homes.

After Pearl Harbor he had, perforce, to declare war on the Axis. And he could not but allow Allied democratic propaganda free scope. To meet this peril, he labored to prove that though to the naked eye his regime might resemble fascism, it was really the higher democracy toward which the United Nations were striving. Some of the definitions that he coined in the process put Lincoln to shame: "Democracy is love"; "Democracy is highways plus well-being"; "Lower forms of democracy emphasize rights, higher forms emphasize duties."

All of which apparently convinced the then United States minister, Robert Frazer, who publicly applauded Martínez when he trampled the constitution and took a third term. Flushed with good-neighborliness,* Washington was determined that insofar as Martínez was concerned its aid must be neither too little nor too late. Lend-lease planes, tanks, and automatic arms were sent to the tiny country until, in the words of a U.S. army officer formerly stationed there, "Salvador became per square mile one of the most heavily armed nations of the world."† Since Martínez could at best be only a most unreliable ally in the event of a Manchukuoan landing, the Salvadoran people concluded that the arms were intended against them. In letters smuggled out of the country, prominent Salvadorans pleaded with the State Department that the arms could be better used in Asia, Africa, or Europe. Their warnings went unheeded.

Martínez was clumsy enough to alienate the staunch sympathies of the coffee planters. Late in 1943 he increased the coffee export tax to resume payment on the foreign debt. The rich were touched in their pouches, and he fell from grace. He had never fitted into their social circle, and now they went out of their way to snub "the crackpot little Indian."

At the outbreak of the European war, a pro-U.S. democratic group had arisen in the Mortgage Bank, headed by a lanky, self-

---

*The so-called Good Neighbor Policy was launched by President Franklin D. Roosevelt during his first term of office, as a means of staunching Latin America's wounds from the armed United States interventions of previous decades, of which the most recent was in Nicaragua (evacuated by United States Marines on January 1, 1933).

†"Lend-lease" was a program launched by President Roosevelt to aid Britain in the early years of World War II. After 1941 it was extended to most Latin American countries, already lined up with the United States in its war effort. Equipment and munitions were supposedly delivered at low cost and with ample payment facilities.

effacing coffee expert, Agustín Alfaro Morán. It succeeded in ousting the Nazi manager and having the bank's statutes revised to prevent it from speculating in coffee and grain. Though educated in Germany and sympathetic to everything German, the new head of the bank, Héctor Herrera, surrounded himself with bright young men of democratic bent. With this new leadership, Martínez clashed head-long.

A series of foolhardy things began happening in a land which for over a decade had been trained for discretion. Acción Democrática, an organization founded to support the Allied cause and suppressed by Martínez, bestirred itself again. Three hundred citizens signed a petition to the Supreme Court asking that Martínez's constitutional amendments be declared illegal. An anonymous anti-Martínez pamphlet went into circulation at a prearranged zero hour throughout the republic. The writer was the dreamy-eyed economist Alfonso Rochac; the organizer of its distribution, a former football star, Ricardo Arbizú. Rochac, become definitely persona non grata with the regime, left to organize farm credit in the Dominican Republic shortly afterward. At the farewell banquet given him, the speeches had overtones of a call to arms. Arbizú and Rochac had already made a beginning of contacting young army officers of democratic leanings.

In December Martínez ordered the arrest of some twenty-five oppositionists charged with conspiring to assassinate him. Arbizú was amongst the twenty-five, but for eight days he barricaded himself in his house, until hunger and the promise of legal guarantees induced him to surrender. While holding the police at bay, he received the visit of Alfaro Morán and turned over to him the names of his army contacts.

Arturo Romero, a thirty-three-year-old doctor who had studied dermatology in Paris and dabbled with psychoanalysis, began calling regularly at Alfaro's home. To ward off the suspicions of the family and the servants, he brought along his hypodermic needles and injected Alfaro with vitamins while they chatted in hushed tones. A lyrically sincere, simple person, Romero was worshipped by the humble folk of the capital for forgetting to send bills when he treated them, and for his articles in the press on malnutrition. Most of the liaison with the army fell to Romero; his clinic was a good blind for visits from officers. Besides, Alfaro's doctor had forbidden him to drink, and in chats with military men it was customary to examine the political situation through the bottoms of glasses.

Before December a Coordination Committee of seven had been set up with Romero representing Acción Democrática, Alfaro the Mortgage Bank group, and the others the students, white-collar, and labor elements. The air force was wholly with the conspirators. In the First Infantry Regiment located in the capital's center, the commanding officer, General Tomás Marroquín, and his aides were in on the plot. It was there that all six lend-lease tanks were stationed, but there were only crews for three of them. Martínez was distrustful of the new gadgets and had dispersed the U.S.-trained crews to other duties. In Santa Ana, second city of the republic, where Romero's professional duties took him on frequent visits, the officers were wholeheartedly with the movement.

Early in February civilian and military leaders gathered at Alfaro's finca on the outskirts of the capital to put the final touches on the plans. The choice for military leader fell upon Marroquín, who, with his pro-German half-brother, Colonel Tito Calvo, had distinguished himself in the 1932 butchery of the peasants. Dealing with reactionary and often pro-Axis militarists was distasteful, but since Washington had armed the soldiery to the teeth, the civilians had no alternative. The uprising was fixed for April 2, a day after the troops would return to the capital from Easter maneuvers in La Paz department.

Alfaro had been entrusted to raise a fund for the support of the victims' families in the event of defeat. He collected $40,000, mostly from his own relatives. It was impossible to deposit such a sum in a bank without arousing suspicion; most of it was therefore entrusted to Dr. Enrique Molina, the eighty-two-year-old head of the Supreme Court, who would have been president in 1922, had the ruling clan not forced his rival down the nation's throat with a dose of lead. On receiving the money, Molina uttered prophetic words: "I distrust the military. They may betray us, or they may fight well and then take over. Frankly, I don't know which is worse."

The military did not fight well. Marroquín was haunted at once by the fear of Martínez and the dread of the civilians coming out on top. Foreseeing just that, Alfaro and a few other civilians went to Marroquín's barracks when the revolt began at 3 P.M. on Sunday. Troops were dispatched to protect the Ilopango airfield. A Captain Montalvo, employed in the War Ministry, had charge of the official seals and by forging the minister's name to an order obtained control of the telegraph and telephone exchange without firing a shot. Meanwhile Captain Montalvo's seventy-year-old father proceeded to the Sesto barracks near the cemetery and arrested the commander without complications.

During the first hours of fighting the key Zapote fortress alongside the presidential palace did not declare for either side. Telephone calls from the revolutionaries brought evasive replies, and emissaries sent to make the point more forcefully were arrested and later shot.

Only the Police Comandancia, housed in a fake gothic building reminiscent of a North American college, adhered resolutely to the government from the beginning. At 5:30 rebel planes dropped their bombs over it, but their appalling markmanship merely started fires blocks away. Rifle and machine-gun fire was trained on the Police Comandancia from the First Infantry headquarters, and the duel sputtered along all Sunday. Only in the evening was Alfaro informed by a subordinate officer of the First Infantry that there were mortars salted away in the barracks. The following morning they were brought out and tore a hole in the wall of the police building.

Instead of moving out his tanks and seizing the offensive, Marroquín shut himself up in his fortress. Arms were refused the civilians on the pretext that there were not sufficient to go around. Marroquín sat pat within his walls and eyed his civilian guests with mounting hostility.

And as though this were not enough, civilians started broadcasting a round-by-round report of the events from radio station YSP, which served to inform the enemy. One speaker announced Arturo Romero as chieftain of the revolution, and thus strained the tenuous arrangement between civilians and militarists.

YSP had an attentive listener. Martínez had gone to the port of La Libertad with his family that Sunday. Apprised of what was afoot, he deposited his wife with the British consular agent, and headed for San Salvador. From YSP's broadcast he knew that the police were holding out, and went there directly. For their part the revolutionaries dispatched a truckful of men to lie in wait for him on the road from La Libertad, some five kilometers below Santa Tecla. But instead of sticking to the left and blocking the road, the party, with a high sense of traffic regulations, kept to their right. Martínez's car swept past them. Before they could turn their truck around, the bird had flown.

At the Police Comandancia, Martínez's unworldly sangfroid gave new heart to his men. In a taunting drawl he urged a frightened officer to get behind a pillar so he wouldn't shake so. He himself walked leisurely amidst whizzing bullets and reminded the boys to aim well because munitions cost good money. He exaggerated: it was lend-lease stuff.

With a mind for every detail, he consulted an electrician, then dispatched parties to shoot up the transformers and plunge the capital into darkness. Next he passed to Zapote fortress, where his presence had an even more decisive effect. "If you are not with me," he quietly told the officers, "then go right ahead and shoot me." They were with him. On Monday an artillery duel boomed on for hours between Zapote and the First Infantry. The latter was a creaking building with a wooden superstructure, and Marroquín was obsessed with the idea of its catching fire. In order to surrender, he had first to shoo away his civilian visitors. He gave them the assignment of occupying the Normal School across the road.

By three P.M. Monday the main shooting was over. Only the Sesto

Barracks fought to the bitter end. What arms they could spare were distributed amongst civilians. They were promised reinforcements arriving from Santa Ana—some three hundred men, mostly civilians. These reached Mejicanos, a suburb of the capital, on Monday afternoon and were met by Tito Calvo in a tank. He ordered them to wait while he surveyed the terrain to the Sesto, but he never returned. The Santanecos hung around till Tuesday morning, and then started back home. At San Andrés, a few miles out, they were ambushed, and most of them slaughtered.

On Monday afternoon, after leaving the Santanecos to cool their heels, Tito Calvo proceeded in his tank to the U.S. embassy. The diplomatic corps, in session there, assumed that he had come to announce the victory of the revolution. He was like a person bemused. "We are beaten," he muttered. "But the fighting is still going on," the diplomats countered. U.S. Ambassador Walter Thurston declined asylum, because the State Department regulations did not permit it. He turned to his Latin American colleagues, whose governments practiced the thing. One by one, they excused themselves. This one had a sick wife, another had not yet presented his credentials. Besides, Calvo was an officer on the active list to whom the right of asylum did not extend. Calvo nevertheless stayed on, for almost four hours. Members of the embassy who went out to examine his tank found that it had plenty of gas and oil to carry him to the frontier, with munitions to boot. Finally, Thurston informed Martínez of Calvo's presence, and troops were sent around to arrest him. He was shot a week later. Others who reached the embassy in quest of asylum, both officers and civilians, were likewise turned away.

Romero and Alfaro were at the radio station at four P.M. on Monday when they learned that a white flag had been hoisted over the First Infantry. They escaped by way of the back door. Hidden by his devoted patients, Romero stayed on in the capital, moving from home to home, till Friday, when he headed for the Honduran frontier, disguised and equipped with false papers. Alfaro made his way to Santa Ana, where he found the city in the hands of drunken civilians who had taken the celebration of their effortless triumph too seriously.

It was Easter when I arrived at San Salvador. The figures of Christ bearing His cross, paraded through the city, were poignant in their symbolism. You could sense the taut nerves of the people who were swarming the streets; the women wore black, even those with no relatives of their own to mourn. An eight o'clock curfew had been slapped on, and each morning there were telltale pools of blood on the pavements. The nights were hideously staccato with rifle fire. Platoons of heavily armed police patrolled the city. Prisoners were rounded up and herded to the police station, from which grisly tales of torture emerged.

It was there that Jorge Pinto, editor of the *Diario Latino,* arrested in December, was shot point blank by his guards as soon as the fighting outside commenced. The bullet had ripped his bladder and come out through his leg, so that he urinated through his haunch as he lay in a pool of his blood. It was a fitting accolade for Pinto. No other journalist was so hated and feared by the dictator. The previous December, the *Latino* had appeared with a remarkable back page, made up of sardonic headings and texts: "Corn Prices Within Reach of All. Thanks to Energetic Action of Government"; "Street-Cleaning in Capital Superb"; "Water So Plentiful in Villages That It Flows in Veritable Cascades," etc. The censors did not dare suppress anything so laudatory, and the whole country chuckled for months over the malicious intent. For a whole year Pinto had to be confined to his bed in a plaster cast, until he was well enough to be flown to the United States for a series of operations.

Most of the rebel leaders had headed for Honduras, fearing the reception that they would be accorded in Guatemala by Ubico, dean and pacesetter amongst Central American dictators. Yet no harm befell the few that did reach Guatemala. They had, of course, to report to the police three times a day, but that was merely an augmented dose of one of the amenities of Guatemalan life of the period. They were received at all only because Ubico had fallen out with his neighbor. The aristocratic Ubico, who had always despised Martínez as an addle-pated little Indian, was offended by the asylum that Martínez had given some Guatemalan exiles a few months earlier. When Ubico asked that they be gagged and shadowed in accordance with the 1934 secret police treaty of the four Central American dictatorships,* Martínez replied loftily that Salvador was a free country whose constitution permitted no such thing. Then, too, there was El Salvador's recent denunciation of the free-trade treaty between the two countries. All this redounded to the advantage of the bedraggled fugitives who crossed the Paz River into Guatemala without knowing just what to expect.

---

*The four dictatorships were those of Maximiliano Hernández Martínez (El Salvador), Jorge Ubico (Guatemala), Tiburcio Carías Andino (Honduras) and Anastasio Somoza García (Nicaragua).

2

Anticlimax Becomes Climax

I LEFT SALVADOR TO FILE MY STORY to *Time* and got back to Guatemala shortly after the first fourteen rebel leaders had been sent before the firing squad. At the court-martial their lawyers were grudgingly conceded two minutes each to defend them; a claque shouting for the death penalty provided a backdrop for the proceedings. Martínez went about the killings with a gourmet's finesse. Marroquín's son was brought to witness his father's death. Martínez not only executed two sons of the Gavidia family, which had helped him out of the gutter, but with a fine sense of propriety penned a note to their parents expressing his condolences.

Disguised as a peon and carrying false papers, Arturo Romero made for the Honduran frontier with a guide. At the very border he was surprised by a group of National Guards, who began hacking away at him with machetes. They would have finished him off there and then; but his cries, emerging from his shattered jaw as much as from his mouth, had so macabre a ring that the Guards froze in their tracks. Romero was taken to the hospital at San Miguel, where two weeks passed before his real identity was discovered. Already condemned to death in absentia, his execution awaited only his recovery. But the doctors attending him were resolved not to pronounce him well until the last possible moment. In the incredible events that were to follow, snatching Romero from the firing squad became one of the compelling motives of the people.

The incident of Tito Calvo and the shut embassy doors preyed on the public mind. The institution of asylum has deep roots in Latin America as a means of assuaging the effects of frequent revolutions. During the Spanish civil war, Latin American legations rented entire hotels to house Franquistas in Madrid, while their consulates in Franco territory sheltered antifascists. At the Pan-American conferences of 1928 and 1933, the United States, because of some obscure State Department tradition, refused to adhere to treaties regulating the conditions of asylum. But there is no need of treaties to extend

18

asylum: it is recognized as part of unwritten international law. In 1929 the United States legation in Guatemala felt free to give haven to Jorge Ubico, pursued by his foes, before the same legation imposed him on Guatemala as dictator.

I quote my letter to *Time* on the matter:

"The issue stands out all the more clearly because Thurston, the U.S. ambassador here, is a well-intentioned man who from the first tried limiting the carnage. But his hands were tied. After imposing a good many brutal dictators in Pre-Good Neighbor days, the State Department might at least have tempered the enduring effects of their conduct with the humanitarian institution of asylum. No amount of comic strips published by the Rockefeller Office can remove the nasty taste left in Salvadoran mouths by the role of the U.S. embassy in recent days.*

"The people here drank their sedition directly from the slogans of the United Nations. It was possible for the *Diario Latino* to conduct an anti-Martínez campaign for a whole year merely by featuring phrases of Roosevelt and Churchill on the Four Freedoms.† These words were inspiration and promise to the people. Perhaps naively, they believed them. They were convinced that by its utterances the United States could not look unkindly on their efforts to unfurl the Atlantic Charter on this bit of Pacific coast.‡ Their leaders botched matters, and the first thing they knew, the embassy doors were slammed in their faces when they sought asylum from their hangmen.

"If Washington's hands are tied by its nonadherence to asylum treaties, it should get busy and negotiate a few of the things. For the sun hangs low, and a lot of chickens are coming home to roost. A few more episodes like that of last week and Nelson Rockefeller can close shop and go back to the oil business.

"Besides, are there no Pure Food Laws that would require the

---

*The young Nelson Rockefeller functioned at the time as "Coordinator of Inter-American Affairs" in the State Department, which was headed by Cordell Hull. His office distributed gratis throughout the continent Allied propaganda in the form of comic strips.

†President Roosevelt set forth the Four Freedoms for which the Allies were fighting in a speech before Congress on 6 January 1941: freedom of speech and worship, freedom from want, and freedom from fear. The latter included general reduction of armaments so that no nation could commit an act of aggression against its neighbor in any part of the world. Note that the Four Freedoms were proclaimed eleven months before Japan's attack on the United States.

‡President Roosevelt and Prime Minister Churchill signed the Atlantic Charter on a British warship on 14 August 1941. Its eight points were the basis of the future United Nations Declaration in 1942.

Coordinator's outfit to attach the following note to their publications: "Warning: The High Principles Expressed Herein Are Purely Propaganda, to Be Taken Seriously Only at Your Own Risk"?

"On Tuesday Thurston saw Martínez and told him that the Allies would judge him by the moderation he showed in his reprisals. The following Monday, the mother and sister of a prominent man amongst the arrested asked Thurston to intervene to save his life (he is the son of an American). Thurston declined because the son is Salvadoran. Besides, he added, Martínez had assured him that there would be no executions. The sister jumped up and told Thurston he had been lied to, and the executions had begun in the graveyard at that very moment.

"She was right. One civilian and ten officers were shot that afternoon. The officers included Julio Sosa, second-in-command of the air force, who had taught the entire force to fly, and with whom Martínez was merely settling an old grudge. The one civilian was Victor Marín, 33, who had acted as liaison between the civilian and military rebels. During a whole night he was tortured to wrest from him secrets that could have sent dozens to the firing squad. He didn't break . . . apart from the small matter of bones. When they took him to his execution, he had to be propped up—both arms were fractured, an eye gouged out, his shoulder dislocated, his knee smashed, his hands a bloody pulp. When the priest asked him: 'Victor, are you afraid of death?' he replied: 'No, padre, it is my body and not my spirit that is shaking.'

"Fourteen have thus far been executed officially—but no auditor goes over the accounts. Workers and private soldiers just don't rate a court-martial or a full-dress execution. I have yet to find a Salvadoran, high or low, who is pro-Martínez. Priests have lent their robes to help refugees in their flight. Protestant missionaries have done their bit.

"When the *Time* bundle arrived, it was whisked to the police headquarters and shot, beg pardon, expurgated. Nevertheless people have been circulating from hand to hand, translations of your piece along with the fine editorial of the Panama *Star-Herald* of the 13th."

The lad who carried this letter out of the country had two brothers executed by Martínez. He himself was arrested at the U.S. embassy and escaped a similar fate only because of the left-handed intervention of Ambassador Thurston, anything but proud of the conduct forced upon him. My letter served as the basis for a couple of columns in *Time,* which drew an anonymous reply by the embassy in the *Diario de Hoy.* In it was quoted chapter and verse of a State Department circular laying down the regulations governing asylum. In essence they set forth that asylum might be extended to those threatened by mob violence, but never to anybody pursued by the constituted authorities. In less stuffy language, a dictator fleeing the retribution of his people would find embassy doors ajar, but for democrats hunted by the dictator's goons they would be bolted. It was an elucidation that could not fail to impress the Salvadoran public.

I was later to meet Chencho Castellano Rivas, who earned his living as radio announcer. Before the revolt he used to broadcast the following spot several times daily for Sterling Products, an American firm manufacturing Mejoral aspirins and Glostora hair goo: "You don't ask for liberty, you conquer it. United, the United Nations will triumph." Sterling Products had the slogan from the Office of the Coordinator of Inter-American Affairs, which was blissfully unaware of the dynamite it was sending into Latin America's tyrant-ridden lands. On the day of the revolt, Chencho had continued broadcasting, and announced Martínez's overthrow to the country. When the debacle came, he was one of those who fled to the U.S. embassy, only to be refused. He was hidden, however, in the embassy building without the official knowledge of the staff. In those trying days Chencho's mind wandered with frequency to the second part of his Sterling Products spot: "For your headaches take Mejoral." Both Mejoral and the United States of America lost much popularity in El Salvador in that dark period. Finally Chencho was smuggled out of the embassy disguised as a monk. Accompanied by two bona-fide friars, he walked through the police lines to the Peruvian legation, where he shed his cassock.

I was also to learn of the escape of young Captain Montalvo, who had taken over the telegraph office for the rebels. Smarting under the role forced on them by Washington's rules, members of the U.S. embassy had hidden him in a crate of files and driven it over the Guatemalan frontier under the protection of a diplomatic license.

The behavior of the Mexican ambassador, Francisco Mora Plancarte, was even less prepossessing than that of the State Department. Mora, a pushing young lawyer from Michoacán, had served a term in Congress before being appointed to El Salvador; he naturally spoke a wicked revolution, and had even been in on the plot for Martínez's overthrow. Yet at the same time he collected his rake-off on the illegal export of cattle to Mexico that Martínez and his friends were carrying on. His loyalties were thus divided, and when the revolt failed, he grew panicky at the thought of the consequences he might suffer. Mexico has always recognized the right of asylum, and befriended democratic movements in Latin America. Yet when the worsted revolutionaries reached the Mexican embassy—a good eight miles beyond the city limits—they were turned back on one pretext or another: he couldn't be expected to run a hotel; Martínez would batter down the embassy with his tanks and artillery.

I paid two visits to the Mexican ambassador to ascertain the facts. He swore that he had offered shelter to all who came knocking. In order to convince me he even brought to his embassy one of the revolutionaries he had previously dumped in a downtown boarding house. (When I left, he redeposited the fugitive in the boarding house). In my hotel lobby, I found a Mexican journalist who was making one of those periodic tours through Central America that offer lush pickings for certain sections of the Mexican press. For fantastic prices which bear no relation to what such articles fetch in Mexico, the dictators are done up rosily—in pages that few people read. Feeling that it would be better for a Mexican to break the story of Mora Plancarte in Mexico, I suggested to my colleague that he look into the role of his embassy. He did—to the extent of blackmailing Mora for $200. On my return to Mexico I gave the facts to *Excelsior* and *Universal.* Mora was recalled and retired from the diplomatic service.

The one diplomat who covered himself with glory was the Peruvian chargé d'affaires, Julio Noriega Pasos. A former journalist with an undiplomatically impish grin, Noriega threw the legation gates wide open. I visited the legation and found some fifty-odd fugitives living *en famille* with the chargé and sleeping sardinelike on the floors. Hams, cheeses, fruit, and sundry provisions poured into the legation from well-wishers outside, so that Noriega's pantry, at least, was not picked clean, though he should not have minded that either. The place was a besieged fortress with no other ramparts than the tenuous principles of international law. The guests roamed the spacious grounds while the police in full force kept menacing watch outside. Now and again they would encroach on its property, and Noriega would have to argue the matter with the Salvadoran Foreign Office. For the first couple of weeks Martínez refused the fugitives a safe-conduct with which to leave the country. When he finally yielded to the firmness of the Lima government, he insisted on the letter of the law and demanded that the fugitives go to distant Peru. Without spending a penny of its taxpayers' money to bribe the Salvadorans into loving it, Peru had acquired fabulous popularity in this remote little land.

The Spanish chargé scored a touchdown for Franco's blood-runs-thicker-than-politics propaganda by receiving two democrats turned down by the Americans. Ubico not only sheltered three revolutionaries who reached the Guatemalan legation, but even sent a special man to bully Martínez into recognizing sanctuary for another two who had ducked into the consul's private residence.

Martínez's bloody instincts betrayed him. Killing seemed to him a mystic purifying rite. When he might have consolidated his victory with a show of clemency, he crowded the prisons to the point of suffocation; some eight hundred were rounded up in the capital alone. Though there were only forty-four death sentences, Salvadorans knew only too well that in Central America being court-martialed is in a way a mark of social distinction to which few ordinary citizens can aspire. Groups of trucks could be seen leaving the city filled with humbler folk and returning empty. The archbishop went to Martínez and told him that too many of his parishioners were clad in mourning; he appealed to him in God's name to stop further executions. The rumor ran the rounds that Martínez replied: "In Salvador I am God."

A mass was announced at San Francisco Church for the souls of the dead; the vast square before the church was thronged with women in black. Spies stood at the church door jotting down the names of those who entered. Some defiantly spelled out their names to the informers. And when the church was jammed, with thousands overflowing, the outraged faithful were informed that the police would not permit the mass.

Countless anti-Martínez leaflets circulated with the request that each reader make ten copies to pass on. In a mechanized age the typewriter was to prove mightier than the machine gun. Children flaunted the seditious sheets before the police and dared them to make an arrest. At first the police obliged, but they tired of the game soon enough. It was a groundswell of popular indignation that dwarfed anything ever hatched by politicians. Suddenly, no one knew at whose prompting or how, it broke as a general strike. The people, who from time immemorial had served as a doormat for hobnailed military boots, now reared up, fierce, towering, and a bit incredulous of their new might.

The doctors were in the forefront. They submitted a memorandum to the government demanding liberty of the press, amnesty for civilian rebels, and reinstatement of doctors dismissed from the hospitals. When this ultimatum was delivered to Martínez, he would not even touch the paper, but ordered his secretary to burn it. Fifty members of hospital staffs signed the document, but when the time limit expired, one hundred and thirty-five of Salvador's one hundred and fifty practicing doctors closed their offices. Emergency clinics were kept open for urgent cases; rich patients paid through the nose, the poor only nominally, and the proceeds went into the strike fund.

Bank employees marched out, and only the central bank maintained nominal operations in the shadow of machine guns. The strikers had difficulty persuading some of the smaller food shops to keep open to supply the population with essentials; students volunteered to bake bread. Justices of the peace and most government employees failed to show up at their offices. Parodying Martínez's famed definition of democracy, the strikers sported "The strike is love" on their placards.

The university students were everywhere, the soul of the movement. It was they who helped push the doctors into a defiant attitude. In agreement with their professors they padlocked the university. Secondary and primary schools were not far behind. After the military coup Martínez had suspended the independent papers, but now he pressured vainly to get them to publish again. Paralysis overtook the railways. The staff of the Interamerican Sanitation Project filed out.

To discredit the strike, the police released criminals with instructions to foment disorder. But bystanders, seeing a leather shop broken into, restored the stolen articles to their owner and thrashed the culprits.

Money was contributed by the fistful to the families of the strikers. For once, El Salvador's wealthy eased their pursestrings. If ever a nation marched united, it was the Salvadorans battling to cast off their twelve-year-old tyranny.

In the midst of this engulfing tide, I interviewed Martínez.

The presidential residence nestled on a hill beneath the Zapote fortress's brow. A creaky two-story structure, it had served as a normal school before Martínez's day. The original presidential palace was near the center of town, but Martínez, preferring his loving people at arm's length, transferred the school to the palace, and himself went up the hill to huddle under the fortress. In the spacious patio three deers nibbled and cavorted—an incongruous pastoral scene. The corridors were lined with waiting officers and civilians, including a delegation from the striking doctors, but Martínez received me almost at once.

You would never have suspected this lean, loose-slung, droopmouthed vegetarian of being a sinister killer. He created the impression of a benign, boneless grandpa. The bees in his bonnet had honeyed his tongue; and Spanish became mush in his mouth. His only comment on the strike was that schoolchildren didn't like going to school the world over. The revolt, he explained, had been the work of malcontents that exist in every country. "Our intellectuals read a lot of books, and then try remaking the world according to their favorite author. The workers have no part in the present sedition."

He seemed embittered at the desertion of a good part of the

propertied classes. He painted a heroic picture of the Communist leader Farabundo Martí, whom he had had executed in 1932: unselfish and disinterested, Martí was a magnificent organizer who had made his life amongst the peons, eaten their sorry fare, shared their hard mats. In part, of course, this was intended to limn Martínez's own role as dragon-killer, but one could detect a note of regret at having thrown in his lot with the privileged against the poor from whose ranks he had risen. When we discussed the Communist revolt of 1932, he insisted that the army had killed "only" two thousand peasants.

On concrete political matters he was somewhat reticent, but when the conversation veered to "transcendental" topics, he mumbled on in mellifluent tones with no notion of the passing of time. "Scientists, having split the atom, found it to consist of energy. And what is the mind, what are emotions? Energy. Science has now only to realize that mind, matter and the emotions, all revealed as different forms of energy, are but aspects of the universal mind. Science is being forced to adopt the theosophist position." And then abruptly: "I know what you are thinking at this moment."

I started in dismay, but his further rambling set me at ease. "For telepathy sends waves from your mind to mine."

I asked whether his thirteen years of spiritual missionary work had yielded any visible results. He pondered the question, and replied: "Yes, there is more spiritual life in El Salvador than you think. Why, just a few weeks ago I spoke before the primary teachers of Santa Ana on transcendental themes, and you ought to have heard what spiritual questions they asked."

He assured me that ether waves informed him of the thought processes of Churchill and Roosevelt at that very moment. Grizzled and bent, he appeared perfectly unruffled by the tempest gathering around him; the words oozed from his mouth endless and unhurried. After an hour, when my struggle to keep a straight face was becoming too difficult, it was I who closed the interview. I left under the spell of a rarely addled but powerful personality.

Martínez did manage to give a thought to worldly things. All day Friday, May 5, trucks were transferring munitions and armament from the First Infantry barracks to Zapote. The First Infantry Regiment, which had been with the revolution in April, was disbanded and replaced with conscripts from the eastern part of the republic. In the east, where peasants raised grain, cotton, henequen, and cattle on modest lands of their own, there was not the same seething discontent as amongst the rural proletarians of the West. While driving to the airport the following afternoon, I could see recruits being herded into the capital, tied by their thumbs in pairs. That was an old Salvadoran custom. Apropos of it there is the anecdote of a general reporting to headquarters during one of the Central American wars: "Am sending batch of volunteers. Please return the rope."

Feeling that the bulk of the coffee-planters had abandoned him, Martínez directed a demagogic appeal to the poor. He broadcast to the nation, blaming the unrest upon the rich, whose frivolous troublemaking he contrasted with the law-abiding labors of the peasant tilling a straight furrow and irrigating it with his sweat. His opponents were resorting to a "war of nerves, borrowed directly from the Nazi arsenal."

The strikers indeed did what they could to rob the nerveless dictator of his sleep. When the United States military authorities, evacuating the bulk of their troops from their Guatemalan base, asked the strikers to allow two trains of empty coaches and tank cars to move from La Unión on Fonseca Gulf to Guatemala, they cheerfully consented. But care was taken to let word of this reach Martínez, to create the impression that Washington was sending troops against him from Guatemala.

Later, in exile, Martínez was to complain bitterly that the strike had provided him with no targets to shoot at. But it was not that he hadn't tried. His appeal to the peasants fell flat; their memories of 1932 were too vivid. But this did not prevent him from bringing hundreds of ugly, machete-wielding desperadoes into the capital, all primed for action against the "rich." On such occasions the term "rich" is defined to include anyone outfitted with shoes and a necktie.

As the scene was set, Martínez could have slaughtered thousands, without the regulations of the State Department (which had given him the lend-lease tools for the job) permitting Ambassador Thurston to crook a little finger to restrain him. For that, as the sequel was to prove and every Salvadoran knew in advance, was all that was required to stave off the bloodbath. Then a miracle occurred. Merciful chance had it that Martínez's first victim was seventeen-year-old Joe Wright, son of an American family resident in El Salvador for a couple of generations. Young Wright was shot through the back of the head by a policeman while standing in front of his home. He had been mistaken for an elder brother who was active in the student movement.

Given this opening, Thurston became a lion rampant. He visited the scene of Wright's assassination and then paid a formal call on Martínez accompanied by his two secretaries and the uniformed military attaché. With an icy regard for protocol, he insisted on being introduced to Martínez, though they had conversed hundreds of times. In turn he presented each member of his staff. He announced in biting tones that he had ordered the suspension of the Pan American Airways service to Salvador. It was his duty to protect American lives. One had already been lost. What could he inform his government?

His eyes on the floor, Martínez mumbled: "You have strikes in your country too."

"They are economic strikes. Is that all I can inform my government, Mr. President?"

"I can only add that I lament very much what has happened."

"Very well, Mr. President, I will inform my government that Your Excellency laments very much what has happened."

The inflection of a U.S. ambassador's voice in Central America is often enough to make the leopard change his spots and the buzzards sing like canaries. Central Americans had often seen these vaudeville tricks practiced—in the olden days as black magic, more recently to occasional benign effect. That is why they are unimpressed by the fiction that the United States ambassador, like the minister of Panama, is without power to influence internal politics. Some of Martínez's ministers had already been urging him to pack and leave. Martínez was no quitter; he would brave the elements of heaven and hell. But when Thurston turned on the faucets of his cold ire, he decided the jig was up.

He offered to resign the presidency, and pleaded for thirty days to wind up his interests before leaving the country. The strikers, however, announced that the strike would continue until he left Salvadoran soil. He deposited power in his War Minister Andrés Menéndez. A few days later a black limousine whizzed across the Guatemalan frontier. It carried the Maestro into exile.

Poems, some moving, others wordy, have been dedicated to young Wright's memory. When a popular regime comes into being in El Salvador, his sacrifice will be recorded in bronze.

3

Man on a Horse

DURING THE DRY SEASON the Suchiate is not much of a river; you are hard put to believe that it has washed away so many bridges linking Mexico and Guatemala. Yet when the barefooted boatman rows you across, it is clear at once you have passed into another world. The dust and dryness of the Mexican side give way to lush frond; spanking banana leaves tell of breezes that don't choose to cross the Suchiate. Lizards the size of small dogs dart under shacks on stilts, and langorous coconut palms sway with pride at having put out a bottled beverage that holds it own against Coca-Cola.

You climb to the highlands and find cedar and pine with purple overtones against a crystalline sky; cactus is pleasantly scarce. Guatemala is a well-watered land, and the people, too, reflect the change. While the Mexican peasant in his dust-colored sarape has borrowed something of the aridness of his fields, the Guatemalan Indian strips the rainbow for his dress. The landscape has none of Mexico's harsh tragedy. It greets the eye with a warmth and gladness that do not extend to human relationships. In the background, drowsy rather than extinct, the volcanoes are ever present.

The Spaniards did not bring the feudal system unchanged to America, as the Normans had carried it across the English Channel. European feudalism had developed on spacious plains; however wretched the roads, the wheel served as the basis of land transport. In Central America the *conquistadores* found tight valleys and tossing mountains. The wheel that they brought with them meant little in such a setting. Besides, subject labor was plentiful, human lives cheap. For centuries in Guatemala's highlands, the wheel remained of secondary importance in transport. The first luxury automobiles that came to the country three decades ago were carried over mountains on sturdy Indian backs to the coffee plantations. The dirt roads were used far more by load-lugging pedestrians than by rolling vehicles.

Feudalism in Europe implied a certain equilibrium: mutual responsibilities of lord and vassal that the new commercialism, creating urgent money needs, was just beginning to corrode. In the New World the conquerors encountered none of the trammels that tradition set back home. With no great mineral wealth at hand in the Kingdom of Guatemala, they attempted to grind from the bones of the Indians the treasures that geology had denied them. Even the women, spared elsewhere, were reduced to slavery; thousands of Indians were sold into bondage in Peru and Panama. Their resistance is one of the neglected epics of humankind. First came armed uprisings. Then the refusal to sow crops in the hope of starving the Spaniard out of the country—a campaign that, hardened into blind custom, has endured partly to our century. Soon the Indians abstained from begetting new slaves; mothers killed their babes at birth. Waves of suicide alarmed the slavemasters. Overwork and disease did the rest. During the first sixty years of Spanish rule, the Indian population in Central America declined by a third. Resistance, beaten down in its open manifestations, found refuge in the hidden recess of the soul.

This heritage of four centuries still weighs heavily: the Guatemalan Indians do not bear their burden blithely. There is something tenebrous and foreboding about their tight-lipped sullenness in the presence of whites. They are a tiny folk, the women often standing no more than four feet; and their unsmiling faces contrast with the cascade of color on their backs. Left little incentive for working, they applied their wits and passion to cheating their taskmasters of as much labor as possible. They were content to plant their corn and beans by poking holes in the near-vertical plots that had been left them, and worked no more on the coffee plantations than was unavoidable. On the whole they lived outside the pale of money economy. Two societies existed side by side, the Indian and the Ladino (mixed-breed, but generally applied to anyone wearing European clothes): they came into contact only when they rubbed against each other. In the highland towns there were even two municipal administrations—the Indian and the Ladino. Sealed off from the Ladino by language, culture, and festering memories, the Indian lived under the despotism of his tribal elders.

The servitude of the Indian had suffused its venom throughout society as a whole. There was a deep-seated inclination for man to treat his fellow with the toe of his boot. Since independence from Spain, the Ladinos had periodically aspired to setting up within their own ranks a democracy nestling cozily on the Indians' backs. But to keep the Indian in his place, a ruthless military machine not creaking with scruples has been required. And having that at his beck, the ruler has usually come to crack the whip over Guatemalan society as a whole. For their part, the Indians, with no interest in Ladino politics,

have been easy dupes of tyrants for use against the libertarian stir-
rings of the towns.

After independence the Liberals tried breaking the power of the
absurd colonial aristocracy, descendants of muleteers and petty merchants become so blue-blooded that "the rats could run under the
arches of their feet." But in the fanatical Indians the clerical Conservatives found an anchor for their rule. An illiterate swineherd,
Rafael Carrera, roused the Indians with the charge that the Liberal
government had brought on a cholera epidemic by poisoning wells.
Doctors sent by the authorities to combat the disease were made to
swallow entire bottles of their drugs. Twice the barbarian hordes took
and pillaged the capital, and for a quarter of a century Carrera
guided the country's destinies.

In 1872, after Carrera's death, the Liberals came to power under
the former horse thief Justo Rufino Barrios. Church and State were
separated, clerical property confiscated. But that was the extent of
Barrios's liberalism. The old export staple, cochineal, had been finally
ruined by parasites and analine dyes, and Barrios promoted the
spread of coffee to fill the gap. For the Indians coffee proved a bitter
brew. They were driven off their lands to make room for the new
crop, and the vagrancy laws were tightened to exact more forced
labor needed for the blushing berries. It was no atmosphere condu-
cive to liberty. Barrios ran the country like a feudal domain. His
favorite executioner, Sixto Pérez, haunted the nightmares of a generation of Guatemalans, until Barrios finally had him soaked in petroleum and burned. In every essential Barrios set the pattern for
Guatemalan dictators of the coffee era. When a race track opened up,
betting lagged because Barrios's horses invariably carried off the
purses contributed by the government. Legions of poets and courte-
sans danced attendance on the gruff despot, who would receive
visitors stretched out on a couch with his face toward the wall. The
millions that he accumulated through his control of the liquor trade
and other enterprises were later to enable his young widow to marry
into the Spanish aristocracy. He differed from subsequent dictators
only in his economic vision. He built the first railway, brought quinine
from the East Indies. In 1885, he died at the head of his troops while
trying to unify Central America by the sword.

Under the next long-term president, Manuel Estrada Cabrera
(1896–1920), large-scale U.S. investment appeared on the scene; his
rule rested not only on the needs of the coffee-planters, but had the
active backing of the State Department. Around this provincial lawyer
of humble origins rose a swelling chorus of international praise. He
had a mania for laying cornerstones of hospitals and schools. With
those single stones he killed more than the proverbial two birds: his

speeches on such occasions, reproduced in the international press, earned him a reputation abroad as a progressive ruler, though that was as far as the construction ever got. A Chilean mission sent to study his celebrated system of trade schools found nothing, not even buildings. But he did throw up Attic temples to Minerva throughout the country, in honor of learning. He consulted witch doctors with regularity, and spent long hours in meditation before a mirror in the habit of a Dominican monk.

If your business took you past ten booths on election day, you voted ten times for Estrada Cabrera, sole candidate, at the risk of imprisonment, torture, and assassination. On one occasion the recorded balloting was three times the country's population.

He fingered poison vials with the deftness of a Borgia, and once tried the technique on a U.S. minister. His assassins tracked opponents to the farthest corners of the earth.* After each of the periodic attempts to assassinate him, hundreds would be done to death. Indians were herded to work on the plantations of his friends, and the army officers who rounded them up kept four-fifths of their pay.

Guatemalan tyrants have, by tradition, a deep dread of earthquakes. For they betray to the people that there are after all forces beyond their control. When a quake and volcanic eruption destroyed dozens of highland towns in 1902, Cabrera dispatched criers to proclaim that the epicenter of the disturbance was in Mexico and that nothing serious was afoot. Amidst the rubble that had been Quezaltenango the crier had to hold a lantern aloft at noonday to read the manifesto, so blackened was the sky with volcanic ash. But read it he did. Then as an afterthought one of Cabrera's palace poets admitted in doggerel that the earth had trembled, but that Cabrera, seizing it by the poles, steadied it.

President Wilson's Fourteen Points, though beamed on Europe, penetrated the fog of this tyranny.† Oppositionists, seeking cover under the century-old ideal of unifying the Central American states, organized a Unionist party for Cabrera's overthrow. The movement took on such momentum that in 1920 the dictator's hand-picked assembly declared him insane and accorded him an indefinite leave of absence abroad for a cure. In reply Cabrera bombarded the city from the surrounding fortresses for six days. Civilians had to conquer it inch by inch, and the streets were strewn with more than a thousand

---

*As in the case of former President Manuel Lisandro Barillas, assassinated by his order in Mexico City in 1907.

†On 8 January 1918 President Wilson announced a program of fourteen points for peace following World War I, which *inter alia* laid the foundation of the League of Nations.

dead. When he surrendered, Cabrera was confined to a room of the military academy until his death three years later.

The so-called Unionist regime, headed by Carlos Herrera, was born with the mark of death on it. Four of the six cabinet members were former Cabrera men; only two were Unionist. By cancelling two onerous contracts granted by Cabrera to U.S. concerns—one transferring the former German power company to Electric Bond and Share, and the other with the International Railways of Central America for the building of a spur line to the Salvadoran frontier—the Unionist regime ran afoul of Washington.* The wartime decree confiscating German properties was repealed, but some of them had meanwhile been purchased for a song from their German owners by people close to the regime. A treaty of federation was signed with El Salvador and Honduras, and a Federal Congress and Council set up in Tegucigalpa, Honduras. Then, on December 2, 1921, the army under General José María Orellana overthrew the Unionist government. At once the State Department announced that it would tolerate no military action by the other two components of the Central American Federation to reestablish the legitimate authorities in Guatemala.† Recognition of Orellana was not long in coming, and the United States railway and power trust got back the concessions.

Orellana died before he could help himself to a second term. There were several contenders for the succession, and to permit General Lázaro Chacón a headstart before the death became known, the corpse was brought back seated upright in a limousine between the widow and the police chief. Chacón won the following elections against General Jorge Ubico.

Ubico had become a sort of perennial aspirant to the presidency. The bald spot on his head was growing bigger, and with it the uneasy feeling that history was passing him by. By a happy coincidence, the United Fruit Company was languishing with similar unfulfilled desire. Because of the ravages of disease on the Atlantic coast, it had planned

---

*Both International Railways of Central America (IRCA) and Electric Bond & Share were to be integral parts of the transnational United Fruit Co. (UFCO), which penetrated Guatemala and grew like a giant in the subregion thanks to limitless concessions by Estrada Cabrera. The overthrow of Herrera and the dictatorship of Orellana were part of UFCO's colonizing project in Guatemala with collaboration of the local army and external support of the U.S. State Department.

†Under the terms of the Unionist pact, any steps that signatory states might take to restore the head of one of them to his functions after overthrow by military coup were completely legitimate. Thus the United States's action not only installed another military dictator in a Central American nation, but also dealt a death-blow to the project of unifying the isthmus republics.

starting operation of the Pacific side. But its proposed concessions for such a plantation, and the building of a modern Pacific port, stuck in the throat of Congress. The deputies were critical of sweeping tax exemptions, and the likelihood of independent banana exporters being crushed. Congress, however, was not to stand in the way for long.

Chacón retired in 1930 due to failing health, and his first substitute, an inept businessman, stepped into his shoes as provisional president. Eight days later came a barracks coup headed by a hard-bitten militarist, General Manuel Orellana. Washington, alleging a 1923 treaty against Central American regimes originating in violence, refused to recognize him. U.S. Minister Sheldon Whitehouse, applying pressure and blandishment, was instrumental in negotiating a deal whereby Orellana withdrew for the sum of $40,000, the promise of a consular job for his son, and the building of an iron bridge on the road to his farm. For good measure, the gallant general helped himself to the national lottery treasury; no prizes were distributed that month. For provisional president, Minister Whitehouse picked José Reyes, an illiterate septuagenarian general much esteemed at the U.S. legation for his loyalty. When Cabrera was toppling, he had, as commander of San José fortress, bombarded the capital. Reyes, indeed, was of sterling presidential timber, not only brave under fire but sage in council. To Cabrera, who had asked his advice on how to dominate the revolution in those memorable days, he had offered a simple solution: "Shoot the diplomatic corps."

A parliamentary commission called on Minister Whitehouse. Deputy Jorge García Granados reminded him that in the United States illiterates were denied the vote, and it was not fitting that a U.S. minister should impose an illiterate president on Guatemala. Whitehouse yielded on the matter of provisional president, but on one thing he was adamant: only General Jorge Ubico would be recognized as president after the elections. Besides, Ubico had promised him that he would not seek reelection after his first term, and would be respectful of civil liberties.

In a hastily improvised polling, Jorge Ubico was elected, and assumed the presidency on February 14, two weeks before schedule.* The United Fruit Company obtained its concessions, and Guatemala a worthy successor of Cabrera.

Ubico made no bones of the fact that he considered himself a

---

*His term should have started on 15 March 1931, to end on 15 March 1937. He began it ahead of time by force, and remained in power several years over the limit also by force, despite the credulous trust of Minister Whitehouse.

local edition of Napoleon. During his youth there was, indeed, a certain facial resemblance that he did his utmost to bring out. A Napoleon with Guatemala for a field of operations was bound to develop psychoses. Yet no layman could pronounce upon whether Ubico's sadism was the product of frustration in later life: at the age of eight his favorite sport was throwing kittens from the roofs of houses.

Ubico was born in the capital in 1878, the lone pampered son of Barrios's dread minister of the interior, Arturo Ubico. His father was a sour misanthrope who quoted Schopenhauer and never tired of the refrain: "All men are scoundrels. The only language they understand is the stick."

He was a backward child at school. Despite his father's powerful influence, he flunked during his first semester at the military academy, and deserted. Ubico Sr. obtained the necessary pardon from the government, and Jorge went to work in a German bank.

When the war broke out with El Salvador in 1906, Ubico left his bank for a cushy post as lieutenant attached to the general staff. But here, too, he got into difficulties; he narrowly escaped court-martial for refusing to approach the line of fire to see why a certain hill had not been taken. Again his father saved the day.

His laurels from the 1906 war still fresh, he was appointed commandant of the department of Alta Verapaz, and then of Retalhuleu. In Retalhuleu his talents unfolded for the first time. Unaudited tallies credited him with hanging and shooting hundreds of Mexicans: some were cattle rustlers, other just citizens of a country that had begun heaving with revolution. Before long, his official biographer boasted, shopkeepers were able to leave town without latching their doors. In his less sanguinary moments, Commandant Ubico organized the Boy Scouts.

But however cruel, he proved an exceptionally capable administrator and won the lavish praise of the Rockefeller Foundation for his vigorous cooperation in the campaign against yellow fever. That extraordinary energy, like his mania for speed, was to remain with Ubico throughout his political career. Whether at his desk or dashing about the country on a motorcycle, he created the impression of trying to escape from himself.

Ubico's career had hit a snag when dictator Cabrera toppled in 1920. He was sent to the United States "to continue his studies." The Unionists, however, proved too forgiving, and he was soon back in Guatemala as chief of staff. Together with Orellana he organized the coup that overthrew the democratic regime. But later, when they fell out, Orellana was to remind him publicly that during the armed action he remained hidden until word came that the danger was over.

Against Orellana, Ubico proceeded to organize a network of secret "groups of five" which soon penetrated all departments of the government. The number five was raised to a symbol and used to plague Orellana on all possible occasions. Five letters in each of Ubico's names (ran the theology of the number); five the basis of his organization. What Ubico's supporters did not suspect was that their leader, once in power, would be content with no less than five terms.

Power gave Ubico full scope for his latent talents. What follows is the portrait of a country as much as of a man. Paranoiacs occur the world over, but there are few other lands so readily convertible into a spacious private madhouse.

For thirteen years Ubico ruled over Guatemala. A grimness descended upon the landscape: the nation became morally stagnant. From the husky whispers to which the people confided their conversations, it seemed as though an epidemic of laryngitis had hit the land. On the streets you were never out of sight of at least two uniformed minions of the law, and no one ever knew how many plainclothesmen. High government officials would have ignorant police barge into their offices to inspect their libraries. Guatemalan diplomats home on leave, foreign visitors, the most unlikely people, would be trailed by detectives. The very walls grew ears.

Indians were shot for stealing a few pennies. Contrabandists operating on the Mexican frontier were executed in the public squares in batches of twenty and forty. "Communists" (i.e., anyone thinking dangerous thoughts) were punished by death, often preceded by fanciful tortures. Heads were deformed by contracting iron crowns to squeeze out evil notions and information useful to the police. Women prisoners were immersed naked in electrolytic baths. Men were hung by their wrists with a weight on their feet and beaten on their testicles. Official photographers were usually on hand to take shots of tortures and messy corpses. Fingering such pictures gave Ubico a rare pleasure.

He had at last found an adequate means of self-expression. The coward of former years was now washing away his own lack of valor in the blood of others. The former backward student blossomed forth as an expert in widely divergent fields. He advised the engineers installing the government radio station on technical details. And whenever the completed station broadcast music that the Great Man did not like, he would phone to order "that junk taken off the air at once." There would be a frantic pulling of switches, and the mousy announcement: "Owing to circumstances beyond our control, we will go off the air for five minutes." When a symphony was organized (its members militarized and paid nine dollars a month), he told the conductor how much woodwind and how much brass to include, what to play, and how to play it. He himself boasted of his musical attainments, and would turn the radio on full blast and accompany it on the cello with a single finger. In his office he kept a set of jazzband drums and traps, and when not striking his ministers, he liked beating the drums.

Twice a year he would go on a tour of the country. His companion on these trips was the "Virginio Gayda of Guatemala," pudgy, sharp-tongued Federico Hernández de León, editor of *Nuestro Diario*.* Hernández's accounts of these trips were published in two volumes as fat as the author himself.† To future generations they will serve as a source on Ubicoland as invaluable as Homer on the Achaeans.

Ubico would start out on his trips with a mobile radio station, a couple of cabinet ministers, Hernández, a military escort, and in later years a Mexican guest or two—the ambassador or a visiting newspaperman. He thus derived full satisfaction from taking as many digs as possible at Mexico. Those he overlooked, Hernández put into the copy.

He fancied himself a sort of Solomon on wheels. Dashing through villages, he decided complicated cases of land ownership, family relationships, municipal disputes, in one minute flat. He fired judges right and left, reversed decisions of the courts, released prisoners and put judges in jail. And on the whole was mighty proud of himself.

He would go over the account books of the local officials and visit his beloved prisons, but rarely set foot inside a school. The only time he talked of educational progress was when he boasted of the numbers of criminals taught to read in the jails, or the soldiers who learned their alphabet in the barracks. For him those were the fit settings for accomplishing things.

Rain or shine, Indians would be lined up along the highway, at times a day or two in advance, to await his arrival. Landowners who neglected to put up floral arches were courting trouble. Ubico would hear the Indians' petitions. If they asked for a saxophone or a marimba, they stood a good chance of getting it. But if they begged for a bit of land, they received a lecture on the sanctity of property; on occasion, for the mere request, he would have them sent to do military service in the unhealthy Pacific lowlands "to rid them of their

---

*Virginio Gayda was dictator Mussolini's press spokesman during most of the Fascist regime in Italy.

†Published in Guatemala as *Viajes Presidenciales*, in 1944, just before Ubico's overthrow.

communist notions." From the way in which the Indians would crowd around the car, some swinging censers, some kneeling in prayer, others touching the fenders for luck, one might have imagined that some primitive Maya-Quiché deity had come back to his people via Detroit.

The keynote of these little jaunts was the General's stamina as well as his wisdom. *El Imparcial* of January 24, 1944, carried the headline "President Ubico Has Returned after Covering 2,018 Kilometers, 67 Meters" and the subheading "The 13th Was the Day of the Greatest Mileage by Auto—223 Kilometers 33 Meters in Five Hours 18 Minutes." He continued running around administering justice, knitting his brows, biting off people's heads, until his cortege was winded and famished. You were reminded of Mussolini leading his cabinet at a trot.* Then when they were finally seated before the groaning boards, the gourmand Hernández de León was able to appraise the fare for his readers: "The steak was so thick I thought it had been cut from my own buttocks."

From Hernández's pages emerge the General's powers of prophecy. He would predict when the car was going to break down, when the wharf would collapse (it was always the rest of the party, never he, who fell into the water), when it would rain, when a chair would fall apart. Hernández could not help indulging in cracks too subtle for the megalomaniac: "I think, my General, that you are not really endowed with powers of prophecy, but that even inanimate objects don't dare disobey you." By merely looking at a criminal he could tell what his crime was and, of course, whether he was guilty or innocent. En route, he pontificated on cooking, fishing, agriculture, engineering, military science, literature, and economics. He taught the lake Indians of Atitlán how to operate their boats.

His one refrain to local administrators, punctuated with dismissal, scoldings and insults, was "Collect more taxes. Don't be a softy. Make them pay through the nose."

In the evening a concert would be broadcast over the president's private mobile radio station. It consisted of local marimba bands and a description of the tour by Hernández. Then they would pitch tents for the night. Before turning in, Ubico would call down the person in charge for having set up the tents in a clearing: "They should be in the woods, military style. You would be a fine one in war with the

---

*Mussolini made his cabinet members do gymnastics and sports to keep in the athletic condition necessary to "better serve Fascism."

possibility of enemy bombardments." Naturally he was the first to get up in the morning. Hernández de León made a big point to be the last.

Early in his reign Ubico set the pattern to be followed by the other Central American dictators by putting an end to municipal elections and the autonomy of the municipalities. Before long he was working twelve hours a day signing decrees authorizing this or that Indian village to appropriate one dollar and thirteen cents for the repair of the village oxcart. This gave him a great sense of being indispensable.

Post office employees, schoolchildren, and the symphony orchestra were militarized—drilled by martinets and subject to martial law. Guatemala became a vast game of tin soldiers at which the Great Man amused himself.

After his fall I spent an intriguing morning browsing around in one of his several residences in the capital. In four rooms I was able to count no fewer than seven bits of statuary of Napoleon, and eight unspeakable paintings showing Napoleon on various fields of battle. Five cigarette lighters in the form of miniature cannon went off with an infernal bang. Of the three gaudily fitted bathrooms, two had two bathtubs apiece in lush colors; the third, with mirrored walls, boasted an enormous sunken bubble bath.

All this blood and circus was justified by uplift. Transiting journalists were much impressed by the cleanliness of the capital and the buildings Ubico threw up. But these lavish piles consisted almost exclusively of administrative buildings, police stations, and barracks, statues of his predecessor Rufino Barrios, and an absurd imitation of the Eiffel Tower in the capital with a bell that rang on Barrios's anniversary. You would search far and wide for a new school. Though Guatemala's population increased by about 20 percent during the first decade of Ubico's rule, the total enrolment in government primary schools between 1931 and 1941 rose only by 6 percent, from 98,065 to 103,860; the number of primary schools decreased from 2,139 to 1,563; the number of teachers from 3,485 to 3,318. The highest wage for teachers in the capital was $33 a month; in rural centers it was as low as $7. For such pittances they taught classes of fifty and sixty children.

Shortly after Ubico's overthrow I visited the school in the Indian lake village of Santiago Atitlán. The school was a wooden shack crowded with a hundred pupils. In the town there were another two thousand children of school age without accommodation. The blackboard had long ago split into two pieces. In the entire school there were a dozen slates. I was shown the filthy ragged texts that had served an entire generation of pupils, the disjointed wooden frames that once held slates. Under Ubico the school would receive a dozen pencils and a dozen pieces of chalk a year. It was hard enough on a salary of eight dollars a month teaching Indian kids, first the elements of Spanish in the Kakchiquel tongue and then the three R's in Spanish, and putting them through the inevitable military drill besides. But when neither teachers nor pupils even had the necessary writing materials . . .

Hospitals, which he considered mollycoddling institutions, fared as badly. Overcrowding in the capital's general hospital was so bad that hundreds of patients were bedded on the floors in the aisles and corridors. Hospital trustees were reduced to soliciting donations in kind—beans, corn, squash—to feed the patients, because whatever monetary contributions would be received were at once deducted by Ubico from the meager state allowance to these institutions.

Four months before Ubico was overthrown, *Readers Digest* carried an article that held up Ubico as a master of anti-inflationist technique because he had got the United States government to lower the wages for the building of its Guatemalan air base from a dollar to fifty cents a day, and on the emergency military highway from one dollar to twenty-five cents. In his haste to catch the mail for Pleasantville, the author overlooked that away back in 1934 when the world's statesmen were concerned with raising prices, with "reflating," Ubico had similarly forced the United Fruit Company to reduce pay of the workers engaged in laying out their Tiquisate plantation on the unhealthy Pacific coast from sixty cents to thirty cents. Ubico's wage policy in reality had no relation to the economic cycle. Like the pyramids, it sat pat for all time. It was but an aspect of the basic political philosophy which he formulated on more than one occasion: "If the people have money in their jeans, they will kick me out." Keep their minds concentrated on their next meal and you will have political tranquillity.

He had studied the patterns of previous revolutions and was much impressed by the fact that a serious revolt in 1897 and the revolution of 1920 coincided with prosperity due to high coffee prices. The whimsical tax system and his labor policy were calculated to achieve a desired end: to have the state coffers overflowing and the citizens' pockets empty.

He had as absolute a faith in his fist as an economic corrective as had Adam Smith in free trade. While discussing the Wall Street crash with a friend shortly after coming to power, he exclaimed: "Why, these North Americans are imbeciles. In their position, I would shut the stock market down, and have the state fix the stock quotations. I'd set things right!"

Ubico passed a decree abolishing debt slavery—the system whereby the Indians were tied to the coffee fincas by money advances.

On the strength of this he even made the Indians contribute five cents each toward erecting a monument expressing their gratitude to him as their "liberator"—in Spanish and Kakchiquel. Ever since the conquest the rulers of Guatemala had amused themselves revamping the legal formula for the Indians' forced labor, but forced labor it remained. Ubico instituted a labor booklet to be carried by every Indian in which his working days on the fincas would be recorded. If he owned less than a certain minimum of land, he was compelled to hire himself out on the plantations for 150 days a year or go to jail as a vagrant (schoolchildren playing truant were liable under the same law). Ubico did everything in his power to prevent the planters from paying more than the prevalent wages, varying from six to twenty cents per day according to the region, plus rations of corn and beans, and sometimes with the use of a plot of land thrown in. Yet it was only by offering the Indian some real economic incentive that industrious habits could be encouraged.

In addition, all adult males were made to contribute two weeks' unpaid labor on the national roads and one week to the municipalities. This could be commuted to a money payment of one dollar per week's work—but the Indians never had that much money. They were even required to provide their own food during their working period. Many hundreds of Indians died while working on the road in the fever-ridden Petén district, for not even the most elementary sanitary precautions were observed. And when road workers were urgently needed, the first police official could tear up the Indian's receipt for work done and pack him off to repeat his slavery.

Sixty years earlier Barrios had also introduced unpaid labor on the roads. But that was merely three days a year redeemable by a payment of something more than a dollar. The Indians' position had clearly deteriorated during the intervening decades.

But as harsh as Ubico was in his treatment of Guatemalans, he showered tender attentions on the United States monopolist interests operating in Guatemala. No sooner had the United Fruit Company obtained its concession for a west coast plantation, with guarantees against tax increases until 1981, than it lost all interest in the modern Pacific port that had been offered as bait. For $50,000 it secured its release from the obligation to build the port, which had already served the company as a bargaining point in acquiring 40 percent of the stock of the International Railway of Central America.* For a modern Pacific port would have short-circuited much of the railway's

---

*International Railways of Central America was a simple United Fruit-owned company, as was the White Fleet, which transported the bananas to ports in the southern United States and Europe.

traffic. Subsequently, the railway and the fruit company continued a profitable and intimate collaboration. The bulk of Guatemala's coffee is grown on the mountain slopes overlooking the Pacific; its logical outlet would be the Pacific ports. But the railway charged more to haul coffee to the nearby Pacific than to Puerto Barrios on the Caribbean, twenty times the distance. The United Fruit Company, with steamships operating only out of Puerto Barrios, stood to gain much from this incredible rate structure. In addition, Ubico hounded trucking lines competing with the railway.

Ubico's honesty was sung far and wide. His *Ley de Probidad* compelled all high government officials to declare their property on assuming office and to register all new acquisitions. If the rate of growth were more than was justified by their legitimate sources of income, they had a criminal suit on their hands. But this did not prevent the president and his close friends from putting ridiculously low values on their properties. Restrictions and monopolies, which operated to enrich the ruling circle, were introduced in the production and distribution of salt, sugar, meat, liquor, and cigarettes. Farms that were foreclosed by the banks were bought up by Ubico at a quarter or a fifth of the value of the mortgages on them, and Guatemalan banks rarely extend mortgages in excess of a third of the value of the lands. Somehow nobody chose to bid against him, and there is no law in any country to prevent people from taking advantage of deserted auctions. In this way he became the third largest landowner in Guatemala, with holdings of about 150,000 acres.

As Ubico's domains grew, he became more savage in repressing the slightest infringement of property by a starving people. A decree passed in 1944 absolved landowners and their lawful representatives from all responsibility even in killing persons found poaching or stealing fruits or firewood on their estates.

The official presidential salary was $33,800 plus a liberal allowance for household expenses. In 1933 Ubico had the assembly vote him a life pension equal to his salary. This was supposedly a reward for the solution of the boundary dispute with Honduras, although the boundary commission had accomplished most of its labors under the previous regime.* In 1941, "for his services in the domain of public

---

*Between 1927 and 1928 Guatemala had a "near war" over ownership of lands in the Motagua River Valley. Actually it was a war between United Fruit (backing Guatemala) and the Cuyamel Fruit Company (backing Honduras). Shortly afterwards United absorbed Cuyamel and there was no reason for war. The owner of Cuyamel shares, Samuel Zemurray, became vice president of United.

finance," the assembly voted him a gift of $200,000 quetzales (the quetzal, named after Guatemala's national bird, was on par with the dollar). It was no accident that Ubico was Supreme Head of the Order of the Quetzal.

His one great sorrow was that he had no offspring, legitimate or otherwise. "I slave for nothing," he would complain, "for I have no heir." In a similar fix Napoleon discarded Josephine, but Ubico knew well enough that for him there was no such solution. Eager to avenge themselves as they might, Guatemalans enlarged picturesquely on this deficiency. Ubico set about to prove them wrong. As was to be expected, he used the entire police force for his courting—to shoo away rivals and to bring to the capital any comely provincial lass who caught his fancy. The whole country felt the stale breath of the senile dictator hot on its neck.

On coming to power, Ubico had sworn to respect a constitution which barred a second presidential term. When he decided to stay on in power for another six years, he encountered violent opposition even in the ranks of his own followers. Former Ubiquistas hatched a conspiracy for his overthrow. Colonel Roderico Anzueto, Ubico's police chief, feigning participation, kept him informed of the conspirators' every move. And then, when Anzueto had gathered all the threads into his hands, the massacre began. On September 9, 1934, scores were seized in their houses, taken to the outskirts of the town and murdered. A wave of arrests swept the entire country. In the town of Zacapa, lawyer José León Castillo pleaded for an immediate death, but the police proceeded to smash his bones leisurely. When they were through, they were able to slip him into a sack and dump him into a ditch. When the body was found there, Ubico's coroners gave a verdict of suicide.

In the central penitentiary, lists of death sentences were read every few moments to hundreds of assembled political prisoners. Executions were carried out in the presence not only of the prisoners but of groups of public employees and members of all army units, to inspire the desired terror. Before the volley rang out, the condemned men tore off their clothes to show spectators the marks of torture. In two days Ubico snuffed out three hundred lives.

A group of women visited U.S. minister Hanna to beg him to intervene to stop the slaughter.* He politely expressed his regrets. He was unable to interfere in Guatemala's internal politics.

*This was the same Matthew Hanna who, as minister to Nicaragua during the presidency of José María Moncada, had a certain Anastasio Somoza García installed as head of the National Guard created and trained by the United States—the first step toward installation of the Somoza-dynasty dictatorship.

This was the most ambitious bit of carnage in Ubico's career. Subsequently, his opponents were so terrified that conspiracies for his overthrow seemed to melt of their own accord. In December 1940 there was a plot to get the officers of Fort Matamoros drunk on Christmas Eve, take over the fortress, and proclaim a new regime. Shortly before zero hour the military leader of the plot telephoned Ubico and denounced the scheme. That did not save him from facing a firing squad along with his accomplices.

In 1936 Ubico held a plebiscite to see whether the "difficult situation" did not justify a second term for himself. The question of the third term was settled with greater finesse. A series of petitions from individuals and "groups of workers" was published in the press urging that the only legal party—Ubico's Liberal-Progressives—amend the constitution to allow a third term for Ubico. "This added up to little less than a referendum," commented an official publication. In September 1941 the legislature extended his lease on the presidency to 1949.

It was the best of all possible worlds, and there was no visible reason why it should not spin on for all time to come. Guatemala seemed frozen into a grand equestrian statue: Jorge Ubico held the reins, and the rest of the country chewed on the bit.

4

Sheep Turn Lions

F ROM ACROSS THE SEA Ubico followed Hitler's career with gnawing envy. If destiny had but assigned him Germany as a pedestal! You
could strike a Napoleonic posture in a place like Guatemala, but the
chances were that the outside world would dismiss you as scratching
for fleas. Yet such gloomy thoughts did not hinder his loyal collaboration in a common cause. He was on Martínez's heels in recognizing
Franco. Long-resident Spaniards who refused to fall in with the Spanish Falange were expelled or persecuted; the Falange acquired a
semiofficial status in Guatemala.

Whenever Roosevelt or Wallace spoke on the "forgotten man,"
Ubico would fly into a rage and denounce them as "Communists and
madmen." His own anti-Communist campaign rivaled Hitler's for the
dust and din kicked up, with the disadvantage, of course, that there
were no Communists worth mentioning in Guatemala. That short-
coming was repaired by sticking the scarlet label on anyone who incurred his wrath—Indians begging for a piece of land, former political pals who winced at his reelections. His cabinet contained several
notorious pro-Nazis. The fossilized minister of foreign relations, Carlos Salazar, was attorney for the blacklisted German banking firm
Nottebohm Bros.*

Throughout Latin America the State Department was trying to
induce governments to confiscate or expropriate Axis property, but
Ubico resisted fiercely. Only in the fall of 1941, when the Americans
presented a virtual ultimatum on this and related matters, did Ubico
have his foreign minister draft a bill for the custodianship of German

---

*An old firm not only engaged in banking, but also chief intermediary in
the purchase and export of coffee, especially to Germany. After the war it
recovered its assets and retains until today its great importance in the coffee
business.

and Italian properties. The German minister was consulted in the formulation of its exceedingly generous terms. The central bank was placed in charge of the German banks for the duration of the war, allowing the owners only enough money for operational expenses. The rest was deposited in trust for them until after the war.

The ousting of the pro-Axis president of Panama, Arnulfo Arias, at about this time, was ominous.* Members of the U.S. embassy went out of their way to cultivate friendship with Guatemalans of anti-Ubico tendencies. Ubico was alarmed. His energetic representations caused the State Department to change the first secretary and commercial attaché at Guatemala. He was less successful in his efforts to rid himself of the naval attaché; the Navy somehow had a truer grasp of Latin American realities.

Ubico devised his own means of taming the unfriendly United States ambassador. That worthy diplomat, aging and excellently connected in Washington, was a great man with the ladies. After much shadowing, the police caught him in Minerva Park in compromising intimacy with the wife of a prominent American businessman. Unceremoniously they dragged the couple off to the police station. When his attempt to bribe the police failed, the ambassador tried another tack: he was the U.S. ambassador and they just couldn't do that to him. The police feigned disbelief: "Why, the ambassador is a gentleman, incapable of such immorality." Ubico himself was brought in, and after making the best of the dramatic situation, tendered his too profuse apologies, and ordered the diplomat released. The following day a little item appeared in the press announcing that the parks would henceforth close at six P.M. because of immoral abuses committed there by certain individuals. That particular ambassador caused Ubico no further trouble. Shortly afterward he was reassigned to another post.

The most important German property in Guatemala was the Central American Plantation Corporation (CAPCO), registered in New Jersey but 53 percent controlled by Germans. CAPCO not only produced a tenth of Guatemala's total coffee, and much sugar and cattle, but there was a vague recollection that cinchona (the source of quinine) had been planted on its El Porvenir Farm by President Justo Rufino Barrios in the eighteen-seventies. Even before Guatemala established custodianship for Axis properties, the United States government had taken over CAPCO through its New Jersey main office.

---

*The civilian Arnulfo Arias, at that time with nationalist convictions. Later he again became president of Panama (1968) and was again overthrown a few days after taking office.

Ubico did what he could to prevent the dismissal of its German administrators. He apparently reached some agreement with the Germans for the eventual restitution of their property in return for two of CAPCO's best farms, Palo Gordo and Chocolá. In any case, one of the classic petitions was already circulating in Congress to donate these two estates to the dictator "for his services to the nation." Ubico thus had a vital interest in keeping the North Americans at arm's length from CAPCO's affairs.

Carlos Mirón, Jr., American-educated son of a large landowner, had earned Ubico's hatred by his outspoken democratic sympathies and his curiosity concerning cinchona. Working with the United States embassy, he went to CAPCO's El Porvenir farm and found some four million cinchona trees that the German administrator had taken great pains to hide. Even after Pearl Harbor, cinchona logs were being used for the construction of fences and cabins.

Eventually, the cinchona of El Porvenir contributed substantially to the quinine needs of U.S. armed forces in the Pacific. But Ubico delayed the permits to ship the bark out and vetoed plans for the erection of a plant in Guatemala to treat the cinchona. Washington paid for El Porvenir's cinchona by making Guatemala a gift of CAPCO's properties after compensating the nonblacklisted shareholders. In addition, the Coordinator's Office adduced it as another reason for peddling Ubico to the American public as a great democrat.

Carlos Mirón, Jr., who had stuck his neck out to help the North Americans get their cinchona, did not fare so well. In March 1943 the police arrested his ailing brother and extracted from him a signed statement that Carlos was conspiring with members of the United States embassy to overthrow Ubico. Carlos was picked up and held incommunicado for several months. His defense was undertaken by a brave lawyer, Juan Córdoba Cerna. To be recognized as Mirón's attorney, Córdoba approached the state attorney and convinced him that he merely wished to mulct the wealthy Miróns and would work loyally with the prosecution. Once he had the case, he astounded the government by subpoenaing every member of the U.S. embassy, from Ambassador Boaz Long to the last office boy, to testify to whether Mirón had conspired with them as the indictment charged.

Even in the storybooks such things had never happened in Guatemala before. The country rocked on its hinges, and the U.S. embassy was indignant. Ubico summoned Córdoba and tried bludgeoning him into withdrawing the subpoenas. "Many a time, while smoking a cigarette like this, I have decided upon the life or death of a man. And you know, I have never been bothered by remorse. It is for the good of the Fatherland." And then whimsically smacking the arms of his chair: "What you people want is this. When you get it, I will watch from afar what a mess you make of things."

Córdoba stood his ground. Having let himself in too deep, Ubico released Mirón and expelled him, his father, and Córdoba over the Salvadoran border. The case ended not with a bang but a whimper.

There were gremlins everywhere. Ubico had always been obsessed by the pattern of previous revolutions. Before Cabrera fell in 1920, there had been a war, and an earthquake that flattened the capital. Now there was a war again, and in the fall of 1943 a severe quake shook the Totonicapán area. Frantic, Ubico suppressed all accounts of the destruction and declined the assistance of the American Red Cross.

The presence of U.S. air forces in Guatemala was demoralizing. The sight of free men talking in unsubdued tones was having a seditious effect. The nightclub that opened to accommodate the American troops was even deadlier. For the first time Guatemalans could meet and discuss politics in hushed tones without arousing too much suspicion. To an extent, Guatemala's revolution was hatched in that lone night club.

In April the military revolt against Martínez flared forth in El Salvador. This was no longer handwriting on the wall; the wall itself was caving in. Ubico had always prided himself on his earthy *bons mots*. In the past his epigrams had been of a cheerful sort: "If I have to abandon the presidency, I will leave wading up to my knees in blood." Now a melancholy note crept into his witticisms: "A ruler must do his thinking not only with his head, but with the seat of his pants—to know when it is time to get up from the chair."

What his trousers failed to tell him, his loving people did.

The dejected fugitives who had reached Guatemala from El Salvador were suddenly decked out with majesty. Martínez had fallen. As they packed their bags to return, they filled the Guatemalans with envy. And ideas.

A chain reaction had begun. Once every quarter of a century Guatemala's lambs become lions. Forty-five lawyers signed a petition asking Ubico to remove a notorious judge who handled political cases. Two hundred schoolteachers asked for wage raises, and their leaders were forthwith indicted before a court-martial for sedition. In reprisal the teachers refused to attend rehearsals for the annual parade in Ubico's honor, and were dismissed in droves. The students pitched in to demand reestablishment of the University's autonomy, abolished by Ubico thirteen years before, unrestricted freedom of speech, and a printing press to publish their opinions. More incredibly still, they gave the dictator a twenty-four-hour ultimatum before going on strike.

Ubico countered with a round of persecution that sent scores of students scampering for asylum in the Mexican embassy. The constitutional guarantees, always a bad joke, were suspended on the pretext that "Nazi-fascist" elements were disturbing the peace; 311 citizens signed a round robin asking that Ubico not only restore those guarantees but take measures to put them into effect. Popular delegations called at the National Palace for bootless conferences with Ubico's ministers.

On Saturday, June 26, the students, dressed in mourning, marched down the main street, their arms crossed behind their backs as though shackled. The cinemas lost their clients to them and shut their doors. Swollen to gigantic proportions, the demonstration spilled onto the plaza where the troops were massed. Cries of "Resign, resign," issued from thousands of throats like the roll of thunder.

In the big wedding-cake of a national palace crouched Ubico, sniffling with a cold. Outside the people entoned the national anthem, discovering in it new virile strains.

That night there was a fair in the workers' suburb of San Pedrito, with dancing and merriment amidst booths and bunting. In the early hours of the morning bands of toughs, previously liquored in the police stations, were let loose to sack and wreck the stands. That was the prearranged signal for the police to swing into action. Rifles blurted, victims fell. The provocators were not molested, but peaceful citizens were rounded up and herded through the city. The official radio screeched "Communists," the magic word that for long years served Central American dictators in every scrape. An indignant mass of citizens that surged through the streets in protest was dispersed by the police with phosphorus bombs.

When an oppositionist delegation visited him that afternoon, Ubico offered to resign at the end of the war. But he warned that as long as he remained president there would be no freedom of speech or association. Guatemala needed a "strong hand." He was at a loss to understand why the people disliked "a government that had always been just." Nobody was capable of taking his place; he had had so much experience. Shots outside interrupted the discussion. The troops were charging a procession of women leaving San Francisco church. A schoolmistress was killed, and the streets were littered with wounded. Many were horribly mutilated by dumdum bullets. The just government had laid on its strong hand.

At a meeting of the diplomatic corps, U.S. Ambassador Boaz Long was unwilling to hear an eyewitness's account of the massacre, but the Mexican ambassador and other colleagues overruled him. To citizens who beseeched him to do something to stop the carnage, Mr. Long tendered his regrets; however, he assured them that he prayed for them every night.

The students had been on strike since June 22. Lawyers and doctors came in during subsequent days. The strike swept all embankments before it and engulfed the economic life of the land. Most of Guatemala's large stores were foreign-owned, and Ubico decreed deportation for any foreigner who closed his shop. The police went from door to door browbeating the merchants to remove their shutters. Martial law and nine o'clock curfew were slapped on.

Ubico's police chief, a pompous fool with a handlebar mustache, summoned the strike leaders. He informed them that they already "had a foot in the grave" and that any further demonstrations would be dispersed with lead. But before the interview was over, they had convinced him that he ought to urge Ubico to resign for his own good. As a result he was dismissed and replaced by dread Roderico Anzueto, minister of agriculture and organizer of the massacre of 1934. Ubico was putting forth a last bold stand. Prominent oppositionists had their cars seized, and were trailed by plainclothesmen with ominously bulging jacket pockets.

The tension was becoming unbearable: something was bound to snap. José González Campo, the pro-Nazi finance minister, sent in his resignation from the Mexican embassy, where he had taken asylum. Clearly the ship was sinking. Ubico began toying with the idea of handing the presidency over to a distant civilian relative.

A frantic S O S went forth to the gods that shape Central American destinies. With an eye on Washington, Ubico suddenly expropriated Axis properties, a measure that he had resisted for three years. He also paid off a huge block of long-defaulted British debt at par, not so much to impress Whitehall as to leave his successor with empty coffers.

The fruit was ripe, and many who had done nothing to shake the tree scurried to catch it as it dropped. Federico Ponce was an impoverished, bibulous general, retired by Ubico years earlier for his excesses while political chief of Petén Department. His one asset was a cousin who served as Ubico's chief of staff and kept him informed about the state of the Great Man's nerves. With two other retired generals, Ponce called on Ubico on June 29. They offered him their services. In a saturnine mood, Ubico growled: "I no longer need anything. I have just signed my resignation."

More articulate than his companions, Ponce caught the ball on the fly. "That is just what we have come to see you about. We cannot tolerate a civilian assuming power."

Ubico flung his resignation on the floor. "Here you have this bit of s- - -."

Ponce picked it up. He had acquired another asset.

Ubico retired to seclusion in his home alongside the Spanish legation. A triumvirate was set up with Ponce cracking the whip.

An epoch had ended. Ponce, however, did not see it that way. On

July 3 troops armed with tommyguns stalked into the legislature, drove the people out of the gallery, and suspended the session. The deputies were summoned to the presidential palace, and forced to swear that they would vote for Ponce as provisional president. Ubico's hand-picked assembly was not given to heroism. The following day it named Ponce president to replace the triumvirate. United States recognition came at once. Several months later Ambassador Long quaintly explained to me that he had believed Ponce's promise to give the country fair elections.

The big plum in the presidential pudding was the expropriated German properties, which included a third of Guatemala's coffee acreage. Before his unexpected ascent to the presidency, Ponce had been pounding the pavements looking for gainful employment: a clothing store was dunning him for thirty dollars that he owed for a suit. Now he prospered. Instead of being put to public auction, as the law required, the coffee crop of the expropriated plantations was sold to an American firm for $200,000 less than the market price. Ponce's two former fellow triumvirs inserted advertisements repudiating the shady transaction. Basking in the good, new life, Ponce got dead drunk almost every afternoon and evening, while his slithery secretary, Manuel Melgar, would shove state documents before him that he later had no recollection of signing. During these libations, he boasted that he would kill this and that one of his opponents with his own hands.

A group of democrats advanced the candidacy of Juan José Arévalo. Strapping, handsome, and forty, Arévalo at the time occupied a chair of pedagogy at Tucumán University in Argentina.* He was the son of humble white farmers, and had taught primary school in Guatemala, written various texts, and studied abroad. For a while he had held a post in the education ministry under Ubico, but finding the atmosphere stifling, he had expatriated himself and taught at various Argentine universities. His campaign was launched at once, and even before his arrival he had become a symbol. Guatemala had had a former swineherd and a horse thief as presidents, and unlettered militarists galore. That it now aspired to a pedagogue was a sign of the changing times. An effective orator, Arévalo toured the country preaching a humanitarian socialism. His utterances resounded like blockbusters: "I'm not against the army as such, but there are too many bandits in military uniforms."

---

*Argentina was governed at the time by Gen. Edelmiro Farrell, whose vice president was Juan D. Perón: a government classified by the United States as sympathetic to the Nazi-Fascist Axis.

The reactionaries rallied behind the candidacy of Adrián Recinos, a foxy lawyer who had played a key role in the overthrow of the democratic regime in 1921. Recinos had served as Ubico's minister to Washington, and was smiled upon by the State Department.

For a decade Ubico had kept wages at depression levels; now that the iron heel was no longer there, trade unions, previously unknown in Guatemala, mushroomed throughout the land. The movement was completely spontaneous: at this stage there were neither walking delegates nor professional organizers. Toward the end of July six thousand workers of the United Fruit plantation at Tiquisate struck and obtained wage increases of as much as 50 percent. Ponce sent three trainloads of soldiers armed to the teeth to provoke an incident, but the strikers' discipline offered them no opening. Guatemala was catching up with itself after fourteen years of suspended animation. But higher wages lent a dizzy momentum to the spiral of inflation. Had Ubico allowed wages to find their natural level in peacetime, this might have been largely avoided.

Thirteen hundred people signed a petition for the resignation of the Ubico cabinet ministers whom Ponce had retained and for the dissolution of the old assembly.

Alarmed by the Arévalo boom, Ponce launched a smear campaign denouncing him as a fascist agent of the Argentine government. In reality Arévalo had almost lost his post at Tucumán University for his outspoken democratic sympathies. Ponce was laying a smokescreen for the terror ahead.

Drawing from the classic arsenal of Guatemalan dictators, he tried stirring up the Indians against the towns. Five thousand Indians were brought to the capital and camped in Aurora Park on its outskirts. They were marched through the streets of the city, with pictures of Ponce about their necks and brandishing sticks. After an incident involving a North American woman, the diplomatic corps prevailed upon Ponce to send them home. Bricks crashed mysteriously through windows displaying Arévalo's photo. Prominent Arevalistas were warned to travel abroad for their health. Guatemalan politics were reverting to type.

Alejandro Córdova, bald, genial publisher of the daily *El Imparcial,* had spent long years in Ubico's harness. But the transformation of his countrymen did not pass him by. "For fourteen years," he explained, "we have been immersed in dung. Only the tip of one heel, where they held us for the dunking, remained clean. We must cherish that little spot, and make of it the point of departure to regain our dignity." When a constitutional reform to allow Ponce to remain in the presidency was broached, deputy Córdova fought it tooth and nail. He paid no heed to threats. Early in October he was shot down by

Ponce's gunmen. At his funeral half the town marched in awful silence.

War was on between Ponce and the Guatemalan people.

I landed in Guatemala on October 17 to cover the dénouement. Arévalo and scores of his followers had taken asylum in the Mexican embassy; the Mexicans had rented part of a hotel to accommodate the overflow. The atmosphere was clammy with terror. The police had fired into an Arevalista crowd in Quezaltenango, leaving dead and wounded. The prisons were brimming; tales of torture were about. Ponce's gutter-rag gloated over the collapse of the Arevalista movement, and poured ridicule over the "cowardice" of the "romantic candidate." The general was sitting on top of the world, with the delightful sensation of digging his spurs into its sides.

In five local elections he had brought his candidates to triumph with Goebbels-like majorities. A congress of his Liberal party was scheduled to draft the constitutional amendments that would give him the presidency for keeps.

The efforts of the democratic forces to react had fizzled. A general strike in the capital was beaten down; scheduled uprisings in the provinces and an invasion of refugees from Mexico failed to come off. Demoralization bit deep. But the opposition had one final trump up its sleeve.

Jorge Toriello, a breezy young man in business as a radio distributor, had never troubled his head about politics. He did play polo, however, and in that way met Captain Jacobo Arbenz, thirty-two-year-old son of a Swiss pharmacist and instructor at the military academy. Toriello and Arbenz were in the gallery together when Ponce sent in troops to intimidate Congress. Arbenz smarted so with the shame of the army's role, that he resigned his commission and began contacting democratic-minded officers. Wisely, he concentrated his social calls on the Guardia de Honor fortress, where most of Guatemala's lend-lease equipment was stored. Fourteen active officers, headed by Major Francisco Javier Arana, were thus pledged to a military coup, if the efforts of the civilians failed.

On the night of October 19, I sought out Jorge García Granados, Arévalo's right-hand man, in his hide-out. Together we awaited zero hour, set for two P.M. To lessen the suspense, we chain-smoked and discussed obscure episodes of Guatemalan politics a half century ago. Our hosts, awake with twitching nerves, plied us with coffee and rum. Liaison men with the outside world came and went, sporting theatrically long pistols.

A full half-hour before the appointed time, a single cannon shot ripped the silence. Had the plan gone haywire? At five to two the rhythmic crackle of machine guns began, punctuated by rifle fire and the chesty boom of mortars. A lone plane droned overhead. Echo played havoc with our attempts to make out the direction of the firing. The streets adjoining our hide-out were deserted, except for clusters of North American night-club patrons savoring a new thrill from safe doorways. After forty minutes the shooting came to a full stop. We took it for a bad sign: the four fortresses could not have been captured in that time. Hugging buildings and dashing across roads, I made my way to the central square where the palace stood. A soldier lay dead in a pool of blood; here and there mortar shells had littered the sidewalks with rubble. The broad plaza was deserted. Above the eery quiet I could hear the whispers of the palace guard on the battlements. Whistling a silly air and clomping my feet to make it clear that I was a carefree gringo, I ventured across the exposed square.

No sooner was I back in my friend's lair than the telephone rang. The revolutionaries had taken the Guardia de Honor fortress and were asking for civilians to bear the captured arms. Under a gently falling dew, I accompanied a student on his rounds to inform his friends that they were needed at the barracks. Heads in ridiculous nightcaps popped out of windows. Excited clots of people enquired what was afoot; when told, faces lit up, and feet started in the direction of the Guardia de Honor. At the home of a student leader we were served steaming coffee, while a grim, dry-eyed mother bade farewell to her son. We headed for home while stray bullets whizzed overhead. A power cable snipped by a mortar shell dangled dangerously on the road. A dead policeman sprawled in the gutter. Under a rosy silver heaven, the city was awakening to a new dawn.

The Guardia de Honor had been taken from within. At 11 P.M. fourteen students gathered at Ciro's night club and elaborately made merry. The band played "*Adios mi vida. . . .* Today I must leave for the front." The night-club owner, who, like night-club hosts the world over, knew many things, came over to the roisterers and told them that their drinks were on the house that night. At one o'clock, feigning great drunkenness, the students staggered into three taxis. As the cars approached the U.S. embassy on the wooded drive, the passengers sobered up. The chauffeurs felt cold revolver muzzles in their backs; they were given the choice of joining the revolution or being killed then and there. Discreetly, they rallied to the cause.

The students had been carefully coached by Captain Arbenz. They would recognize the revolutionary troops by the missing left sleeves of their uniforms. The students were to obtain thirty automobiles to transport arms from the Guardia de Honor to other parts of the city. If any of them showed the slightest sign of weakening, he was to be killed by his comrades. Anybody with knowledge of the plan who was in danger of being captured was to commit suicide. "*Constitu-*

ción y Democracia" was the password. The students were to be brought into the fortress as prisoners and, once within, would help the military conspirators take over.

But the Guardia de Honor was in the revolutionaries' hands before the students arrived. Fearing betrayal of the plot, the rebel officers had acted ahead of schedule. The commander had been killed when he resisted. The students were armed, assigned ten soldiers each, and dispatched to the siege of Matamoros fort at the other end of town.

Some 105-millimeter mortars were wheeled out of the Guardia de Honor to bombard the government strongholds. The marksmanship on either side was excellent: of twenty-one shells fired by the loyal troops, twenty found their mark in the Guardia de Honor. Civilians, queuing up to receive arms, impressed the soldiers with their calm as shells burst around them. As a mist settled over the city, the artillery duel was suspended by mutual consent to avoid unnecessary destruction. Besides, the revolutionaries were in a quandary. The artillery officer who had made the calculations for the shelling of San José fortress had lost his nerve and failed to show up. At seven A.M. Arbenz was deeply preoccupied, when his eye fell on a prisoner being brought in. It was an artillery officer from the San José regiment recently returned from an artillery course in the Panama Canal Zone. Arbenz jumped at the windfall. The prisoner was given the alternative of being executed or directing the artillery against his comrades in San José. As he trained the guns on his regiment, his cheeks were moist with tears. But his third shell found San José's munition dump and converted it into a pyre. By nine o'clock the whole city was in the streets gazing incredulously at the hissing column of flame and smoke. Crazed with horror, soldiers fled the holocaust carrying what belongings they could. A hundred or so were trapped inside and roasted.

Jeeps dashed to and fro under the white flag of parley. Civilians disarmed the fugitives from San José. From the crowds on the streets came husky cheers of "Viva Arévalo." The news spread that Matamoras fort, too, had been reduced.

The lend-lease armament had backfired murderously. An automobile flying the Mexican flag drew a wild ovation "Viva Mexico!" The U.S. embassy car was received with stony silence.

Sniping continued from the police station. After crossing the city on foot, I entered the national palace at noon, just as the white flag was going up over it. A delegation of the diplomatic corps that had arranged the surrender was leaving in the British legation car. In the sun-drenched patios, Guardia de Honor soldiers were stretching for a nap. A colonel of a loyalist regiment was pleading volubly with a skeptical civilian: "I did no more than my duty. I have to earn bread for my children."

The government troops were in no hurry to vacate the palace, although the surrender had been signed. Early that morning Ponce had radioed a frantic appeal to Honduran dictator Tiburcio Carías, to send his vaunted air force, and he was slow to abandon hope.

I picked my way to the office of Manuel Melgar, bosom friend of U.S. Ambassador Long, and the power behind Ponce's throne. Sleek and smart, he was hastily tearing up documents as he spoke to me. He made a heroic stab at smiling: "General Ponce has agreed to resign to avoid bloodshed. Our lives have been guaranteed." Ponce and Melgar took asylum in the Mexican embassy across the road, where they were put up in rooms freshly vacated by Arévalo and his friends. That evening Arévalo danced his first tango since leaving Argentina. "Now I can do so without being denounced as Perón's agent," he jollied.

Ambassador Boaz Long had left for Washington a few days before the revolution. But his spirit hovered over the scene. General Miguel Ydígoras Fuentes, Ubico's director of highways, tried shoehorning himself into the provisional presidency on the strength of his excellent connections with the U.S. embassy.* But a revolutionary junta consisting of Toriello, Arana, and Arbenz took over. One of their first acts was to get Ydígoras out of the country by naming him military attaché in Washington. They cancelled his appointment while he was en route to his post.

Formerly the hemisphere's most heavily policed city, Guatemala now did impressively with no police at all. The old police had been rounded up by soldiers and civilians and imprisoned pending an investigation of individual records. Until the new Civil Guard was formed a couple of weeks later, students and workers took over. Boy Scouts—some of them eight years old—directed traffic. In good-natured travesty of the old omnipotent police force, a legless man and a dwarf were also assigned this work.

For a couple of nights phantom cars dashed through the city firing at random; the Poncistas were trying to stir up disorder to delay foreign recognition of the revolutionary regime. Tracer bullets festooned the sky—the armed civilians could not resist trying out their

---

*The same Ydígoras Fuentes who in 1954 would participate in overthrowing constitutional President Arbenz, in "Operation Success" directed and financed by the CIA and State Department. See Gregorio Selser, *El Guatemalazo, La Primera Guerra Sucia* (Iguazú, Buenos Aires, 1961) and, *inter alia,* Stephen Schlesinger and Stephen Kinzer, *Bitter Fruit: the Untold Story of the American Coup in Guatemala* (Garden City, New York: Doubleday & Co., 1982).

novel toys. When shooting was reported from Ubico's home, a tank was brought up, and armed civilians broke into the house. There was some looting until responsible leaders got things under control. Almost the entire block of buildings belonged to Ubico, and it was found to have been made into a warren of escape passages. Ubico himself had gotten away to the Spanish legation next door. From there he was transferred to the British minister's residence. Though accommodations were uncomfortably cramped, Ubico was loath to leave the country. "It is all a boys' escapade," he kept repeating, "and can't last more than a few days."

When finally persuaded to board a plane for New Orleans, he spoke his last lines nobly: "It is an injustice to cast me out like a dog. But now that you have let yourself in for this adventure, show that you have the courage to go through with it. But beware of the Communists and the Conservatives!"

The morning after the revolution the Indians of the town of Patzicia, fretted by Ponce's demagogy, rose and butchered off every Ladino in sight, men, women, and children. Over three hundred Indians were killed before the district was pacified. Panic gripped the scattered Ladinos throughout the highlands. The chasms in Guatemala's racial structure yawned wide.

The abundant generals of the army were corralled in a sixth-class hotel and dispatched into exile in parcels. Each member of the Ponce government was allowed to take out one thousand dollars with him. Ponce shed scalding tears when an additional sixteen thousand dollars were found in his baggage and taken from him. He had also lost a son in the fighting.

The revolutionary junta set about cleaning the stables of the dictatorship. The fortunes of the Ubico and Ponce cliques were frozen pending an investigation of their origins. The Ubiquista assembly was dissolved and a new one elected. A constitutional congress started drafting a new basic charter. The schools were demilitarized, and the autonomy of the university was restored. The pay of schoolteachers and the army was doubled. Work on a one-thousand-bed hospital in the capital was begun. The junta introduced a profit tax favoring small concerns. But the large foreign companies, the United Fruit Company, the International Railways of Central America, and the Electric Bond & Share Company, had written into their concessions guarantees against further taxation for decades to come. To cope with that, the new constitution authorized the revision of prerevolutionary concessions.

When labor difficulties threatened to paralyze the railway, the junta deported one of its executives who had overlooked that native workers could no longer be treated as inferior beings.

The army was subjected to a military council and granted a high degree of autonomy. Many civilians considered this a dangerous innovation.

Relations were broken off with Franco, and several months later the Spanish government-in-exile was recognized.

No member of the Arévalo parties was included in the junta's cabinet. The presidential elections that in December 1944 gave Arévalo an 85 percent majority were the fairest Guatemala had seen.

Throughout Central America the pundits were sure that the junta, having captured power with guns, would never surrender the presidency to Arévalo merely because a certain number of ballots had been cast. Such a thing could never happen in Central America. Yet on March 15, in a moving ceremony, the junta handed over power to Arévalo. The law of the jungle was giving way to something more civilized.

In Arévalo's cabinet Arbenz became minister of war and Arana became commander of the army.

Few rulers have had a more difficult task than Arévalo. He was faced with the job of prying Guatemala out of a forgotten century and bringing it abreast of contemporary times.

Foreigners in Guatemala are amazed by the high price of land. It isn't the soil that you take into your hand, spit on, and rub, that goes to make up that extravagant price; you are asked to pay for the de facto slaves that go with it. In normal times, paying the Indians ten or twenty cents a day, the agriculturists earn huge profits. These earnings, regarded as the yield on an investment, determine the value of the land.

Arévalo and the leftist-inclined Congress considered the Indians citizens who awaited redemption: to the old-fashioned gentry, on the other hand, the brute state of their peons is a cherished patrimony. When the government launched a modest campaign to reduce the country's 80 percent illiteracy, letters appeared in the press warning that teaching the Indians to read would be detrimental to agriculture. One of these, appearing in *El Imparcial* of July 25, 1945, exposed with the boldness of a surgeon's scalpel what goes on in the head of a reactionary planter. "What benefit would the Indian and the country as a whole derive from his knowing to read and write? Could he afford to buy newspapers or magazines? Certainly not. . . . He would use his superiority as a literate to convert himself into the chieftain of other Indians and create all sorts of difficulties for the plantation owner. . . . The Indian, due to his atavism, prefers his primitive life. . . . If he shows an apparent interest in any suggestion that he become civilized, it is due to his sensing the possibility of material and not spiritual gain from such a step."

Most prosperous citizens wanted the revolution to remain a respectable political affair, leaving untouched the economic foundations of the land. Mexico, too, under its sainted president Francisco Madero, aspired to a purely political democracy that would not meddle with the peons' bondage. In Mexico, essentially a land of racial mixture, the chasm separating exploiters and exploited was never so deep as in Guatemala. Yet Madero's feeble tinkering was engulfed in hell and high water. A decade of blind, destructive peasant revolt left little of the stiff-necked feudalists, and played havoc with the country's economy. If the wrong thing happened in Guatemala, it would make Mexico's civil strife seem tame by comparison. Because of this, responsible liberals urged that an orderly program of agrarian reform be undertaken from above.

On the face of it Arévalo was in an excellent position to carry out just that sort of program. One third of the coffee acreage, plus cattle and sugar lands to boot, were in the State's possession as a result of the expropriation of Axis properties. The planters were eager to have these lands put on the auction block, but the constitutional assembly blocked any such move by inserting Article 93 into the constitution prohibiting the alienation of state properties. Instead, these lands might be rented to cooperatives, families, farmers working the lands themselves, or to joint stock companies in which the state was a shareholder. This article unfurled a banner of agrarian reform that struck fear into the hearts of most planters.

The person who drafted this clause was the brilliant president of the constitutional assembly, Jorge García Granados, a little capsule of a man who during his long years of exile had studied what was worthy of imitation and what had best be avoided in Mexico's land reform. García Granados drew upon himself all the hatred of the reactionaries.

Though his own sympathies were nebulously to the left, Arévalo detoured, free-wheeled, and played for time. A law on cooperatives, backed by a very limited budget, was passed to permit cautious experiments in the spirit of the constitution. The army was of traditional outlook, and unfriendly to any rescrambling of social relationships in the countryside. Prominent leftists like García Granados were later sent out of the country to diplomatic posts; peasant organizers more unceremoniously whisked off to prison or thrown across the Mexican frontier. In the spring of 1946 the Agricultural Ministry, run by a rightist planter, was inserting large advertisements in the press, reminiscent of the crude anti-Bolshevik cartoons in the early twenties, showing labor agitators inciting drunken peons and raking in their dues.

Cartoons, however, are frail ramparts. To cope with possible Indian uprisings, the country was divided into military zones and the army's lend-lease gadgets distributed amongst them.

For the first time in Guatemalan history, the workers entered upon the political scene. With perhaps 75,000 members, two trade union centers sprang into existence and later fused to meet the challenge of reaction. When the threat of a farm labor strike hovered over the critical coffee-picking season in 1945, the government suspended further agricultural unions until the passing of the labor code the following spring. The labor unions tended to offset the power of the army and constituted a factor in the system of political equilibrium without which no real democracy is thinkable.

Though Arévalo's achievements, in the light of liberal expectations, seemed patchy and compromise-ridden, he had a plausible theory to justify his opportunistic course. If he challenged the conservatism of the wealthy frontally, there would be a danger of alienating the army and being overthrown. By keeping the roof from falling in, though it requires deft flexing of the back, he hoped to make it possible for the new democratic institutions to take root. More daring things might perhaps be attempted during his successors' terms.*

Arévalo, indeed, threw the windows wide open. Guatemala, which had lived hermetically sealed off from the century and the world, was being aired by gusts from without. The educational budget was more than doubled in a single year, though the increase in the teachers' salaries swallowed up most of the new allotment. New schools were built, the curriculum of primary and secondary education revised, co-education introduced experimentally in the secondary schools. A faculty of humanities was added to the university. Lecturers were brought in from Mexico and Argentina. For the first time in years there was no longer an index for prohibited books and periodicals. Art shows began to come; concerts of well-known artists were organized with state support. The government was bludgeoned merrily in the independent press. The movies, empty in Ubico's time, were full: for despite the high cost of living, workers now had a few coins in their jeans.

---

*In effect, his presidential successor Jacobo Arbenz attempted something so daring by implementing the agrarian reform which Arévalo thought himself unable to put through—immediately generating conspiracies to overthrow him, which culminated in June 1954. Moderate and cautious as Arévalo was, however, his administration inspired some thirty attempted military rebellions, *coups d'état* and risings, the most serious of which occurred on 18–20 July 1949.

Of course, when windows are opened, there are always people who complain of the draught. The reactionaries sighed for the good old days when every man was frozen on his rung in the social hierarchy by fear and strikes were a capital offense. Arévalo's civilized blandness encouraged the diehards to plot his overthrow; three major military plots were unearthed in a single year. After the last frustrated coup, several noncommissioned officers were sentenced to death by court-martial, but Arévalo commuted their penalty.* That served as further proof to old-timers that he was not a serious ruler.

Privilege had long grown rank and ugly in Guatemala and resisted every move to trim it. Landowners and merchants had inherited something of the mentality of the Spanish conquerors four centuries ago. When Congress adopted a provisional labor code and a subsecretariat of labor was founded to enforce it, one might have imagined from the outcry of employers that the end of the world was at hand. When Leon Henderson prepared a report for the government on price control, the Chamber of Commerce charged him with ignorance of the elements of economics and hoisted the moth-eaten banner of free enterprise. Meanwhile the same profiteers, banded together in the reactionary Partido Nacional, used the rising cost of living as a club against the regime. The clergy, Falangist Spaniards in large part, employed pulpit and confessional to rouse the faithful against "communism." By identifying every aspiration for social betterment with communism, the reactionaries were rendering a priceless service to the handful of Communists.

Ubico had gone, but the country still footed the bill. Under his rule a generation grew up with no other norm of public behavior than fawning on a deranged dictator and keeping their voices low. Fourteen years like that scar the soul of a nation. With few exceptions Guatemalan politicos remained as green as bay trees. In every branch of the administration you found officials with more than nature's quota of thumbs.

The experience of Guatemala, where the social setup was perhaps knottier than in any other Latin American land, exemplified the headaches of most fledgling democracies. Overthrowing the tyrant is but the flashy prelude. With the new political freedom, tangled social problems, the legacy of Spain's colonial system, come to the fore.

---

*Among the officers whose sentences were commuted was Col. Carlos Castillo Armas, who soon afterward, with his guards' complicity, escaped and sought asylum in the Colombian embassy. Returning later to Honduras, he planned from there with U.S. support the military rising which overthrew Arbenz in 1954.

Callow democratic statesmanship is sorely tried, but it is only under a democracy that these issues can be honestly faced.*

---

*The professor Arévalo tried with complete honesty to apply models of representative democracy and ample freedoms, in the way desired by William Krehm. However, the semifeudal oligarchy allied with foreign economic interests frustrated most of his plans. In this connection, three important books by Arévalo are recommended: *The Fable of the Shark and the Sardines; Guatemala, la democracia y el emperio;* and *Antikomunismo en América Latina* (the last two only in Spanish).

5

Backslide

On leaving El Salvador Martínez deposited the presidency with his war minister, General Andrés I. Menéndez. A man of sixty who had begun life as a carpenter, Menéndez was neither stung by ambition nor noted for the firmness of his spine. These qualities equipped him superbly as a caretaker of the presidential palace during momentary vacancies. When Martínez was preparing his first reelection in 1934, he had handed over the presidency to Menéndez for six months and recuperated it intact. Now Menéndez's good intentions served to throw the democrats off their guard: they accepted the vessel as seaworthy due to the honest face of the figurehead on her prow.

The army had come out of the political upset unscathed. Fascist-minded generals continued in command of the forts that encircled the capital like an enemy town. On their return from exile the officers who had taken part in the April revolt were not reinstated into the army, but were given civilian posts. The army was thus purged of the few democratic elements that had escaped Martínez's vigilance. The old police, too, stayed on, and were soon engaged in an underhand campaign to discredit the revolution. Citizens who reported robberies were taunted: "You wanted freedom, didn't you? Go ask the doctors and students to investigate the theft."

The peaceful revolution had left an unbroken legal continuity. That ensnared the democrats in their every attempt to safeguard their conquests. Martínez's assembly was preserved as the lawmaking body.

The popular gusts, however, blew mightily and swept some less sheltered refuse before it. Citizens invaded the legislature and guided the debates with their boos and cheers; there is no gallery in El Salvador's parliamentary chamber, and the massed audience literally breathed down the red necks of the deputies. Now and again a worker or student would ask for the floor and participate in the discussions to powerful effect. Thus prodded, Martínez's legislature dismissed many officials of the old regime. Yet at most a whisk was applied where a vigorous broom was needed.

A half-dozen candidates bustled about launching their presidential campaigns. For the bulk of the people there could be only one president now that the tyranny was prostrate. Disfigured for life by the machetes of the soldiery and rescued from the firing squad by the revolution, Arturo Romero had come to personify their martyrdom and their hopes. The civilian leader of the April revolt, Agustín Alfaro Morán, more mature and with a greater gift for handling people, quickly stepped back to become the organizer of Romero's party, the Partido de Unión Democrática (P.U.D.). Romero himself left for Rochester, Minnesota, for a series of surgical operations.

Romerismo swept the land as something fervent, mystic, compelling. Romero—in Spanish the word means "pilgrim"—would lead his people in quest of the grail: release from hacking poverty and groveling servitude. Practically the entire medical profession was behind him. While the other candidates distributed liquor and tamales in the time-honored fashion, Romerista medical and dental brigades, assisted by students and stocked with free samples from pharmaceutical firms, toured the countryside each weekend. Without fee they treated the ailing as a token of the health services that would be available to all once Romero was elected. When Romero returned from the United States for a brief visit between operations, eighty thousand people packed the central square of the capital to hear his evangel of "fewer machetes, more schools." A lyric warble filled the air; men's souls were big with hope and warmth. Skulking in their fortresses, the militarists were not at all happy.

Given this state of affairs, the reactionaries did not dare advance the candidate of their hearts' desire. The best they could do was throw their weight behind General Salvador Castañeda Castro. Castañeda, a former interior minister of Martínez's, wore a dim halo for having been imprisoned by the dictator for a few months in 1934 and then retired on full pay. A well-meaning man, notoriously henpecked by both his wife and mistress, he was far too ineffectual to have made many enemies. The younger officers remembered him fondly as a humane director of the military academy. He had been offered the military command of the April revolt, but begged off: "I am too old, and besides, the police keep their eye on me." Yet when Martínez was reeling under the thrust of the general strike, Castañeda felt rejuvenated: he headed a self-appointed "strike committee" that called on Martínez and tried to cull the laurels. Behind Castañeda the militarists and rightist planters rallied with something less than enthusiasm.

The campaign was speckled with violence. When Romero addressed a meeting in San Miguel, the Castañedistas opened fire, and in the resulting skirmish several victims fell. Here and there Romeristas were beaten up and their homes sacked. The popular beast, subdued in 1932,* was again on the prowl and had to be worried until he could be enchained once more. The reactionaries saw El Salvador poised at the brink of their flat, medieval world, an inch removed from the bottomless void.

On June 30 the commanders of the capital forts visited President Menéndez and ordered him to move the elections forward from August to January. The elections were postponed. The democratic police chief in May was dismissed for excessive decency and replaced by the hard-drinking Colonel Osmín Aguirre, one of the artisans of Martínez's December 1931 coup and the 1932 butchery. With Osmín in charge of the police, the government was shorn of effective control. Soon it was worth a man's life and liberty to be found shouting "Viva Romero." Informers, who had disappeared during the honeymoon days of the revolution, returned to inhabit the shadows. The army was gathering up the powers spilled in May.

Sprawling and undisciplined, the Romerista P.U.D. was without a sense of tactics or maneuver. With Romero and Alfaro absent from the country, the P.U.D. had a big pulsing heart, but no head. The most disparate elements clambered onto the bandwagon. The independent papers that mushroomed throughout the country hit upon a brilliant business principle: the shriller their headlines against the clergy and army, the quicker their editions were snatched up. It mattered little that Romero himself moved cautiously and couched his social program in terms of the papal encyclical *Rerum Novarum* to avoid needlessly provoking the more neutral priests and officers. As a final straw the reaction circulated leaflets scurrilously attacking the army and signed by fictitious Romerista committees: there were so many of the latter that the public could not keep track of them.

The Communists were no great help. Those who had remained in El Salvador throughout the Martínez dictatorship and suffered persecution for their views collaborated loyally with the Romeristas. But when the highly politicized exiles began dribbling back from Mexico, difficulties ensued. Many of these had backed the Mexican fellow-traveling trade-union leader Vicente Lombardo Toledano in his denunciation of the anti-Martínez revolt as "fascist-inspired." Because of the Soviet-American war alliance, Communists were trying to

---

*The author is again referring to the massacre of peasants set off by Gen. Hernández Martínez in 1932.

ingratiate themselves with the State Department by aping its support of Latin America's dictators. When the revolution broke in El Salvador, Lombardo Toledano had made a grandiloquent appeal: "Central Americans, you have waited a century for your liberties. Wait a bit longer until the war is over."*

It is an oddity of the bureaucratic mind to imagine that sweeping social movements can be started or stopped by pressing a button or issuing a ukase. But once Martínez had fallen, and the golden harvest beckoned in the breeze, the Communists hurried back from Mexico to bring it in. One of these, Alejandro Dagoberto Marroquín, obtained control of the Unión Nacional de Trabajadores (U.N.T.), a trade union center organized after the dictator's exit. He used it less as a trade union than as a ladder for his personal political ambitions.† The U.N.T. received financial and moral support from the Romerista party, and on the strength of that recruited Romeristas in the provinces. But once it had grown sufficiently, Dagoberto began bargaining with the Romerista party for the vice-presidential nomination, and even announced a U.N.T. convention to pick a presidential candidate. The Romeristas discontinued their financial subsidy. Unlike the Guatemalan unions, the U.N.T. was too enmeshed in political scheming to do much about improving wages and working conditions.

Pro-Franco Spanish Capuchin monks agitated intensely from pulpit and confessional against the "ungodly and Communist" Romeristas.

The Honduran exiles who flocked into El Salvador were warmly received by the local democrats. These *émigrés* used El Salvador as a base for armed expeditions against the Honduran dictator Tiburcio Carías; the Honduran and Nicaraguan tyrants were riddled in the Salvadoran press. With reason, Carías and Somoza saw in El Salvador and Guatemala democratic foci that imperiled their own regimes, and took steps to eradicate them. Honduran and Nicaraguan money circulated freely among Salvadoran army officers. Intrigues were spun in Managua, Tegucigalpa, and Washington. The counteroffensive to

---

*This position corresponded with the so-called Browder line, or "Browderism," named after U.S. Communist leader Earl Browder. The CPUSA maintained it to the end of World War II, and most Latin American Communist parties agreed to postpone their own programs till after defeat of the Axis, under the prevailing tactics of the period.

†One of the earliest fighters against fascism and imperialism, the late writer Vicente Sáenz, has come to the rescue of the "lofty vision and good faith" of Marroquín, although, according to a note in the first Spanish edition of Krehm's book, the Central American Democratic Union which Sáenz directed was always against Marroquín's "tactics."

recoup Guatemala and El Salvador for law and order was closely coordinated and under the very best auspices.

By mid-October, when dictator Ponce in Guatemala was gloating prematurely over the pulverization of the Arévalo party, the Salvadoran militarists, too, were ready to act.

On Friday October 20, ten thousand Romeristas, having finished their weekly meeting in Libertad Park, marched through the streets of the capital to deposit their party banners in their headquarters. As they wheeled by the Castañedista offices, they were fired upon. The crowd stampeded, leaving a couple of dead and many wounded. When Menéndez's interior minister phoned Police Chief Osmín Aguirre to enquire what the shooting was about, Osmín assured him that it was of no importance and urged him to return to bed: charitably enough, for Menéndez's cabinet was to get little sleep that night. In synchronized raids the police rounded up hundreds of Romeristas in the provinces. At two A.M., Menéndez and his ministers were pulled out of their beds and taken to the Zapote fortress alongside the presidential residence. Menéndez's aged mother-in-law was rudely handled when she protested; his wife, of known Romerista sympathies, was locked in her room and escaped by sliding down a drainpipe.

In the fortress Menéndez was made to sign a prepared statement abandoning the presidency because of ill health. His interior minister, a medical man with a prickly professional conscience, refused to add his signature to the document unless the reference to the president's health were omitted. Under pressure, however, he gave way.

Menéndez was allotted a $37 monthly pension and released the following day. A few weeks later he slipped out of Guatemala and told the world that his resignation had been extracted under duress.

With Menéndez out of the way, the legislature was convoked in the Zapote fortress and Osmín Aguirre sworn in as provisional president "to save the country from anarchy."

While Menéndez was being dragged to the fort, the police had attacked the Mortgage Bank guards and seized the building. The Mortgage Bank was cordially loathed by the reaction as the hotbed of democratic sedition, and many of its executives were arrested the following morning. New bank directors were named by the Aguirre government, but the personnel refused to recognize the usurpation and declared a strike. For days the police worked with acetyline torches to get into the bank's vaults. When it opened its doors a week later, there was a run on it. Public confidence, laboriously built up over a decade, was shattered. For months thereafter the private banks, vulturelike, did a record business.

The foreign legations were bursting with refugees. Once more the Peruvian legation picked up its laurels of April and housed nearly fifty. When I visited there, I was greeted like an old friend by the warm-hearted chargé d'affaires and his guests. The latter included an atrociously mauled student whose arm had been broken by the police in two places and whose head, back, and legs bore gruesome marks of rifle butts. The police prowled on the fringes of the legation grounds and insulted the relatives of the inmates who came with their food offerings. For many weeks the siege continued while Osmín Aguirre stubbornly refused to grant the refugees safe-conducts to leave the country. A month later, during the absence of the chargé, the police seized his five-year-old son and, holding a rifle to his head, threatened to shoot unless two of the refugees gave themselves up. The refugees surrendered, and several blistering notes from the Lima government were necessary before they were restored to their sanctuary.

On the night of the coup nine Romerista leaders, including Alfonso Rochac, former manager of the Mortgage Bank, were kidnapped, placed on army trucks, and driven over the Honduran frontier. With no hint as to where they were being taken, they resigned themselves to the fate of many of their comrades: shots in the dark and a shallow grave. At the border a Honduran colonel and troops were on hand to receive them. Calmly, the colonel pointed his Thompson gun at each of them in turn as he checked off their names on a list. For two more days the suspense continued, until they reached the Ojo de Agua fortress near the Nicaraguan boundary. There they were left to the care of Colonel Tomás Martínez, one of Carías's sanguinary rustic satraps. Martínez was the soul of solicitude. His wife cooked their meals, and when they declared a hunger strike some weeks later, dictator Carías phoned daily from Tegucigalpa to ask why they were not eating. For a week nobody in the outside world knew what had befallen them or where, until the Mexican ambassador at Tegucigalpa loosened the tongue of Carías's obtuse chief of protocol and learned their location.

During their confinement, bands of armed Honduran exiles irrupted into the country from Nicaragua, and seized some dynamite sticks from the nearby Agua Fría mine. The Salvadorans could hear the bombing by the government planes and see the ragged barefooted troops being rushed up to repel the revolutionaries. As zone commander, Colonel Martínez shouted his orders to the commander in the field into a telephone outside their rooms: "Don't be cowards! Let 'em have it! Hit 'em hard! If I weren't looking after these gentlemen here, I would show you how to do it."

Dictators Carías and Aguirre never clarified under what principles of international law Honduras had become a prison for Salvadoran democrats. Not until six weeks later, when they had started a hunger strike, and the Mexican ambassador at Tegucigalpa threatened to leave the country, were the last of the nine released.

Bruised and jolted, the Salvadoran people rallied to meet Aguirre's challenge. In staggered fashion, wheels stopped turning, and the country's economic life was hobbled. The banks led, and the university and many government offices followed. Railway mechanics were lodged in foreign legations beyond police vengeance, and the railroads were able to maintain minimum operations only by importing Nicaraguan blacklegs. Confidently, the Salvadorans were treading familiar paths.

The government radio blared the charge that "Jewish capitalism" had organized the strike. Tough peasants were brought in from the East to reinforce the capital's barracks. Heavily armed soldiers patrolled the city in force on foot, in jeeps, and trucks, and intimidated shopkeepers.

Soon it was clear that no government would recognize Osmín Aguirre, except his accomplices, the Nicaraguan and Honduran dictators, and Franco Spain. The lines were too clearly drawn even for the U.S. State Department to overlook them. Aguirre's subsecretary of the interior, Ramón López Jiménez, had achieved notoriety in diplomatic circles a decade earlier with a book defending Martínez's recognition of Manchukuo. In its way the volume enjoyed great success and was even published in a Japanese translation. Other pro-Axis lights graced Aguirre's cabinet.

The new American ambassador, John S. Simmons, had not yet presented his credentials, but won great popularity by circulating unaccompanied through the streets and observing what was going on. Thirty thousand women streamed to the embassy and were permitted to sign a petition to the State Department against recognition of the Aguirre regime. At the beginning they were manhandled by the police on their way out, but the embassy prevailed upon Aguirre to withdraw the massed police from its gates.

News of Ponce's overthrow in Guatemala trickled in and heartened the people. The Supreme Court, headed by the octogenarian Miguel Molina, declared the Aguirre government unconstitutional. As Menéndez's legal successor, Molina issued a manifesto announcing that he had set up a constitutional regime "somewhere in El Salvador." In reality Molina, smuggled out in the car of a friendly diplomat, was already in Guatemala, and the copy of his manifesto that I brought out of El Salvador was the first that he saw.

Aguirre had reserved posts in his cabinet for representatives of the minor parties to give his coup a purely anti-Romero aspect. All but one of these groups declined the ministries.

I visited Aguirre at the height of his troubles. I mistook him for a minor palace flunky as he shuffled into the room, chinless and shifty; when he corrected the error, I inadvertently blurted out: "So you are the president!" Ravaged by liquor and disease, he looked more decrepit at fifty-five than Molina at eighty-two. He seemed the sort of inarticulate, mediocre person for whom brutality is the only possible medium of self-expression. He had killed on a monumental scale in 1932, and now was at it again. Nevertheless, caught between the popular fury on the one hand and the diplomatic boycott on the other, he played the reasonable fellow. He assured me that he had acted against communism, but would give the country free elections.

Under Aguirre's repression the strike petered out. It had been an adequate weapon against the dictator in May. Clumsily, Martínez had alienated every sector of the nation: the bulk of the planters and the Church had backed the strike. When the situation became critical, the military had jettisoned Martínez and sat tight. In the intervening months democracy had been sorted from greedy privilege; the coffee barons and the pro-Franco Spanish priests fell in behind Aguirre. Now the people were face to face with the military caste as such. A peaceful strike was unequal to the task of ousting a martial machine bristling with modern armament.

Though the strike folded up, the Mortgage Bank employees refused to return to work, and the independent newspapers did not resume publication until the end of the year. Guatemala closed its railway to Salvadoran goods in transit to and from Puerto Barrios on the Caribbean. The cost of living leapt violently. Business was at a standstill.

The opposition turned to terrorism. The previous summer Salvadorans had helped Guatemalan exiles fabricate bombs for use against the Guatemalan dictator. Now that dictator Ponce had been laid low, the positions of Guatemalans and Salvadorans were suddenly reversed. Bombs that had been earmarked for export began popping in the homes of prominent Aguirre supporters. Digging deep into its arsenal for a war of nerves, the democrats began propagating fanciful rumors of mass lynchings of Ponce supporters in Guatemala, and of an underground Committee of Public Safety functioning in Salvador that passed sentences on the enemies of the people. The password of the terrorists was *Pitos y Cohuetes*, "Firecrackers and Whistles." Three barrels of fireworks went off in one of the town's central squares one afternoon, and the police panicked and shot two civilians. Aguirre ordered all fireworks manufacturers to declare their gunpowder stocks. His deputies took to sleeping in the Zapote fortress, where the country's official political life was fast becoming concentrated. Government members wore faces longer than those of the vanquished democrats. It looked increasingly as though Aguirre had caught a bear by the tail and was at a loss how to let go. The Salvadoran ministers and ambassadors in Washington, Guatemala, Mexico, and Costa Rica pronounced themselves in favor of Molina's government-in-exile. His peacemaking envoy was snubbed by Guatemala's revolutionary junta and returned in double-quick time. Guatemala refused to visa Salvadoran passports.

All hopes were pinned on Guatemala, once the darkest hole of Central American tyranny. The day after the Aguirre coup the revolutionary junta there had sent a plane to San Salvador to bring certain leading democrats to Guatemala. As soon as these arrived the Guatemalan junta promised them all aid to overthrow Aguirre and reestablish democratic government in El Salvador.* Troops were dispatched to the Salvadoran frontier.

Aguirre refused to permit the hundreds of refugees in the foreign legations to leave the country, lest they swell the army of Salvadoran exiles that was training in Guatemala. Instead he implored them to return to their homes with full guarantees. Few accepted the offer. Bombs continued going off in the most unexpected places. Aguirre's police entered the French legation with drawn revolvers and shot down some of the democrats sheltered there. Practically without a foreign service, he had his hands full with the ensuing diplomatic incidents. The broadcasts of the exiles assured the martyred nation that the day of reckoning was close at hand.

It seemed that the merest shove would suffice to bring Aguirre's regime to the ground. The bear was as good as dead, and there was a rush to divide his pelt. Many oppositionists had not warmed to Romero's candidacy, which was, indeed, the accidental outcome of his miraculous escape from the firing squad. The bright young lawyers were inclined to be a bit condescending about his lack of political flair and his lyric social program. Some, too, were resentful of his readiness to fill all panels of the triptych raised to him by the worshipping people, without reserving a corner for his comrades in the hazards and travail of the April revolt. In general around the government-in-exile the liberal coffee planters, lawyers and old-school politicians gathered, while labor, the doctors, students, and school teachers and above all the women swooned for Romero. Romero, however, a rather ingenuous soul, allowed himself to be surrounded by a few calculating

---

*On the plane was Alfaro Morán with his family, and the Guatemalan junta member Jorge Toriello personally met him and promised his help against Osmín Aguirre.

politicians, and by young army officers who had little sympathy for his aspirations of social reform but judged him a good horse to ride.

Cold logic would have dictated that the military expedition against Aguirre be entrusted to the government-in-exile, so that it might appear not as a partisan enterprise, but an attempt of all democrats to restore free institutions. Besides, the Molina government had the few experienced military men in oppositionist ranks. On his return from the United States, however, Romero was influenced to view the men around Molina with distrust. After its first heroic impulse, the Guatemalan junta was stricken with caution, and preferred treating with Romero, who was after all but a private citizen, rather than with the government-in-exile. As a result the invasion became a purely Romerista venture, and the few older officers who had acquitted themselves well in the April revolt were not consulted in its organization.

Despite Romero's fabulous popularity, the terrorist leaders within El Salvador were close to the government-in-exile. They toyed with the idea of forestalling the Romerista incursion and overthrowing Aguirre alone by a coup in the capital. Nevertheless Alfaro Morán, who throughout had tried bridging the rivalries of the two groups, persuaded the internal *maquis* to synchronize their action with that of the Romeristas. The date was set for December 9.

Over eight hundred Salvadorans had been training in Guatemala at Jalpatagua, some sixteen miles from the frontier. Some had escaped from El Salvador only a few days before they were to return with the liberating expedition. The Romeristas had signed an I.O.U. for $135,000 for provisions and arms received from Guatemala—rifles for the most part, a few automatic guns, and four machine guns. There was neither artillery nor aviation. Aguirre, they knew, would receive them with every modern weapon on land and in the air, but they trusted in the justice of their cause. It was as touching in its madness as the Children's Crusade.

The plan was simple and betrayed the generalship of lieutenants. The main column of 460 men was to march on Romero's home town, Ahuachapán. Another hundred and fifty men were to cross from the Guatemalan side to the village San Antonio Pajonal to divert the Aguirre forces. But Ahuachapán, a town of ten thousand, had been the center of the Communist disturbances in 1932. Its wealthy citizens had never since forgotten the blind violence of the Indians, while its humble classes, remembering the bloody reprisals of Martínez, were not eager to hurl themselves into another adventure. It would have been wiser for the invaders to have chosen Santa Ana for their objective. For Santa Ana, second city of the republic, was staunchly pro-

Romero and the hub of a thickly populated region. They decided against Santa Ana because of the strong garrison stationed there; yet that same garrison could rush reinforcements to Ahuachapán by railway or over an excellent road. Ahuachapán offered all the drawbacks of Santa Ana without a single of its advantages.

The officers in charge were familiar with the Salvadoran side of the frontier, but had not bothered reconnoitering the Guatemalan stretch from their Jalpatagua camp to the border. On the map it was a mere sixteen miles, and they hoped that setting out at four in the morning their column could reach the dividing River Paz shortly after dawn. Enough provisions were taken along for a snack before entering El Salvador; after that it was expected that the grateful liberated population would provide the victuals. However, when the expedition broke camp on December 8, the sixteen miles turned out to be scabrous goats' trail. Starved and exhausted, the men reached the boundary two days later. Then they had to fight continual skirmishes on the way to Ahuachapán.

Known Romeristas had been evacuated from the town by the government, which was kept apprised of the invasion plans. The liberators found all doors bolted, and could not obtain so much as a glass of water. Without difficulty they took the police headquarters, the town hall, and the telegraph, but the barracks held out. Four planes swooped low, bombing and machine-gunning the Romeristas. Troops poured in from Santa Ana and Sonsonate and began encircling the town. To avoid being cut off, the Romeristas fell back. The air force straffed them during their retreat; government troops lay in ambush. Many dropped in their tracks from inanition, and were finished off by the enemy. For three days the trickle of ragged, bone-weary boys continued across the frontier.

At the last moment a third column was improvised to march against Santa Ana under the war minister of the government-in-exile, a colonel with a thorough French training. But by that time the Guatemalan junta, alarmed by the extent of the disaster, began calling in its arms.

The uprising in the capital had been timed for the ninth to coincide with the invasion. At various points throughout the city *maquis* groups waited breathlessly for the signal—carnival fireworks set off from a rooftop. Outside the National Palace a cluster of boys, their pockets bulging with hand grenades, scanned the heavens and sweated in cold suspense. No flares appeared, the person assigned to light them had wilted at the last moment. Only in one suburb, San Miguelito, did the *maquis* strike. Thirty men seized the police station, carried off rifles and ammunition, and barricaded themselves in the local church. When it was clear that they were doomed, the son of a

Supreme Court judge held off the police from the belfry while his
companions escaped. An excellent sharpshooter, he nicked off ten or
so police before he died. It was a futile, heart-rending muddle. Only
on the following day did the weary column from Guatemala enter El
Salvador.

Still without word from his expedition, Romero on the twelfth
dispatched a messenger to Ahuachapán to find out what had become
of it. He returned and reported glowingly that the town had risen to
welcome its redeemers. That was the origin of the optimistic reports
flashed to the world from Guatemala. Later it was discovered that the
cowardly man had never reached Ahuachapán, but invented his
pretty tale after crossing the River Paz. On the strength of this fabrica-
tion Romero sent on a portable radio station with a crew of twelve
who fell into the enemy's hands and were killed.

I arrived in Guatemala on December 14 and on the same night
joined a party of Romeristas who were taking a load of bread and
cheese for the defeated army. Once we left the Pan-American highway, we had to get out every few miles to remove boulders that the car
was not equal to clearing. By dawn we were at Jalpatagua. Two hundred and fifty haggard, disheveled men huddled in the porticos on
the central square to escape the biting night wind. The region around
Jalpatagua is arid and sparsely settled, and food was nowhere to be
found for so many mouths. They queued up to receive their rations
from the provisions we had brought: two slices of dry bread and a
couple of ounces of cheese per man. Some had gone for three days
without nourishment; their clothes were in tatters. In a nearby hut the
Guatemalan Red Cross ministered to a few wounded. Survivors still
dribbled in. Each drew hysterical embraces reserved for those
snatched from the jaws of death.

One hundred and fifty men were still missing. On the other side
Aguirre boasted of having killed six hundred. The discrepancy was
not entirely due to martial bragging: in the wake of their triumph the
Aguirre forces had rounded up and slaughtered Romeristas who had
not come from Guatemala. From the wan lips of the men at Jalpatagua came stories of a hopeless fight of rifles against planes and machine guns. But they were still unrepentant. Nobody entertained the
idea that Osmín Aguirre could stay in power.

The Guatemalan junta was apprehensive of international complications arising from the fainthearted aid that it had given the
Romeristas. Rifles bearing the Guatemalan crest and captured from
the invaders were gloatingly exhibited in San Salvador. Already the
Salvadoran radio flatly charged Guatemala with organizing the incursion. In tones of admonishment a member of the Guatemalan junta
replied that the outcome would have been very different if that had

been so. There were hurried consultations between Honduras, Nicaragua, and the Aguirre government, and talk of a military alliance against Guatemala. To calm the storm, the junta whisked Romero out of circulation and packed him off to Costa Rica, an embittered and dazed man. Before he left, the junta persuaded him to issue a manifesto withdrawing his candidacy in the Salvadoran presidential race. Aguirre had already effectively done this for him, but the government-in-exile hoped that Romero's declaration would unleash the latent antagonists in Aguirre's camp, hitherto cohibited by a common dread of Romero. But amongst the Salvadoran people Romero's manifesto exerted a demoralizing influence.

Aguirre had come out of it all better than he had dared hope. He even began caressing the thought of staying on in the presidency himself instead of putting in Castañeda, the candidate that the reactionaries had sullenly accepted when their backs were to the wall. Tension set in between the government and Castañeda, and for a while it was uncertain that the elections would take place at all. The hostility of the U.S. embassy, however, enjoined caution upon Aguirre. The elections were held in January. Alleging fraud and intimidation, the small independent parties withdrew from the running. Peasants were brought into the capital in army trucks and given vouchers for food and drink each time they cast a vote for Castañeda. Nobody was surprised when Castañeda was swept to victory on a high flood of ballots.

In January the independent press, which had suspended publication in protest against the Aguirre coup, reappeared. Its vitriolic indictment of the regime was permitted: because of the repudiation of the governments of the hemisphere, Aguirre was on his very best behavior. Basking in the wintry sun of this tolerance, the people licked their wounds, took heart once more, and steadied themselves for a final push. Then, suddenly, they were stabbed in the back by an unexpected hand, and their hopes turned to ashes.

On February 18, 1945, a little more than a week before Castañeda was scheduled to be inaugurated, the United States of America extended its recognition to the government of Osmín Aguirre.

Traditionally, El Salvador has been the most independent of the Central American republics. Foreign capital plays a relatively minor role in its economy. Imperialist aggression anywhere in the isthmus has always aroused the most vocal resentment in El Salvador. During the 1920s when the State Department had five thumbs in the Central American pie, anti-U.S. feeling was so intense in El Salvador that schoolchildren would make it a point of honor to flunk their English examinations. Laboriously, the Good Neighbor policy had assuaged this rancor. Now, overnight, the recognition of Aguirre undid all. Everything connected with the United States became abomination. In the movies Roosevelt was booed when he appeared on the screen. Leaflets circulated with a picture of Roosevelt against a swastika background and the text: "Roosevelt sheds his mask." By every mail the United States embassy received photos of Roosevelt previously used as toilet paper. Neat packages of dung arrived by parcel post. Though it was an open secret that the embassy in El Salvador had vigorously opposed Aguirre's recognition, its members were snubbed in public.

And what were the statesmanly reasons that led Washington to touch off the most violent anti-U.S. outburst that Central America had witnessed in fifteen years?

The official pretext was the need to confront Argentina with a united body of continental opinion at the Chapultepec Conference that was to open in Mexico on February 21.* Yet by taking Osmín Aguirre unto its bosom the State Department stripped its stand against Perón of all moral plausibility; what remained was the mere truculence of power politics.

As so often happens, "inter-American consultation" on the subject of El Salvador consisted simply of Washington ramming its caprice down the throats of the other republics. But all did not run smoothly. United States recognition alone was not enough to bring the Salvadoran delegation to the Chapultepec Conference. As host, Mexico alone could extend the invitation. Washington, indeed, had recognized Aguirre only after receiving assurances that Mexico would follow suit from Ezequiel Padilla, Mexico's rightist foreign minister, loathed by most of his countrymen as a stooge of the State Department. But apprised of what was afoot, Guatemala appealed to Mexican President Avila Camacho directly; Avila Camacho reversed Padilla's decision and promised Guatemala that Salvador would be recognized by Mexico only after Aguirre had handed over power to Castañeda on March 1. The State Department, having counted on Padilla's ability to deliver the goods, was left out on a limb. A Machiavelian Mexican foreign minister, intent on maneuvering the United States into a position of unpopularity, could have done no better than the servile Padilla.

Worse still, Guatemala now refused to attend the Chapultepec Conference. Never had a Central American republic been known to

---

*Argentina, governed by Farrell and Perón, continued refusing to break definitively with the Axis. It only did so weeks before the defeat of Hitler, declaring war on the Third Reich in order to be eligible for participation in the United Nations' postwar arrangements.

behave in so headstrong a fashion. In Mexico City U.S. Ambassador George S. Messersmith summoned the Guatemalan ambassador, Guillermo Toriello, to tell him that while he appreciated Guatemala's feelings, "higher interests" had required Aguirre's recognition. Although Guatemala was the country most vitally affected, Messersmith did not deign disclose to Toriello what these "higher interests" might be.

Guatemala remained adamant right up to February 20, a day before the conference was to open. Early that morning a U.S. Army plane swooped down onto the Guatemala City airport. From it emerged Secretary of State Edward Stettinius, homeward bound from the Yalta Conference. Wreathed in smiles, Stettinius asked to see the president. Gently he was informed that there had been no president in Guatemala since the last one was thrown out four months earlier, but that there was a revolutionary junta of three. He was taken to the junta. When Jorge Toriello, speaking for the junta, gave him a sizzling piece of his mind concerning the U.S. recognition of Aguirre two days before, Stettinius pleaded that that was the first time he had heard of it. But he did turn on the full jet of his charm, and cajoled the junta into allowing him to take a Guatemalan delegation with him to Mexico City.

We can only surmise what went on behind the scenes. Later, Nicaraguan dictator Somoza was to boast that he had brought to bear his influence in Washington to secure recognition for Aguirre. Inclined by a stubborn mental habit to lay all their ills at the door of the United Fruit Company, Central Americans attributed the recognition to its intrigues. Investments in El Salvador—apart from its interest in the International Railway of Central America—the fruit trust did not have. But El Salvador had become the key to the entire Central American situation. Aguirre protected the flank of the Honduran dictatorship; he was a club poised over the head of Guatemala, where United Fruit was having its full share of labor and taxation troubles. Yet there was no evidence, and the fruit trust might well have been as innocent as it maintained.

The person least happy about Aguirre's recognition was the president-elect, Castañeda. For it became doubtful whether Aguirre, emboldened by the tardy accolade, would vacate the presidency at all. Relations between Castañeda and Aguirre grew strained. Aguirre issued an amnesty worded to take in his own group as well as his opponents, but the assembly, controlled by Castañeda, was not eager to allow him feathers for his cap. When the amnesty bill was submitted to it, only five deputies turned up, and there was no quorum.

On March 1 the inauguration did take place. In the blistering Salvadoran midday heat, diplomats in tails, army officers, and a few curious private citizens crowded into the Red Room of the adobe

National Palace. Aguirre, nervously licking his lips, stood alongside Castañeda, but the two studiously avoided meeting each other's gaze. After Aguirre in melancholy tones had bumbled through his speech, Castañeda received the presidential sash. Five military planes and a question mark hovered overhead.

Castañeda excluded from his cabinet Aguirre and his leading collaborators in the October coup. But he failed to follow up this auspicious beginning by attracting oppositionist elements and broadening his government's base. Aguirre rented a house alongside the police headquarters, which he regarded as his stronghold, and went to huddle there. The government-in-exile disbanded, and its members returned to their homes.

Castañeda's position was that of a tightrope walker, with only space beneath him, and exposed to a fatal push from either side. There were so many virile generals, each eager to save his country, that they actually got into one another's way. At first it seemed that the power and the glory would be to him who contrived first to give Castañeda the necessary fillip. On the other side, too, the skulking Romeristas were awaiting their chance.

Reaching for something to lean upon, Castañeda met President Arévalo of Guatemala at the frontier on May 17, and they signed a pact proclaiming the political union of the two lands as their nebulous goal. In reality, it had little to do with union. For Guatemala it was a diplomatic triumph: Salvador had been wrenched out of the orbit of the Honduran and Nicaraguan dictators and at least neutralized. Castañeda, for his part, hoped that it would improve his standing with his own people.

The Salvadoran army was not impressed. On June 10 part of the air force declared against the government and dropped a couple of bombs on the police station. The coup failed, and Aguirre's former interior minister, deeply involved, was shipped into exile.

Again Castañeda fumbled the opportunity for making his peace with the opposition. The Guatemalan minister, Roberto Arzú, offered to arrange a reception at his legation where the president could meet the democratic leaders. Castañeda was enthusiastic and promised eternal gratitude if Arzú were to bring about such a reunion. It was no easy task persuading the oppositionists to attend. Yet on the day of the rendezvous Castañeda phoned to tell Arzú that he had eaten some oysters that were not too good, and would he please excuse him for not turning up. The police, however, had had no oysters and surrounded the legation on horse and on foot. The oppositionists were in a white rage. As a final touch Castañeda complained to his friends about that Guatemalan minister who organized antigovernment meetings in his legation.

A constituent assembly had been chosen in grossly fraudulent elections, and applied itself in secret sessions to drawing up a new constitution. A few months later Castañeda rejected its draft, and instead had the democratic constitution of 1886 adopted in somewhat amended form. That was a substantial sop to public opinion.

Within Castañeda's cabinet, crisis followed crisis. That of September 1945 was typical enough. Carlos Guirola, the finance minister whose rigid honesty was bothersome to certain of his colleagues, was surprised to read in a morning paper close to the government that he had submitted his resignation. When he confronted Castañeda with the clipping, the latter shamefacedly offered him the Ministry of Foreign Affairs. Guirola resigned in a rage. Meanwhile the foreign minister, hearing that his post was being offered to someone else as a consolation prize, also resigned. The rest of the cabinet toppled over like a row of dominoes. Five people in succession were offered the Finance Ministry, but no one warmed to the suggestion. For a month the country was without a cabinet and yawned in boredom as Castañeda made the rounds peddling his ministries.

And yet for all its ineptness the government survived. Nobody was eager to overthrow it. The mainspring of Salvadoran politics had simply run down. The democrats were winded and demoralized, though until late in 1945 the odd bomb went off nostalgically here and there. On the other side the militarists were split into innumerable warring cliques—the academy officers against those risen from the ranks, old officers against young, fascist-minded against the traditional reactionaries. Osmín Aguirre himself had lost much prestige in military circles because of the illegal exports of foodstuffs that had flourished under his regime. Moreover, the dogged resistance of civilians had gradually taught many militarists that it was impossible to govern without a measure of popular acquiescence. More than anything else, Castañeda stayed on in the presidency by default. And as the months slipped by, people began wondering whether he had not been playing the idiot as a tactic, and whether there was not a shrewd streak beneath it all.

All the blood and thunder of 1944 had not been in vain. Liberty of the press prevailed, though now and again a leftist would be run out of the country. Local trade unions mushroomed and in a series of successful strikes bettered the lot of labor. The government was roundly trounced in parliament and wherever Salvadorans talked of politics. The nation felt cheated, for elections, rather relevant to a democracy, were a wretched farce. Yet it was a far cry from the grim days of the Martínez dictatorship. The mountain's labors had produced no mouse.

6

In Quest of a Railway

O F ALL THE CENTRAL AMERICAN REPUBLICS Honduras was the most woebegone. With no other communication to the outside world than planes and mud-tracks, Tegucigalpa breathed a spiritual desolation that one found in none of the other capitals. The national library called to mind a neglected chicken coop, but dictator Tiburcio Carías claimed the role of "providential man" for having cobbled a few streets. In the War Ministry, a Dickenslike setting of broken chairs, high officials were engaged in signing exit visas and playing checkers with pop-bottle tops. All this and much else prompted the visitor to scratch and sigh deeply for humankind. It was like a caricature of a caricature.

Honduras was a mother that had spawned notable sons. Francisco Morazán, Central America's great champion of democracy and union, was born in Tegucigalpa. José Cecilio del Valle, encyclopedic savant and one of the fathers of Central American independence, was from Choluteca. But somehow history cheated Honduras and left it a moldy nook, whose yokel setting made its very tragedy just a mite ludicrous. Even the statue of Morazán on Tegucigalpa's central square, where the band plays every Sunday night, is not really Morazán as the inscription states, but—of all things—Marshal Ney.* A commission was sent to Europe in the last century to order a statue of Morazán, but ran out of funds; they were thus reduced to buying up cheap an equestrian figure of the Marshal, created for a French town that rejected it. That is the sort of thing that happens to all that Honduras sets its heart on.

Between the malarial marshes around the Gulf of Fonseca and

---

*Michel Ney (1769–1815), Duke of Elchingen, Marshal of France: revolutionary and military leader who distinguished himself in Napoleon's Russian campaign, condemned and shot for treason after the defeat at Waterloo.

the Atlantic lowlands, Honduras is a billowing sea of pines. Only the occasional tight pocket of fertility breaks the monotony of the mountains. The impoverished settlements in these secluded valleys were dependent primarily on donkeys for their contact with one another and the world. Even the gold and silver output of the New York and Rosario Mining Company was brought to port by burro train. Only in the north, along the Caribbean, do the puckered wastes of pine give way to good level lands—a broad triangle of alluvial soil that has been washed down by the rivers from the highlands. The swift mountain streams, grown fat and lazy, overflow each year and renew the richness of their valleys.

The rank fertility of these lands meant little but disease before the American fruit companies came to drain, sanitate, and develop them. Today, in the western part of the coast from Puerto Cortés to La Ceiba, one can see what the tropics can become under the touch of modern engineering. Rows upon rows of banana trees spread their frond over a gridiron of steel rails; the administrators' settlements with their neat hedges, screened bungalows and landscaped boulevards cheer the eye. After the squalor of the mountain villages, one comes at last upon something made vital by the breath of enterprise.

Four fifths of Honduras's export consist of bananas from the coast. Yet economically irrelevant though it may be, the highlands are the country; from their amazing barrel chests, you sense at once that Hondurans are a mountain folk.

National unity in such a setting has necessarily been an abstraction. In the last century local chieftains came to wield an absolute authority in their isolated bailiwicks, and warred with one another for the greater spoils of the national treasury. It was in a way the replica of Europe in the darkest Middle Ages: what were called margraves, dukes, and barons there passed under the title of general in Honduras. Honduran generals came in two categories: the *generales gritados* (or "shouted generals," that is, chieftains who had proclaimed themselves generals on the battlefield), and the *generales legales*, elevated to that rank by Congress. The two were equally innocent of technical military training: there was no military academy.* Their equipment was personal valor, manliness, and a lack of scruples. And just as the myriad appetites of the feudal gentry of fourteenth-

---

*Early in the fifties, when the Inter-American Mutual Assistance Treaty began to be applied throughout Latin America, the United States promoted the establishment of military academies in Honduras, as in other countries of the region that lacked them. In May 1954 Washington signed a military mutual assistance pact, then designed to facilitate the maneuvers to destabilize the Arbenz regime in Guatemala, a pact still remaining in force.

century Italy were loosely integrated into Guelphs and Ghibbelines, with vague reference to their attitude toward the Papacy, so in Honduras the generals styled themselves Liberals or Conservatives supposedly because of their anticlericalism or clericalism. But the church question in Honduras, because of its very indigence, never assumed troubled forms. Clericalism and anticlericalism, federalism and centralism served periodically as the gauziest mantle thrown over the hot contest for spoils.

The parochial feuding of Honduras was absorbed and stimulated by the greater rivalries in the adjoining states. Honduran presidents were imposed, sustained and overthrown by the governments of Nicaragua, Salvador, and Guatemala. No matter who was in the saddle at Tegucigalpa, Honduras had everything to commend it as a no man's land. The unhappy republic became a smitten field; towns like Juticalpa, a thriving center in colonial times, sank into abandon.

Honduras was a country in quest of a railway. For a century its sons had dreamed of steel ribbons that would span the isthmus and bring to the scattered settlements the blessings of civilization. In the 1850's E. G. Squier, a United States diplomatic agent, sniffed a cool breeze on the torrid Fonseca shore and had a hunch that it blew in from the Caribbean through a gap in the mountains. Exploration disclosed the passage, and Squier launched a company to build a railway through it, from Puerto Cortés to the Pacific. That and other attempts failed, but Honduras piously reserved the "Squier Route" for its future railway.

Between 1867 and 1870 the government contracted four British loans totaling six million pounds to build the railway. The money stuck to the fingers of politicians and bankers, and to top it all, Honduras made the grievous mistake of paying the contractors by the mile. The railway wriggled imaginatively in the easy lowlands, and got winded before it had penetrated too far inland. By the time fifty miles had been built, the funds had evaporated in the tropical heat. But the debts contracted, with accumulated interest, amounted to $125,000,000 in 1926, and proved a millstone around the neck of the tiny land.

That staggering indebtedness had its sequel. Under President Taft the U.S. State Department had evolved a special formula for bringing the Caribbean lands under its sway: loans for the liquidation of their European debts, guaranteed by an American customs receivership, much as a dentist fits a golden crown upon an enervated molar.* With its backbreaking British debt, Honduras was a natural

---

*President Taft called this device, imposed by the United States on Honduras, Nicaragua, Haiti, and the Dominican Republic, among others, "Dollar

for such an arrangement. In 1910 the Liberal regime of President Miguel Dávila, harassed by the inevitable civil wars, was showing itself amenable to State Department pressure on the point. But just when Dávila was congratulating himself on his excellent relations with the Americans, something that augurs well for any Central American regime, his doom was shaping. For the idea of a customs receivership drew the displeasure of Samuel Zemurray.

Zemurray was a Bessarabian immigrant who had started his career buying overripe bananas from the United Fruit Company and peddling them in New Orleans. In time he began purchasing his bananas directly from Honduran planters, and he learned bananas and Honduras from within. Zemurray had visions of provinces of banana trees soaking up the tropical sun and of railways built to service them. Now the Customs Receivership Agreement contained a clause barring tariff exemptions until the United States loan was paid off; doing business in Honduras would thus have been reduced to the same dull affair as in the United States or any other sovereign land. That was not what Zemurray saw in his trances.

He sought out ex-President Manuel Bonilla, tough Conservative leader, perennially plotting Dávila's overthrow from exile. Zemurray bought him the ship *Hornet* and equipped it with arms. In addition, he helped him foil the vigilance of the United States authorities at New Orleans, who were determined that no expedition should sail against Dávila and the customs receivership. The *Hornet* disembarked men and arms at Trujillo, and after a few stirring weeks of campaigning had Dávila down on his knees. Brought around to see the force of Zemurray's logic, the State Department stepped in to negotiate Dávila's surrender. On October 1, 1911, Bonilla was elected president, and Honduras became a banana republic.

Bananas or plantains are a wonderful fruit. Sliced and added to cold cereals, they make a savory breakfast dish. They are useful in combatting dread sprue disease. One day North Americans may learn to regard the banana as a vegetable and roast it with meats as Latin Americans do. But to Hondurans in the hopeful year of 1911, they promised an interoceanic railway.

The railway will-o'-the-wisp had the Hondurans bemused again, and Zemurray exploited it to the fullest. With an understandable influence over the Bonilla regime, he not only obtained princely concessions for his own Cuyamel Fruit Company, but also for the United

---

Diplomacy." Constituting in effect a protectorate in disguise, it led to no few conflicts in Central America and the Caribbean between the 1910s and the 1930s, until finally President Franklin D. Roosevelt put a stop to it.

Fruit Company, his deadly rival of later years. The concessions covered railway construction and banana farming, and included customs exemptions not only on all materials required for the railways, telephone systems, irrigation works, but during the first ten years even on articles for the personal use of the companies' employees. United Fruit received the Tela and Trujillo regions; the Cuyamel, the western side of the Chamelecon River. Naturally, the terms of these concessions had a marked effect on the Honduran fiscal system; as late as 1927 the government was losing fully one third of its revenue from import duties under such special exemptions.

To obtain such generous franchises, United Fruit agreed to build a railway to Juticalpa, halfway from the north coast to the capital, and eventually to the capital itself. It was all laid out with engaging precision. The Truxillo Railway Company, subsidiary of United Fruit, would build twelve kilometers of railway each year, or pay a fine of $2,000 yearly for each kilometer of railway construction that fell behind schedule. After a certain number of years Honduras's capital would be connected with Puerto Castilla on the Caribbean, or the Honduran treasury would be prosperous enough with United Fruit fines to undertake the construction on its own. The Cuyamel Company made similar promises. Yet the mileage that was laid was little more than what was strictly necessary for the operation of the banana industry. It tended, therefore, to run parallel to the sea instead of climbing into the highlands. For each kilometer of railway built, the companies received from 550 to 1100 acres in lots of 10,000 to 12,000 acres alternating with similar lots reserved for homesteaders. But the companies, through intermediaries, went in for homesteading, too. Illegally, and at a nominal price, they acquired these "alternate lots" so that their plantations might stretch in vast unbroken domains.

Honduras's fateful dream of railways had saddled it with a burden more oppressive than the British debt. Its plight became clear when hostilities broke out between the United Fruit and Cuyamel companies. The bananas were to have brought railways, the railways cohesion and peace. It worked out otherwise: the traditional strife of rival political bands was now geared to the pitched warfare of the banana barons.

And that struggle was nothing to be contained within the borders of a single Central American republic. United Fruit had long been operating along the Motagua River in Guatemala, hard on the sketchy Honduran border. Now Zemurray obtained a concession from Honduras that overlapped upon his rival's Guatemalan holdings. A serious dispute flared forth between the two republics, with United Fruit beating the martial drum in Guatemala and Cuyamel doing cornet's duty in Honduras. Cuyamel struck heroic postures and urged that

Honduras go to war rather than yield an inch of territory. At Honduras's other extremity, where Zemurray held concessions from Nicaragua, Cuyamel backed Nicaragua in her boundary altercation with Honduras. War almost ensued between Honduras and Guatemala; the quarrel, indeed, went on for several years after the rival banana empires had merged and lost all interest in the patriotic issue.*

Due to the absence of an extradition treaty with Washington, there was a steady influx of U.S. scapegraces and cutthroats, who shot straight from the hip and served the highest bidder. For those who could overlook the tragedy of a little land there was much that was droll about Honduran politics. A whole generation of North Americans were entertained by the novels of Richard Harding Davis, without suspecting how much U.S. big business and diplomacy contributed to their subject matter.

In 1920 Cuyamel obtained a weird "antichresis" lease of the National Railway from Puerto Cortés to Potrerillos, in return for $1,000,000 credit bearing 8 percent interest. The loan was to be used for improvement of the line to enable it to haul heavy equipment for Cuyamel's sugar refinery at La Lima. The contract provided that the railway would revert to the government once the million dollar loan had been repaid out of its earnings.

The National Railway runs through the world's best banana lands; its control was the lever to their domination. Cuyamel made sure that the railway would not return to the government in a great hurry. Though Honduran law prohibited the building of private railroads in a zone forty kilometers on either side of the National Railway, Cuyamel proceeded to construct clandestine lines in the Choloma, San Pedro Sula, and Villanueva districts. Eventually it laid a railway along the Ulua River, directly parallel to the National Railway, to syphon off its traffic and revenues. In a pamphlet published in 1928, Rubén Bermudez, former accountant of the National Railway, charged that these "clandestine lines" had been built with National Railway equipment, and included photographs to prove the point. He alleged, too, that National Railway rolling stock was used on the "clandestine lines" without any rental. Since Bermudez was paid by the United Fruit Company for writing the pamphlet, his evidence cannot be lightly dismissed.†

---

*Note that to settle this "near war" between Honduras and Guatemala the U.S. government had to intervene, as if it did not know that the United Fruit-Cuyamel Fruit dispute was the key factor behind all the brouhaha.
†Denunciations of this kind were returned by Cuyamel, which hired experts to perform the same job against United. See Charles D. Kepner and Jay H. Soothill, *The Banana Empire.*

By these and other means the earnings of the National Railway were kept low: during the first eight years of the antichresis lease the debt actually grew to $1,514,711. Meanwhile, the control of the National Railway permitted Cuyamel to break the cooperatives of the independent planters. The entire region became a Cuyamel fief.

After a destructive three-cornered civil war in 1924, the Nationalist Miguel Paz Barahona became president.* In general, Cuyamel was backing the Liberals while United Fruit was betting on the Nationalist (Conservative) horse. President Paz Barahona, however, was estranged from the bulk of his party and soon found himself in Cuyamel's harness. The great issue that agitated Honduran politics of the period was the legalization of Cuyamel's "clandestine lines." Mercenary journalists, retained by one or the other of the fruit companies, were debating the issue in the press with heat and histrionics. President Paz Barahona was exerting himself to have the lines sanctified, while the president of Congress, Tiburcio Carías Andino, was blocking the move on orders from United Fruit. On the outcome of the fight hinged Cuyamel's continued control of the National Railway and the rich acres flanking it. Money circulated freely. It was during this time that Zemurray spoke his winged phrase: "In Honduras a mule costs more than a deputy."

Alfredo Schlesinger, a talented Guatemalan publicist of Austro-Hungarian origins, achieved the unusual feat of serving both Cuyamel and its arch-foe Carías at the same time. In 1927, on his way back from a lobbying mission in Washington on Carías's behalf, he met Zemurray in New Orleans and received the following instructions: "We are going to have Congress convoked to grant us a concession legalizing the clandestine lines. Now, I want you to go and tell Carías that either Congress approves the concession, or we will never let him become president. We will spend all the money necessary to prevent it."

Since Cuyamel was known for its readiness to fling cash around in fabulous quantities, Zemurray's threat packed an awful punch. Yet Schlesinger, having sought out Carías on his tiny farm at Zambrano, received an astounding reply: "Money never wins elections in Hon-

---

*This war prompted the U.S. minister in Tegucigalpa, Franklin Morales, to request intervention by the "Banana Fleet," as the U.S. naval squadron based in the Canal Zone was called. Two hundred Marines landed and remained in the capital for several weeks, without an invitation from any of the three conflicting factions. Finally, President Coolidge sent down Sumner Welles as his personal commissioner. Welles mediated a peace based on a provisional government which called elections. The Conservative—that is, the United Fruit candidate—was the winner.

duras." And the Carías-dominated Congress defeated Cuyamel's concession.

Zemurray got his revenge. There were two Liberal candidates doing setting-up exercises for the 1928 presidential race. With the Liberal vote split, Carías's triumph seemed assured. But Cuyamel set about cementing together the anti-Carías splinters. The two Liberal candidates were induced to retire in favor of Vicente Mejía Colindres, and Cuyamel made a large contribution to Mejía's campaign fund. Carías was soundly whipped at the polls, but Congress, not due to be renewed for another two years, remained under his control.

True to his bond, President Mejía submitted Cuyamel's concession to Congress once more. At Carías's beck Congress killed it again. Mejía referred the matter to the Supreme Court, which upheld Congress. After spending so much of his hard-earned money, Zemurray was foiled. He consoled himself by selling the Cuyamel Company to the United Fruit for cash and 300,000 shares of stock.* For he had foreseen the depression with its perils and promises. The banana war in Honduras was over. As the smoke cleared, only a single mammoth banana concern remained—apart from the Standard Fruit Company that grew bananas around La Ceiba and engaged in banking, soap manufacture, and brewing. But United Fruit feared no competition from Standard: the relations of the two companies were friendly and intimate.†

The physiognomy of Honduran politics was altered overnight. Hitherto the embattled banana companies had often held each other at bay; their rivalry was reflected in the clash of Congress and the executive, which created the illusion of the checks and balances of a democracy. An articulate public opinion had managed to survive as a no man's land of this mighty war. With the banana industry consolidated, it was inevitable that the trend in Honduran politics should be toward stability and toward dictatorship. Revolts would continue to occur as in the past, but there was no longer a rival fruit company to put muscle into them.

---

*According to Kepner and Soothill, in December 1929 when Zemurray received them, the 300,000 United Fruit shares were valued at $32,000,000, while the fixed assets of Cuyamel—including La Lima sugarmill, ships, rail lines, buildings and banana lands—were worth $26,000,000. Thus United rid itself of a fierce enemy whom, in addition, they made a vice president of their company. In this as in other transactions directly concerning them, neither the government nor the people of Honduras had anything to say; they did not even receive a few thousand dollars in real estate transfer tax.

†They had to be: Standard was, and still is, an undeclared subsidiary of United.

Executive and Congress no longer locked horns. In 1932 the irrigation tax on banana lands was reduced from ten to three dollars per hectare: later it was lowered again to $1.50. The $10 tax, against which United Fruit had raised a hue and cry, amounted to about 2.5¢ per bunch of bananas and had been perfectly acceptable to Standard Fruit. Practically, the only other taxation paid by the fruit companies in Honduras was a 1.5¢ export tax per bunch, amounting to one percent of the value. The issue of the "clandestine lines" was amicably settled: they became part of the National Railway, operated by United Fruit under the terms of the antichresis contract. With the independent producers eliminated or subjected, and the rival banana corporations merged, the lease of the National Railway had lost much of its strategic value. For the first time the antichresis debt began dwindling: in 1946 it amounted to little more than $300,000.

The former opponents, Mejía Colindres and Carías, suddenly found themselves working for the same master. Mejía favored Carías in the elections of November 1932. Banana gold was generously on hand for buying up the municipal authorities who ran the elections. Carías emerged triumphant.

But long before then momentous changes had taken place in the United Fruit Company itself. In 1932 its stock plunged catastrophically and its very directors began unloading their holdings. From his Louisiana retirement, Zemurray heard the call of destiny again. Gathering the necessary proxies from frantic shareholders, he turned up at the company's Boston offices. "You've f----- up the company long enough," he told President Cutter. "Get out."

The former fruit peddler found himself at the head of a $200,000,000 organization. Effecting drastic economies and putting his old Cuyamel crew in charge, Zemurray managed to bring the banana trust out of the red.

Honduras footed the bill for some of these economies. In 1933, for $98,000 and the surrender of 60,000 hectares of land that had cost it nothing, United Fruit was released from its obligation to build the railroad from Puerto Castilla to Juticalpa and Tegucigalpa.

That was a mere beginning. No sooner had Zemurray pulled floundering United Fruit out of the crisis than a new menace turned up. The Panama fungus, consuming root and stalk of the banana tree, appeared in Panama in the late twenties and spread like wildfire along the Caribbean coast. Entire areas were ruined for bananas, though the disease in no way impaired the usefulness of the soil for other crops. Throughout the isthmus the grand trek of the banana industry began from the steaming Caribbean coast to the Pacific littoral, where lower humidity is less favorable to the spread of the fungus. In 1935 the company abandoned its entire Truxillo division. For $150,000 it obtained permission to rip up the 125 kilometers of railway from Puerto Castilla to Iriona and ship rails and bridges out of the country. Thousands of Honduran settlers were left stranded as the jungle took possession again. The original concession had provided that the railway would revert to the government whenever the company ceased operating it. The company was likewise permitted to rip up other railways: from Puerto Castilla to Olanchito; from Omoa to the Guatemalan frontier. There was not even a thought given to the feasibility of leaving the bridges so that the right-of-way might be transformed into a road.

Counting the lines torn up and construction from which the company was released, Carías signed away over 700 kilometers of vital railway in a country that had repeatedly pawned its soul in the hope of acquiring railroads. The triangle of the northern coast is the only broad expanse of fertile land in Honduras; without communications it is closed to development. In bygone days Mussolini aroused the admiration of vacationing ladies by making the trains run on time; dictator Carías, more impressively, had done away with much of the country's railway system altogether. Let us take a look at the political setup where such things can happen.

On honest weight scales Tiburcio Carías Andino was far and away the greatest president of the Americas. One was keenly aware in his presence of the triumph of matter over mind: the huge bole of a body tapered off to a stubborn head. In his youth, it was said, he could break a rifle over his knee; now his friendly handshake left your knuckles tingling. He had been born some sixty-eight years before into a numerous family of Indian and Negro blood and fierce clannish ambitions. Young Tiburcio plunged into his country's civil strife at a very tender age. At sixteen he served as a cook for a band of Liberal guerrillas led by his brothers. In the 1907 war, in which the Nicaraguan dictator Zelaya helped the Liberals to power, Carías commanded a Liberal detachment without distinction. He had interrupted his plodding law studies to go off to the wars, and once the Liberals came out on top, they rewarded him with a law degree. In Central America lawyers sport the title "doctor," and by virtue of his spurious degree, Carías assumed the double-barreled prefix *Doctor y General.* Yet his legal career was terse: he took on one case and lost it.

Two decades of revolutioneering as a Liberal were getting him nowhere fast. Still far from midstream, he swapped horses. In 1923 he was Nationalist (Conservative) candidate for the presidency, and though he failed to obtain a majority, he polled the largest vote in a three-cornered contest. From the ensuing civil war, in which Tegucigalpa was bombarded by his planes, he emerged as a legendary strong man backed by the United Fruit Company. But in 1924 and again in 1928 he tasted electoral defeat. The country was in no hurry to recognize its savior.

During these decades of dismal trying, Carías was a poor man. He was supported by his wife, who ran a small roadhouse inn at Zambrano on the northern highway. He spent his days in a hammock, and on the strength of a tiny vegetable patch where he did some hoeing, passed as a Cincinnatus home from the wars.

But Dame Fortune finally leered at him. When he was hoisted to power by the banana trust, several distinct factors conspired to ensure him a lengthy tenure. The spread of totalitarianism in Europe offered him both a model and a propitious backdrop; the doting Good Neighbor threw in arms and underwrote his regime morally and financially. The perennial dictatorships that settled on the isthmus in the thirties coordinated their repression and covered one another's flanks.

And then there was air power. In November 1932, after Carías's electoral triumph, a section of the Liberal opposition rose in arms and marched on the capital from San Lorenzo. A barnstorming pilot from New Zealand, Lowell Yerex, who had set up a small aviation company, Transportes Aereos de Centroamerica (TACA), rallied to the government in its hour of need. Yerex's two planes flew in arms from El Salvador, where dictator Martínez offered his support, reconnoitered over the enemy lines, machine-gunned and bombed the rebels at El Sauce. In the fighting Yerex himself lost an eye. The bombing had dispersed the rebels when they seemed on the verge of victory. For his eye Yerex received a juicy concession that launched TACA on its phenomenal career. His subsequent marriage to the daughter of Carías's education minister fortified his position still further. Flying guns, liquor, merchandise; bringing in heavy machinery for the gold mines; remedying the lack of roads by making tracks in the blue Honduran skies, TACA became a unique institution, first in Honduras, and then in Central America as a whole. Transcontinental and Western Airways—TWA—acquired controlling interest in 1945.

Carías had been elected in 1932 for a four-year term under a constitution that barred reelection. In 1936, however, his Congress extended the presidential period to six years and gave him another term ending 1943. In 1939, by the simple device of "amending" the figure three to a nine, Congress gave him a further lease on the Presidential Palace until 1949. Never before in Honduran history had a president helped himself to a second term and survived to the end of it.

There was no further congressional election after 1932. Legislature and courts lost their independence and became mere tools of the dictator's whim. The autonomy of the larger towns was extinguished.

In 1933 internal passports were introduced. Martial law, with brief intervals, was in force from the moment Carías took power to the spring of 1946, when U.S. Undersecretary of State Spruille Braden put on the screws.* The press was gagged, the prisons jammed.

Tourists visiting police headquarters in the capital to pick up one of the three indispensable stamps for their passports received a rosy if chaotic picture of the Honduran penal system. The air was rent with the clatter of marimbas, the screech of fiddles, the flatulence of trumpets: the prisoners in their cells below were practicing their lessons, and casually letting the visitor know that the forward-looking regime of *Doctor y General* Tiburcio Carías had enlisted the muses to redeem its wayward citizens. But there were other prisons not on display to tourists. In the penitentiary of the capital hundreds of political prisoners rotted in humid dungeons. Some hobbled about in shackles with sixty-pound iron balls attached; others were forced to lie face down in moist sawdust with a weight on their backs, for weeks on end. There was an electric chair with insufficient voltage to kill, but more than enough to make tongues wag; moldy cells where a man could neither stand up nor stretch. Many of the inmates had lost their minds, the more fortunate had died. Murderous beatings were administered with a Freudian sort of whip known as the *verga de toro* made of the sexual member of a bull, distended and dried, with a wire threaded through its canal.

In 1934, when the government began preparing for elections that were never held, the official paper *La Epoca* advanced the theory of "the useful crime," necessary for the health of the state. It was no empty theorising. Carías had tracked down his opponents inexorably at home and abroad. In 1938 the Liberal Generals Justo Umaña and M. A. Zapata were assassinated in Guatemala by Ubico's gunmen, executing orders from Tegucigalpa.

Seen from the capital, Carías affected the role of heavy-handed patriarch rather than sadistic dictator. Oppositionists had often been forbidden to travel in motor vehicles; some, indeed, had had their automobiles "imprisoned" in the penitentiary. Anti-Carías lawyers watched the grass grow before their doors, since their clients were sure to lose their suits. Carías warned off prospective tenants from renting oppositionists' houses, and beaux from courting their daugh-

---

*The same Spruille Braden who, when his diplomatic career ended, moved into the direct service of United Fruit as its public relations chief. In that office he contributed outstandingly to the overthrow of Guatemalan President Arbenz.

ters. In Tegucigalpa the tyranny was as significant for its village-pump connotations as for its severity.

The departmental governors were the scourge of the country and enjoyed a high degree of autonomy. The name of Carlos Sanabria, governor of Colón Department, became the Honduran equivalent of Attila. For Sanabria was not content with the routine functions of a Carías satrap: operating gambling and other vice rings, running the local liquor monopoly, levying tribute on businessmen, jailing and assassinating the odd oppositionist. Surrounded by his tough gunmen, Sanabria wiped out entire villages suspected of oppositionist sympathies and wreaked vengeance on Liberals down to the second and third generations. Many of the leading families of Trujillo fled the country. When a delegation of women came to the capital and pleaded with Carías to remove Sanabria, Carías had a curt reply: "Would that I had seventeen Sanabrias, one for every department of Honduras."

Even *beisbol* (baseball) clubs were outlawed by Carías as possible foci of conspiracy. But in 1943 the dictator's late nephew General Calixto Carías, director of a nonexistent artillery school, returned from a visit to Cuba with a feverish enthusiasm for the sport. He convinced his uncle to permit baseball because it was useful in teaching the soldiers to throw hand grenades. A Cuban professional was imported, and the game resumed its former popularity.

The formula applied by Central American dictators to justify their grip on the presidency was a simple one and varied little from republic to republic. Firstly, they gave the country order, which meant that the jails were full and spies ubiquitous. Then they undertook important public works. It sufficed to point to a highway paid for by United States taxpayers, and an airport built by Pan American Airways, to prove that it has been necessary for the president to remain in office for fifteen years, and urgent for him to stay another twenty "to complete his mission." Bronze plaques marked out every culvert, every sentry box built under the dictator. Frantically added up, these "public works" were supposed to make the regime an "epoch" and an "age." A barracks or a bridge was offered to vindicate hundreds of lives snuffed out, a generation of backbones bent and souls violated. It was a system of bookkeeping common to those parts, and there were always foreign diplomats and journalists on hand to certify that the weird ledgers balanced.

Carías, too, played at this game, but his chips were ludicrously scant. With an air of the utmost gravity, he would confide that the main work of his regime had been the beautification of the capital. Tegucigalpa huddled around the presidential palace like a straggling village around a robber baron's castle. Its drowsy charm derived from the fact that it had changed so little since colonial times. The steep, twisting streets were built for donkeys rather than for motors or men. Not a single one was paved; during the rainy season they were gushing torrents of water and mud. In thirteen years Carías had cobbled a few. He had laid out a tiny square with grotesque concrete imitations of ruins "in the Mayan style." He had completed a bridge, previously begun, to dusty Comayaguela across the river and erected a bust to himself on Comayaguela's central square.

The mud road from Tegucigalpa to the Gulf of Fonseca was in worse shape than it was a decade ago. The only road construction in thirteen years worth mentioning was the Inter-American Highway skirting Fonseca and paid for almost entirely by the United States, and a road along Lake Yojoa financed wholly by Washington. The one new educational institution was the United Fruit Company's splendid agricultural school at Zamorano, in which Honduran politicos had no other part than the crowing. Amidst such desolation, Carías's pretensions as "providential man" were just a little wry.

Doctor and General Carías was a man of simple tastes whose years of power had not altogether interred the rustic guerrilla chieftain. A decade ago a Nicaraguan secretary had taught him to carry a cane and wear a fedora, and even convinced him to trim his fierce mustachios to seemly proportions. The same secretary, too, advised Mrs. Carías on fashions and coiffure. But it was a thin and brittle veneer that chipped readily. Carías had been known to receive diplomats with a two days' growth of beard. He led the life of a stern patriarch, neither smoked nor drank, and imposed the same puritanic code on his henchmen. When possible, he dispatched the state's affairs long before noon, and spent the day at Villa Elena farm, named after his wife. He was legitimately proud of it, as of his La Moderna ranch at Guasculile, and all his other properties along the northern highway. He had stocked them with imported blooded cattle, and introduced advanced methods of husbandry. They were, indeed, his one contribution to Honduras's economic development.

From her days of running the roadside inn at Zambrano, his wife brought a reputation as a goodhearted woman and an excellent cook. Once a week, in the early years of her husband's rule, she would send a note around to acquaintances informing them that there would be tamales for sale at the Presidential Palace on such a morning. Since Doña Elena's tamales were justly celebrated, a brisk trade would be done. But avarice soon dislodged the kindness in her heart. She obtained the monopoly for supplying tortillas to the army. She began collecting farms, and army trucks creaked under the burden of vegetables, milk, and firewood being taken to the capital for sale. Her real passion, however, was buying up entire blocks in Comayaguela, the dirty suburb of Tegucigalpa across the stream. People began calling her *Doña Barrios* (Madame Blocks) and spoke harshly of her. No longer, as in the first years, did she stick her head out of the second story of the Presidential Palace to gossip with friends who chanced to stroll by. She sat on her moneybags and feared her people.

Carías's eldest son, Gonzalo, a dentist by training, was consul-general in New York. In the old days, when dictators could indulge in thoughts of dynasties, Gonzalo was being groomed as heir-apparent. He toured the country distributing free radios to the municipalities and getting to know his people. But that belonged to a distant, dulcet past. An ineffectual man in his late thirties, Gonzalo had dreamed vaguely of doing something big. In September 1939 he obtained a vast concession from the government for the establishment of canning concerns for fish, meat, fruits, etc.; factories for the manufacture of soap, butter, and all sorts of oils; for the building of docks, highways, railways; for livestock and grain farms. Under the concession, he was authorized to import all the necessary materials for such ends without paying other customs duties than one eighth of a cent per kilogram. A new meteor seemed to have swept onto Honduras's economic horizon. Gonzalo had a keen appetite and hoped to repeddle the concession to foreign interests. Actually, he did nothing with it until he formed a partnership with Henry Klapisch, an American of great prestige in the international herring trade. They began buying up the catch of the Fonseca fishermen under monopolist conditions and flying them to the capital in army planes. Partners Gonzalo and Klapisch also carried on a brisk export business to Panama in eggs, chickens, and meat, contributing notably to the high cost of living in Honduras.

A younger Carías son, Tiburcio, lived permanently abroad as consul in Liverpool.

Carías's favorite child was his daughter Marta, who had inherited much more of the old man's grit than the sons. She was the divorced wife of an elegant Guatemalan, who received the post of Honduran minister to France as a dowry. Her six-year-old son was the apple of the dictator's eye; his laughter was the only ray of sunshine penetrating the gloom of the palace.

With Carías, the most rustic elements of a very backward land had come to the fore. There was little of the Attic about the pillars of the regime.

Chief muscle-man was Carlos Izaguirre, burly and fiftyish, who began life as a baker and schoolmaster. Izaguirre fancied himself as something of a Renaissance character in the homespun Honduran setting. It was he who took to the air and did the bombing whenever a revolt broke out; but he also had a maddening literary itch. His first medium was the political essay. In his book *Readaptaciones y cambios,* published in 1935, he wrote: "In Europe the iron figures of Mussolini, Stalin, Laval, and Hitler have come to the fore. . . . These men are fashioning new nations. . . . They have impressed on their peoples the physiognomies required by the circumstances, have brought order where anarchy reigned, social consolidation where dissolution prevailed. And if these men decided to abandon their posts, the people would simply not allow them to do so; they would be committing a crime against their fatherlands. . . ." All, of course, with an eye on the home situation. Later, Izaguirre stuck to atrocious poetry which he published in luxury editions. He operated a lucrative liquor monopoly in one of the departments, and for ten years occupied the post of inspector-general of consulates without once leaving the country.

Izaguirre held the distinction of being the first man to bombard an American city from the air. In 1924, when the Carías forces were besieging Tegucigalpa, he flew over the town and heaved a fifty-pound bomb out of the plane window. Subsequently Honduran planes were fitted with bomb racks: a valuable technical advance, for it allowed Izaguirre a free hand to cock a pistol at the pilot and guarantee his loyalty. Though the bombing was effective in dispersing the enemy, the marksmanship was never notable. In thirteen years the only rebel casualties from air bombardment on record were one mule and one general.

The barrel-shaped president of Congress, Plutarco Muñoz, was a native of Yoro. His political success he owed entirely to the United Fruit Company, which retained him as attorney. On the side he ran the liquor monopoly in Yoro Department. Not only did he pilot United Fruit legislation through Congress, long cleared of every shoal; he was also renowned for the piquancy of his debating. To justify his chief's long stay in the presidency he coined a famous phrase: "God, too, continues in power indefinitely."

General Benjamín Henríquez was an oldish little Indian from Talanga, with a part in the middle of his graying hair, eyes slightly apop, and a strange persuasiveness in his whining provincial intonations. Before Carías became president, Henríquez sold tickets in a movie of the capital. As a symbol of the cultural strides made under Carías, he proudly pointed to the two toilet bowls in the single bathroom of his ample house. Officially he was highway treasurer, but he himself described his key role to me as follows: "We are like the Holy Trinity. Honduras is the Father, Carías is the Son, and I am the Holy Ghost."

When he told you: "Thanks to the peace and order under Carías, we have had plentiful rains this year," you might be inclined to dismiss him as picturesque; yet his illiterate, eloquent letter to the head of the Export-Import Bank convinced Washington to build the highway around Lake Yojoa entirely at its own expense.

With the thirteen percent of the Honduran budget assigned to him for road construction, Henríquez's achievements were less spectacular. When the rains came, the highways not built by the North Americans were treacherous channels of mud that separated rather than joined population centers. Henríquez, though in charge of road building, was not much of a hand at reading maps. While enlarging to me on the marvels of the Northern Highway, and punctuating the high points with golden jets of tobacco juice aimed at the floor, he placed a bony finger on the wall-map—smack in the middle of Nicaragua. Then, jabbing an imperative thumb at an assistant, he commanded: "Come, show him where the Northern Highway is, come on!"

Though in his frequent fits of temper Carías had been known to kick Henríquez around the room, the little fellow was in a real sense the idea man of the regime. Throughout Latin America Roosevelt's third and fourth terms were seized upon by the dictators as a precedent for remaining in power indefinitely *without* elections. Yet nowhere was the "parallelism" exploited so masterfully as in Honduras.

On January 31, 1944, Henríquez directed to all state employees a circular that had obviously been retouched for style: "As partners of the great nation of the North in the armed struggle, we can participate without fear in the civil contest approaching in the United States for the election of a citizen to guide its destinies during the next four years. We therefore proclaim as sole candidate . . . the illustrious patriot Franklin Delano Roosevelt." All Honduran government employees were enjoined to work for the candidacy by unspecified means. The circular was reproduced in the official paper *La Epoca*. When Roosevelt was elected, Henríquez again circularized the state employees, congratulating them on the victory of their candidate. On Tegucigalpa's central square, where Marshal Ney rides his spirited stallion, Henríquez had the band play to celebrate the triumph.

Fernando Zepeda Durón, big, husky, and balding, was the Goebbels of the regime. A former sexton, not excessively literate, Zepeda was memorable for his droll lisp and cagey blandness. He had taken an active hand in shutting down oppositionist papers; for two dreary years Tegucigalpa had no further press than his own hand-set *La Epoca*. The sole paper of the capital of a progressive republic, its publishers did not even make an effort to sell it on the streets. For a reason. The "news" dispatches of its columns marked an epoch in journalism. Some random samples: "San Lorenzo, May 12th – Twenty years ago Dr. Paulin Valladares said that General and Doctor Carías

Andino, if he reached the presidency, would make the greatest president the country ever had. How correct he was!" "Yoro, May 13th – What did the refugees leave behind when they were forced out of power? Ruin, devastation, thefts. Now these people want to come back to undo the work of our beloved providential president." *La Epoca* was financed out of a 5 percent levy on all government employees' salaries "for the Nationalist party."

Zepeda, in close connection with the president's wife, had accumulated considerable real estate in Comayaguela. As he looked back in contentment on his career, he liked to muse what a fine figure of a president he would make. He was a deputy, and his favorite hobby was keeping the outside world posted on Honduras as correspondent of the Associated Press.

Carías maintained a surly discipline amongst his underlings. Even statesmen of Zepeda's and Izaguirre's caliber scurried around feeding and watering the dictator's pet canaries while awaiting their turn for an interview.

In pursuing its ends in Honduras, the United Fruit Company dispensed with the regard for appearances that it showed in other lands. The war minister, Juan Manuel Galvez, the president of Congress, Plutarco Muñoz, and the head of the Supreme Court, were all United Fruit attorneys. There were local commanders on the North Coast who received half their pay from the company. Those not rating a regular salary came in for frequent tips. Before Spruille Braden came to the State Department, journalists who ventured to criticize the banana trust were silenced with bribes, while recalcitrants disappeared into Carías's dungeons.

Hondurans cherish the memory of Lempira, an Indian chieftain who roused his people to a heroic stand against the Spanish conqueror. Their very money is named after Lempira, and bears his likeness. The 1944 rate for lempiras, however, was two to the dollar.

Honduras never had much luck with the United States diplomats accredited to it. It is such an inconsequential nook of creation, and the pressure of political job-seekers in Washington so very great. In 1920 Franklin Morales, a North American of Latin descent, had worked for many years as barman at Tegucigalpa's Agurcia Hotel. During a visit to the States, he saved a drowning girl; as in the fairy tales, she turned out to be the daughter of an influential senator. The senator, understandably moved, asked how he might repay him, and Morales begged to be named consul at Tegucigalpa. After making enquiries, the senator informed Morales that it was impossible for him to be appointed consul, for that was a career job. But he could easily have him made minister. Hondurans swallowed hard as they saw the man who had so long poured their drinks return as U.S. minister. Thereafter Minister Morales could often be seen on the right side of his old bar, debating with the president's brother-in-law, Carlos Lagos, which of the two it was who really ran Honduras.

The ambassador in 1944 was John Draper Erwin. As Washington reporter for a Tennessee paper, Erwin won the friendship of Cordell Hull and was appointed minister to Honduras. He was automatically stepped up to ambassador after the outbreak of war. Pudgy, loquacious, with little knowledge of Spanish, Erwin had reduced diplomacy to its very simplest principles. He saw it all as a football game in which his team was Carías. For the first eight years that he graced the post, oppositionists were not even received at the embassy. He viewed them as a rural Southern sheriff might view trade-union organizers, "agitators and troublemakers." Even when he traveled abroad, he took along Carías's chief of protocol, much as a blind man might his seeing-eye dog.

When Erwin visited Mexico in 1942, Angel Zúñiga Huete, exiled head of the Liberal party, sent him a memorandum on the Honduran situation. It was returned unopened with Erwin's inscription "Refused." In June 1943 when Alfredo Trejo Castillo published some articles in *El Cronista* in favor of democracy and against Carías, he was invited to the embassy by the first secretary, John Bernard Faust. Faust asked whether he did not consider criticism of Carías prejudicial to the war effort, and whether "we do not need strong men at a time like this." Shortly afterward *El Cronista* was suppressed.

The war brought complications for Carías. Overnight he found it necessary to erase from public memory the praise of fascism that had filled the official press and pose as an anxious crusader to make the world safe for democracy. It was easier to impress U.S. diplomats with the farce than the Honduran people. Carías's consulates in Europe had carried on a lively trade selling Honduran passports to Nazi agents. There was some embarrassment in the fall of 1942, when a German spy, who had never seen Honduras but was proud possessor of a bona-fide Honduran passport, was caught in Cuba, tried, and shot.

The propaganda of the Coordinator's Office was raking up the country. The brave new world was portrayed so seductively that Hondurans decided they, too, would like a cut of it. The effects were not long in coming. In November, 1943, the Guatemalan minister at Tegucigalpa denounced to Carías a plot for his assassination in which the palace guard and certain civilians were involved. Sixty men were arrested, and twenty-eight of them lodged in the penitentiary for a lengthy stay. But Carías made a show of clemency: none of those implicated was tried or executed.

On May 27, 1944, the incredible happened. Three hundred

women gathered before the cathedral and, flanking an anti-Carías placard with United States and Honduran flags, marched through the streets of the capital. His nerves frayed by dictator Martínez's recent fall in Salvador, Carías had been caught off guard. There was a confusion of recipes in his mind. The rock bottom of his statesmanship during eleven years had been to smack down all opposition, but, on the other hand, Martínez's sanguinary excesses had clearly had something to do with his overthrow. Finding the just mean between repression and tolerance was obviously the secret of success for a dictator. But how was it to be determined?

He was still pondering the problem when Ubico crashed in Guatemala a month later. Honduras took up the cue. On July fourth another demonstration was organized and called at the U.S. embassy to offer birthday greetings and a bouquet of flowers to the Great Good Neighbor. They found the door bolted, and proceeded to bang away on it for a half hour. Within, Ambassador Erwin paced up and down his office, mopping his brow and debating whether he could receive his subversive visitors. Finally the brave decision was taken, the bolts were drawn, and two of the women were let in. Graciously Erwin accepted their flowers, but no sooner had one of them begun the accompanying speech then he shut her up with a brusque "I can't listen to politics."

From the embassy the marchers, growing in numbers and spirits, made their way to the Presidential Palace. Stones were flung into Carías's second-story window. The crowd charged the iron gates and bellowed denunciations of the dictator. Within there was bedlam. Ambassador Erwin was phoned and begged to come and witness the iniquity of the opposition. Erwin offered asylum to Carías and his family, but daughter Marta put her foot down and urged her father to see the thing through. Though most of the lend-lease armament was kept right in the palace by the distrustful dictator, there was some delay in finding the tear-gas bombs. Finally located, they served to scatter the demonstration. Then the police rounded up Alfredo Trejo Castillo and scores of other oppositionists, women for the most part. The U.S. head of the air force resigned, and, once out of Honduras, told the Associated Press that the lads that he had trained would never lend themselves for use against the people.

San Pedro Sula, second town of the republic, spoke up. Lying in the hub of the banana region, San Pedro is the economic center of the country. A couple of streets were paved; an excellent newspaper, *Diario del Comercio,* owned by the United Fruit Company, provided good international coverage and deftly avoided the reefs of Honduran politics. Not dependent on public posts for their livelihood, San

Pedro's citizens walked more erect than those of the capital. It was the headquarters of Carías's war minister, Juan Manuel Gálvez, a lanky, indolent lawyer, close to the heart and purse of the fruit company. More urbane than his colleagues in the government, Gálvez had up to then kept clear of the regime's atrocities. He was rarely to be found in his ministry at Tegucigalpa, preferring to lounge in San Pedro Sula near his patrons. Carías and his lieutenants viewed him with distinct jealousy.

From Gálvez, San Pedro's oppositionists obtained permission for a peaceful demonstration on July 6. They were assigned an itinerary, and the sole condition set was that there would be no speeches. Again the procession consisted largely of women. They filed through the streets, and at the end of their route, one of the leaders appeared on a balcony and asked them to disband. This the troops, who from the start had breathed down the paraders' necks, took as the signal to open fire. Crazed with fright, the people stampeded for the doorways. Women hit the sidewalk writhing in agony. Volley followed volley until the pavement was sticky with blood. Over one hundred were dead or mortally wounded. The hospital overflowed. Shivers of indignation coursed down the nation's spine. Finding clemency unavailing, Carías had tried another tack. Honduran history is crimson with blood spilled in the heat of battle, but there had never been an instance of cold mass murder on such a scale.

Now it was war without quarter between the dictator and the people. In Tegucigalpa Carías peddled cynical tales: the demonstrators had tried assaulting the barracks, several blocks away from the scene of the carnage; in another version they had broken into a bank. To visiting journalists Ambassador Erwin pleaded lack of information, but he understood that "about four" demonstrators had died. High officials of United Fruit, seeking to cover Gálvez, whispered that he had had no part in the butchery staged by the Carías clique to discredit him. During a visit to San Pedro several months later, the president of Congress, Plutarco Muñoz, had another explanation: "Of course there was blood on San Pedro's sidewalks. The women demonstrators must have been menstruating."

Four months after this excitement I interviewed Carías. Iron gates clicked behind me as I entered the massive castle. I was received by someone whose name I did not grasp and ushered into the presence of the dictator. The small, stuffy, middle-class room was incongruous after the fanfare of turrets outside. The two windows smashed by the populace in July were still unrepaired: in the case against the opposition they were the prized exhibits A and B.

When I enquired why the ailing democrat Alfredo Trejo Castillo had been kept in prison so long, Carías pointed plaintively to the broken panes and replied: "That is what he got the mob to do. They almost assassinated me."

The whine in his voice contrasted strangely with the speaker, who was decidedly St. Bernard rather than poodle. He had, he told me, given the country peace during his lengthy rule. The previous civil wars had left only destruction in their wake. On the lips of a man who had devoted four decades to just such revolutioneering, the words had an odd ring. I asked whether he was not defeating his laudable purpose by staying on as president: for months Honduras had been heaving with demonstrations, shootings, invasions, bombings, all of which could be ended by the simple device of free elections. "They will have their elections," he rumbled, "but in 1948."

Then I committed a frightful boner. I had not caught the name of the third person sitting in on our interview, and I went on to remark that *La Epoca,* the sole paper of the capital at the time, was quite the most absurd sheet I had ever seen. When a cow dies in Danli it is legitimate to print the obituary in a news dispatch: but when someone predicted twenty years ago that Carías would make the best president in Honduran history, that might go to make an excellent editorial, but had no place in a news column. Why, on my previous visit to Tegucigalpa, when it rained hard and we gringos at the hotel couldn't go out, we amused ourselves reading for *La Epoca* and holding our sides with laughter. Carías looked saturnine, and the third party turned beet-red. I asked whether he were by any chance connected with *La Epoca.*

"Zi, theñor, I am Zepeda Durón, its editor."

"A thousand pardons, but *La Epoca* is really an invaluable arm for the opposition."

"Yes, that is what the Mexican ambassador, whom you visited three days ago, always tells me."

"Indeed I visited my friend, Muñoz Cota, but we found other things to discuss."

Carías mumbled that there were different schools of journalism in different countries. I concurred.

Carías told me that were he to leave power, the country would lapse into anarchy like Guatemala.

"But Mr. President, I have just come from Guatemala and saw no trace of anarchy. Why, if you had seen the splendid self-discipline of hungry people, with eight-year-old boys directing traffic and workers policing the city, you, as a Central American, could not help being proud of your people." Pride did not seem his dominant emotion.

I could not resist describing in detail how I had seen dictator Ponce seek asylum at the Mexican embassy, where he was put up in the room freshly vacated by Arévalo, the popular leader. Carías rose to dramatic heights: "That will never happen to me. They can kill me right here, but never, never will I seek asylum at the Mexican embassy."

In a lachrymose voice he dwelt on the moral depths plumbed by the opposition. His wife had suffered a stroke in June. Though the opposition was aware of that, it would not budge from its decision to hold its July 4 demonstration. The doctors had warned that moving the patient would endanger her life, but Carías had no alternative but to send her to New York by plane on July 3. "I told my son, Gonzalo, not to bring the body back if she died. Just bury her there. In that way you will be fulfilling your duty as a son, while I as president will remain here fulfilling mine."

He denied jokingly that tortures were applied in his prisons, but outlined with relish the gruesome details of the torments attributed to his jailers. I was relieved that we had finally touched upon something that Carías could feel lighthearted about.

P.S.

In 1948 Carías's "promised election" took place on schedule and his candidate, Juan Manuel Gálvez, emerged triumphant. The opposition candidate had previously withdrawn from the race alleging coercion and fraud. But the installation of a puppet president by Carías had changed so little in the real political setup of Honduras that I have left this chapter exactly as I wrote it in 1946.

7

Success Story

In Nicaragua the Andes peter out in broad lakes and rolling pampas. In remote geological times this was the widest of four sea channels parting the islands that came to form Central America. Lake Nicaragua, with a spread of over three thousand square miles, was lifted out of the ocean so slowly that its sharks had the time to adapt themselves to fresh water; at the end of this long adolescence the isthmus is still pimply with volcanoes. Here, unlike the other Central American republics, it is no longer the coastal fringe that sweats at sea level while the heart beats more sedately in the cooler uplands.

Nicaraguans are "tropical" in the Latin American usage of that term—too mercurial, talented, and deft-witted to qualify as really serious folk. A goodly tincture of Negro blood imparts an exuberance to everything they do. And the cruelty of the jungle. A century ago the three rival towns of Granada, León, and Managua all but exterminated one another in a series of wars where principles were only the fuzziest pretext for plunder. There was nothing saturnine about politics as in Guatemala. Admiration for sleight-of-hand and nimble fingers relaxed the norms of public morality. In their agony under a ruler who had crammed so much of the country into his pockets, there was still a discernible note of awe at his skill in doing so. The one austere man to achieve real prominence in Nicaraguan politics in this century was, significantly enough, an unbalanced visionary who became more of a symbol outside the republic than within.

The lakes and rivers that contribute so much to Nicaragua's sweltering beauty have brought it care and sorrow. For the San Juan River and Lake Granada almost add up to a natural interoceanic canal. They early caught the eye of the world powers and led to entire cycles of foreign intervention and civil war. Panama and Egypt, with similar experiences, had at least the economic benefits of the canals to console them. But Nicaragua's century-old dream of having the world's commerce flow through its parlor had never been realized. It was in the unenviable position of suffering an acute bellyache without really having supped.

The great Nelson lost an eye while trying to plant the Union Jack at the mouth of the San Juan River; Britain claimed a protectorate over the Nicaraguan north coast right up to 1894. In quest of a slave empire, the American filibuster William Walker seized the country in the fifties, and all Central America rose in arms to eject him. During the lulls in the fighting the Central Americans penned poems on their drumheads, but defeating Walker cost a sea of blood. It would have proved still more difficult had Walker not run afoul of the Vanderbilt interests operating the Nicaraguan interoceanic route by boat and road.*

The really serious complications, however, set in after 1900, when the United States was finally ready to build the canal. There were two possible routes—Panama and Nicaragua. Washington proceeded to negotiate for rights to both. A Nicaraguan postage stamp, showing Momotombo volcano smoking, convinced the American senators of the hazards to which a Nicaraguan canal would be exposed, and tipped the balance in Panama's favor.† A reasonable fellow who had lavished favors on U.S. interests as the price of the canal, dictator José Santos Zelaya was understandably incensed. In retaliation he not only sounded out Japan for the building of the canal, but negotiated a French loan for the construction of a railway to the Caribbean.‡ At the time the U.S. State Department was feverishly engaged in eliminating European financial influence from the Caribbean; Zelaya could not have done a more tactless thing. Worse still, he offended the Fletcher interests of Pittsburgh, prominent in Nicara-

---

*Shipping magnate Commodore Cornelius Vanderbilt ran a shipping line connecting the East Coast with California. In the 1850s when rail and road lines were still undeveloped, the fastest communications were via the interocean Panama railway and the land route in Nicaragua (which also made use of two lakes). The rush to California resulted from the boom following discovering of gold in that state.

†This is one of many anecdotes concerning this option, which in fact was resolved by the lower over-all cost of the Panama Canal, and also by collusion between the House of Morgan and the team of President Theodore Roosevelt and Secretary of State John Hay.

‡If Japan was indeed sounded out—which has not been proved—that country could not at the time have undertaken a work of this magnitude, much less defied the power of the United States, which was already building the canal in Panama. There was also the risk, at the beginning of the century, that the Kaiser's Germany would take an interest in projects of this type or install bases and coaling stations in Mexico or such Caribbean countries as Haiti and the Dominican Republic.

guan lumbering and mining, with whom Secretary of State Philander Knox was intimately associated.

U.S. arms and money were made available to Zelaya's enemies, and in 1909 a revolution was launched. When the government shot two American filibusters caught laying mines in the San Juan River, Secretary Knox declared Zelaya outside the law of nations. The Marines were landed.* Zelaya relinquished power, but Washington continued its intrigues until a regime arose that was entirely satisfactory to Knox.† It was headed by the Conservative Adolfo Díaz, book-keeper of the Fletcher mines.

To maintain Díaz in a vertical posture, the Marines were sent in again. In return Díaz accepted the Bryan-Chamorro treaty giving to the United States the canal rights, renting the Corn Islands on the Atlantic, and permitting the establishment of a naval base in the Gulf of Fonseca. Still very much Fletcher's bookkeeper, Díaz even re-quested a frank United States protectorate in Nicaragua along the lines of the Platt Amendment in Cuba. But that stuck in the gullet of the U.S. Senate.‡

In 1916 Emiliano Chamorro succeeded Díaz with the active goodwill of the U.S. legation. A U.S. customs collectorship was in-stituted.**

Four years later Chamorro made way for an uncle of his, after elections declared corrupt by the American supervisor. The Conservative party, resting on U.S. bayonets, had become "a machine for turning out Chamorro presidents."

---

*These landings, at the small port of Bluefields, were made to exert psychological pressure on the autocrat Zalaya; at least in that year, 1909, the Marines took no physical action. Knox's December "statement of principle" was in any case decisive.

†Zelaya was succeeded by lawyer-jurist José Madriz, who would in turn resign in August 1910, this time definitely from direct pressure by the Marines, who occupied Bluefields and declared that port a "neutral zone." General Juan José Estrada seized power and obtained United States recogni-tion. Secretary of State Knox then pressured Estrada to resign and hand over power to Adolfo Díaz.

‡The Senate was controlled by the Democratic party. Following denunci-ations of irregularities connected with the Bryan-Chamorro treaty, and be-cause of the prevailing revolutionary situation in Mexico, ratification of the treaty was postponed until 1916.

**The collection of customs duties in countries like Nicaragua, the Dominican Republic, and Haiti was a feature of the so-called Dollar Diplo-macy imposed by President William Howard Taft. In effect, the collectorships were concealed protectorates; Taft justified them as necessary to prevent such foreign creditors as Britain, Germany, Italy, and France from seeking to col-lect their debts by force; that is, by landing their troops in these weak coun-tries.

Washington might never have tired of the Chamorro dynasty, but Nicaragua did. In 1924 the dissident Conservatives formed an alliance with the Liberals and elected an inept Conservative as president, and a Liberal U.S.-trained doctor, Juan Batista Sacasa, as vice-president. Yet the Chamorros were not to be ousted as simply as that. On October 25, 1925, Emiliano Chamorro captured the Loma fortress dominating Managua, and the following year assumed the presidency. Washington persuaded him to step down in favor of the veteran Adolfo Díaz, whom they recognized at once. Mexico for its part backed the constitutional vice-president, Sacasa, provided arms, and opened a recruiting office for the Constitutionalist cause in Mexico City. Sacasa landed at Puerto Cabezas on the Atlantic coast and set up his government there.

General José María Moncada, a hard-driving little man with a tongue like a scimitar, took command of the Constitutionalist army, and was soon pushing over the Conservative forces all down the line. Wherever the Constitutionalist beseiged the Conservatives, the U.S. Marines would declare the region a neutral zone.*

Yet the Constitutionalists continued to triumph. Moncada over-ran the departments of Metagalpa and Chontales, and reached Tipitapa in sight of the capital. At this critical point, Colonel Henry Stimson, personal representative of President Calvin Coolidge, arrived and invited Moncada to a conference with the Conservatives. Moncada was persuaded to lay down arms: ten dollars was paid for every rifle surrendered. A treaty was signed providing for elections and a U.S.-trained guard combining military and police functions. To convince those in his ranks who might consider his agreement treachery, Moncada had permitted the Marines to occupy the heights dominating Tipitapa without knowledge of his staff.

Under the workings of the U.S.-drafted electoral law, Moncada became president. The frumpy village of Tipitapa, site of the deal, was renamed Villa Stimson in the first gush of enthusiasm. But no one remembers that today. For all practical purposes it remains Tipitapa, a little dirtier and more abandoned than before. Nicaraguan politics, too, did not emerge from the historic Tipitapa confab greatly transformed.

Some of Moncada's lieutenants were loath to lay down arms while foreign troops continued in the country. The leader of these recalci-

---

*On declaring a port or territory in Central America or the Caribbean a "neutral zone," the Marines decreed that in those area there must be no armed struggles of any kind. Hence, if there was one, they could decide which side they would favor. In effect, the action disguised interventions ordered from Washington.

trants was Augusto C. Sandino, a magnetic wisp of a man whose name soon became a household word throughout Latin America.

Sandino was the natural son of Gregorio Sandino, a citizen of substance in the western town of Niquinohomo, and Margarita Calderón. When Gregorio married another girl, Margarita handed over little Augusto to his wife, and soon sank into prostitution. Augusto's legitimate half-brothers received good educations, but he, as second-class offspring, got only enough schooling to equip him for administering the family farm. While doing so, he was impressed by the fact that the city merchants were exploiting the farmers, and proceeded to organize a cooperative marketing association. Alarmed, the merchants of Granada commissioned José María Moncada to take Sandino in hand. Moncada, an artist at boozing and whoring, invited Sandino to a little party. The liquor flowed freely, and Moncada's plan was on the brink of success. But the tart assigned Sandino was called Margarita. The name and the circumstances reminded him of his mother. In his drunkenness he became violent and killed one of the guests. That made him an outlaw. He fled to the Segovia mountains, worked in a gold mine, and, hounded for organizing a strike, escaped to Mexico.* His having killed a man preyed on his mind. For consolation he turned to spiritualism and theosophy. During the year that he worked in the Tampico oil fields, he devoured all that he could find on occultism and radical labor theory. In his head the two came to form a weird omelet.†

He was obsessed by the parallelism between his country's plight and his mother's turning streetwalker in her misfortune.

---

*I had this anecdote from the Nicaraguan Salomón de la Selva, who for some years was Sandino's camp poet. Having found no confirmation elsewhere, I have been bothered by the thought that Salomón may have availed himself of his poetic licence.—W.K.

Moncada was then already too important in Nicaragua's political life to bother with inebriating young hotheads. True, Sandino got into a shooting incident, but it occurred in the atrium of Niquinohomo church one Sunday at the hour of Mass. Sandino's opponent insulted him to his face, brandishing a weapon. Sandino drew his own gun and wounded him in the leg. He fled in alarm to Honduras, then to Guatemala, and finally to Mexico. In all three countries he worked for concerns owned by U.S. corporations.

†Sandino reached Mexico in full revolutionary fervor and, as an employee of U.S. oil firms, plunged into trade union struggles and read much about his country's political and social problems. At the same time his interest continued in theosophy, spiritualism, and freemasonry. His hasty and disordered studies and Catholic religious feelings produced the confused beliefs reflected in his writings, in which, however, his ethical and moral concerns stand out.

When Sacasa opened up his recruiting office in Mexico City, Sandino spent his savings on red-and-black silk handkerchiefs—the syndicalist colors—and set out for Puerto Cabezas on the Nicaraguan north coast. He arrived just as the Americans ordered Sacasa's government to clear out. With the aid of some women, he managed to carry some rifles into the interior before the ultimatum expired. He soon distinguished himself in the cruel partisan warfare. When Moncada made peace at Tipitapa, he retired to the mountains and rallied all those who felt that the anti-imperialist cause had been bilked.

His mind was clearly unhinged, but it was a noble, disinterested aberration. He had a way of dragging Vishnu and Christ into his military commands, and claimed to be guided in battle by the voice of Bolívar. Soon he took the *C* in his name (for Calderón) as César, and signed his decrees Augusto César Sandino.* Yet his moral force fired his followers to storm the heavens. For five years, with practically no outside assistance, fighting with guns torn from the enemy's hands, hand grenades made out of sardine tins filled with stones, they withstood the aviation and modern equipment of the Marines and the Nicaraguan National Guard. His bitterest opponents have paid tribute to his fantastically well-organized espionage—a sure sign that he enjoyed the warm sympathy of the population amongst which he operated. In the lowland cities, Managua, León, and Granada, he had much less of a following, because the presence of the open-handed Marines there had brought on a business boom.

North American old-timers in Nicaragua will assure you that the Marines were not really eager to crush Sandino; he offered too good a pretext for using the country as a training ground. But there was little that resembled feinting. Some of Sandino's followers were professional contrabandists, tough Robin Hoods of the frontier, and it was impossible to restrain such men. Unspeakable atrocities were committed by either side. One of the Sandino commanders invented the "vest cut," consisting of decapitating the victim, hacking away his arms, and slashing him across the abdomen; the "bloomer cut," hewing off the legs at the knees and traversing the abdomen. On the other hand the photo of a Marine dangling Sandinista heads received wide international circulation.

Sandino repeatedly proclaimed that it was a "war that we are

---

*Sandino never signed any document or letter "César"; he always signed "Augusto C." The attribution of the second name was the work of some Mexican newspapers unaware of his placing the maternal before the paternal name.

bound to lose." His stand was Hispanic quixotry at its purest—to die resisting an injustice from the mightiest country on earth, but to let the world know that Nicaragua did not bow to oppression.

Throughout Latin America Sandino became a legendary David, who, while he could scarcely hope to chop off Goliath's big blond head, did administer a resounding tweek to his nose. For the U.S. press, with the exception of the liberal fringe, he was a vulgar bandit. Never before or since had the two Americas been so widely at variance. Sandino, more than any one man, dramatized the impasse into which the Big Stick policy had led Washington's diplomacy. And by doing so, he cleared the boards for the Good Neighbor Era.

Before the State Department began teaching the Nicaraguans democracy, the police and army had existed as two separate organizations. However ambitious their commanders, they tended to neutralize each other, and the civilian president thus had a chance. The North Americans fused both forces into the National Guard, and trained it to a new efficiency. Nothing was left of the old checks and balances; the National Guard offered a sure ladder which any daring adventurer could scale to power. The first man to plant his feet on the top rungs was Anastasio ("Tacho") Somoza.

Somoza's granduncle, Bernabé Somoza, had been a notorious bandit in the sanguinary wars of the past century. Because he was supposed to need that many rags to wipe the blood from his hands, he passed into local folklore as *Siete Pañuelos* ("Seven Handkerchiefs"). Siete Pañuelos ended his days dangling from a gibbet in Rivas Town.

The grandnephew was born at San Marcos in 1896. After a sketchy primary education, he was sent to Philadelphia and enrolled in a commercial school. But he was not the studious sort, and soon deserted shorthand for gambling. When down on his luck, he worked as an automobile salesman. A handsome gay blade, he made a good impression on a young Nicaraguan lass of excellent family, Salvadora Debayle, and was soon meeting her daily under Wanamaker's clock.

Salvadorita convinced Tacho to return to the little land of big lakes, and they were married there over the opposition of her family. When his father established him in a little general store in San Marcos, his taste for cards proved his undoing. He went bankrupt and paid his creditors two percent. For a while he worked as inspector for the Rockefeller Foundation, checking whether the citizens had poured kerosene into their outhouses to keep the mosquitoes down. His friends dubbed him "the Marshal," for the flashlight that he carried to peek below deck did resemble a marshal's baton. Clever with his hands, he eked out a living installing electric fixtures in León and worked for the power company for a stretch as meter reader. His manual adroitness led him onto more tortuous paths. In 1939 ex-president Emiliano Chamorro published in *Hoy* of Mexico a version known to all Nicaragua: in 1921, shortly after Chamorro had handed the presidency to his uncle, Somoza and his friend Camilo González, later his chief of staff, were found with molds for counterfeiting gold coins. They were prosecuted, but the influence of the Debayle family served to get the proceedings dropped. From these and other cares, Somoza sought distraction umpiring baseball and football games.

No serious Nicaraguan in such straits could overlook politics as a means of betterment. In 1926 Somoza, at the head of a dozen lads, tried seizing his hometown, San Marcos, for the Liberals, received a trouncing, and took to his heels. On the strength of this defeat in a minor skirmish, he promoted himself through all the degrees of the army hierarchy, replacing the "señor" before his name with "general." Because of his command of English, he sat in at the Tipitapa Conference as translator. Then, in tribute to his way with North Americans, Moncada named him subsecretary of foreign affairs. It proved the decisive turn in his career.

The United States minister, Hanna, and his wife were bewitched by Tacho's effervescent personality. Mrs. Hanna, considerably her husband's junior, adored dancing, and Tacho danced so very, very well. Shortly before his death, Moncada related to me how Hanna had urged him to groom Somoza for the presidential succession. Moncada demurred; the Liberal party had nominated Dr. J. B. Sacasa, and he did not get along with Moncada. But to please the doting Hannas, foxy old Moncada did name Somoza commander of the National Guard, when the time came to replace the U.S. commander with a native son.

Sacasa was the uncle of Mrs. Somoza, and what follows is in a sense strictly *en famille.*

On January 1, 1933, Sacasa took over the presidency, and the Marines were withdrawn shortly afterward. At last it was possible for Sandino to make peace with Managua. He came to the capital and, amidst rousing oratory and much liquid refreshment, signed a peace. He was to disband his army, retaining an armed guard of one hundred, and was allotted virgin lands along the Río Coco to absorb his men in cooperative enterprise. Sacasa was by no means eager to liquidate Sandino as a political factor, for that would leave him alone to face his disquietingly ambitious National Guard commander.

Somoza was not happy about the arrangement. He tried playing off both ends against the middle. Though his guards were worrying and occasionally assassinating the Sandinistas, he went out of his way to win Sandino's confidence. When the guerrilla leader arrived at Managua in rags, Somoza graciously had a pair of old britches sent up to him from the National Guard barracks, and then the two were photographed together in a friendly embrace. In December 1933 he proposed an alliance to a lieutenant of Sandino against Sacasa. "The old imbecile is ruining the country. He opposes me only because he knows that Sandino is behind him. Together we could force a new cabinet on him with Sandino as war minister." When Sandino refused to fall in with the plan, Somoza filled Sacasa's ears with stories of an imminent Sandinista coup.

To offset his bumptious relative, Sacasa appointed a Sandino lieutenant in charge of four northern departments. It was throwing down the gauntlet to Somoza.

Three weeks later Sandino came to Managua with a sack of rock samples under his arm. He was convinced that he had struck gold near his Wiwili colony, and was breathless with plans for a cooperative mine. That evening he dined with Sacasa, accompanied by his brother and two aides. As Sandino and his comrades left the Presidential Palace, they were seized by the National Guard and informed that they must face the firing squad. Remembering the enthusiastic back-thumping of his good friend Somoza a few months earlier, Sandino asked to speak to the commander. Over the telephone Somoza was his usual genial self. He was awfully put out to hear about Sandino's plight, but he just couldn't countermand the order of his subordinate. Sandino and his companions were executed near the U.S. embassy.*

That same evening, with slick timing, the National Guard surrounded the Sandinista campt at Wiwili and turned machine guns on the occupants. Three hundred men, women, and children fell under the bullets. Then an amnesty was announced for Sandinistas, on condition that they report at Jinotega for their papers. Those who were trusting enough to obey were butchered as they left Jinotega. Somoza succeeded in eradicating practically the entire Sandinista movement. Nicaragua was swept clean of visionaries and prepared for a type of politics after Somoza's own heart.

Sacasa did not raise his voice in protest against this carnage. With Sandino gone he felt himself a guest in the Presidential Palace.

To justify the deed, Somoza played up the earlier atrocities of the Sandinistas. He burst into authorship and produced a book which,

---

*The crime occurred on the night of 2 February 1934. Sandino was assassinated along with his generals Estrada and Umanzor; at the same time his half-brother Sócrates Sandino was murdered in the house of Agriculture Minister Sofonías Salvatierra. On the evening of that day Somoza had obtained the advance approval of U.S. Minister Arthur Bliss Lane, a verbal authorization that Somoza used to persuade his officers who were involved in the plot.

carefully read, bears more damning witness against the writer than against the villain.* He even had himself triply decorated for his bloody feat with the Cross of Bravery, Medal of Distinction, and Presidential Medal of Merit.

Over the clank of all this hardware, Somoza thought he detected a move of Sacasa to install his foreign minister as his successor. His riposte was a coup carried out from the fortresses of Managua and León in May 1936. When the diplomatic corps intervened to put an end to the fighting, Sacasa was all too ready to throw in the sponge. After all, the presidency would stay in the family. He left the country, and his vice-president, of no sterner stuff, also resigned. Congress elected a trusted Somoza stooge to sit out the remaining months of Sacasa's term.†

On January 1, 1937, after most satisfactory elections, Somoza added the presidential sash to his collection of medals. Washington's recognition came by return mail.

Nicaraguan politics during the previous forty years had wanted nothing in corruption. The thirty years of Conservative rule that ended in 1893 had in many ways been a golden age of progress and honesty in public affairs. Nicaragua's Conservatives of the epoch were a local paradox, as amazing to outsiders as its fresh-water sharks. Though theoretically clerical, the Conservatives had separated Church and state, expelled the Jesuits, founded abundant schools, and imported Masonic and Protestant pedagogues. By peaceful means they stripped the land of much underbrush that in other Central American states had been cleared only by destructive conflagrations. No Conservative president had attempted to perpetuate himself in power. The subsequent Liberal dictatorship of José Santos Zelaya corroded both the civil liberties and morality. The ruling group bled the country through innumerable monopolies—liquor, medicines, soap, tobacco, lumber. But it was only under the United States occupation that venality was really enthroned. With disinterested parties outraged by the intervention, the occupation authorities leaned heavily on unconscionable adventurers. While the North Americans scurried about sterilizing outhouses, the country's public life grew fetid.

But even against this background Somoza felt himself a big-city slicker fallen amongst village yokels. The dreary years of meter-

---

*The book, put together by amanuenses of Somoza, was titled *The Real Sandino, or The Martyrdom of Las Segovias.*

†This provisional president was Carlos Brenes Jarquín.

reading and 2 percent bankruptcy had imparted a Damascus edge to his hunger. He proceeded to organize his territory along scientific lines; the motherland was milked from all orifices.

The oppositionists were able to draw up an alphabetical list of Somoza's enterprises starting with A and running through to Z without skipping a letter (X for businesses unknown to the public). In May 1944 I spent a week in Managua collecting data on these rackets, not from politicians but from businessmen in each specific line.

Cattle, the most mobile and widespread form of wealth in undeveloped lands, have always been close to the hearts of Latin American dictators. But Somoza set a new high in the thoroughness of his exploitation of the cow.

In the early thirties Costa Rica imposed a forty-colon tax per head of cattle imported from Nicaragua. Sacasa retaliated by banning cattle exports to Costa Rica. But that ban was never enforced until Somoza came to power and spied its sweeping possibilities.

In the departments along the Costa Rican frontier, where Nicaragua's best cattle ranges are located, "prohibited zones" were set up. An exact census was taken by the National Guard of the cattle there; when a cow died, the owner had to obtain a death certificate for it in order to convince the authorities that it had not been sold. The National Guard had to be notified in advance of how many kine were being transferred from one district to another; a permit had to be secured to drive your cattle across certain lines. You had, for example, a fattened herd on the rich pampas of Chontales, and wanted to move them to the capital. At Tipitapa between the lakes, the National Guard stopped you for a permit. You wired Managua. You waited, watching your stock grow thin. You started paying for pasturing them. Still no reply. You grew desperate. Then a certain Ponciano Muñoz, Somoza's chief agent in the cattle business, would turn up casually and offer you a ridiculous price for your beeves. You cursed loudly, but had no alternative but to accept. Once you sold, the permit arrived.

The same thing happened at times when you wished to move your cattle from one bit of pasture on your ranch, which had been cropped, to another up the road. Ponciano Muñoz and his aides always turned up at the strategic moment.

Though all this was justified in the name of revenge for the Costa Rican export tax of more than a decade ago, Somoza himself did a rich trade exporting cattle illegally to Costa Rica. They went to Victor Wolf, close ally of the Costa Rican ruling house of Calderón Guardia, who fattened them on his ranch at Chomes near Puntarenas. These exports did not exist so far as Nicaraguan statistics were concerned, but turned up in Costa Rican records. The Costa Rican Statistical

Report for 1943 gave cattle imports from Nicaragua in 1942 as 8,652 head. But the Nicaraguan Year Book for 1942 placed the total exports from Nicaragua for the same year (not only to Costa Rica, but to Panama and Peru) at 1,467. The 7,185 head that entered Costa Rica from Nicaragua, but didn't leave Nicaragua for Costa Rica, were one of the many miracles of the Somoza regime.

In 1943 Somoza sold 5,000-odd head of cattle to Panama at a profit of about $20 a head, and a similar number to Peru. None of these exports appear in the customs reports.

Only occasionally, at the cost of much pleading, did Somoza permit other cattlemen to export under special license. I was shown cancelled cheques on U.S. banks made out to Somoza for his rake-off. In one instance the exporter discreetly left out the name of the payee, but Somoza had shamelessly scrawled in "Anastasio Somoza." There was vigor rather than nicety about these transactions.

The National Guard was known to seize cattle for Somoza without any legalistic rigmarole. Anything in Nicaragua with horns, four legs, and a moo was potentially Tacho's.

Slaughtering licenses were granted only to good friends, who resold them to bona-fide parties. Somoza's natural son, José Somoza, had a lucrative monopoly supplying tallow to manufacturers.

Somoza owned a pasteurizing plant in the capital called, with a fine sense of irony, La Salud (Health). The equipment could not handle more than a fifth of the city's milk supply, but theoretically all the milk had to be marketed through the plant. For the most part the dairymen delivered unpasteurized milk to the customers' homes, collected 1.80 cordobas for "pasteurized" milk, and then handed 60 centavos over to the Salud for pasteurization.

Of all Central America, Nicaragua is the only natural cattle country. But because of Somoza's brilliant "organization" of the industry, the herds grew thin as Tacho waxed fatter.

Gold mining, Nicaragua's most important export industry, ran the cow second place as a source of income for Somoza. Apart from the legal taxation of seventeen dollars per kilo, the mining companies made two further contributions to Tacho, totaling approximately 2.25 percent of their production or about $175,000 annually. These remittances were made out to "General A. Somoza" or to "the President of Nicaragua, General A. Somoza." Somoza owned a gold mine in his own name, El Albino, acquired by a series of brilliant maneuvers.

In approximate terms Somoza was the proud possessor of 51 cattle ranches and 46 coffee estates within Nicaragua, and was by far the largest coffee producer. Some of this real estate he came by legitimately through shrewd buying ("My father taught me that it was wiser to buy from heirs"). But there were other ways of gathering in the rolling acres. In 1942 the Bank of London and South America put to auction the farm Alemania belonging to Julio Bahlke, who had hidden Somoza on his plantation in 1926 after his defeat at San Marcos. At the announced hour, Somoza's chief of staff, Colonel Camilo González, arrived with an entourage of machine guns to discourage competitive bidders. Somoza bought the farm for $60,000, about a tenth of its real value.

When the Airfields Development Project (the U.S. government and Pan American Airways) began planning their new airfield at Las Mercedes, near Managua, Somoza embarked upon energetic land purchases in the vicinity. One citizen called Murillo who was unfortunate enough to have a strategic holding was beaten up by the National Guard and informed through his lawyer that the drubbings would continue until he sold his land. He sold to Somoza, and Somoza passed the property on to the North Americans at a good-neighborly profit.

Alongside the Mercedes airport Somoza retained a farm known as Mercedes. As you got off the plane, you could recognize it by the iron railings that enclosed it. They were removed from a public park in the capital for that specific purpose. Many of his other properties were fenced in with ties provided by the state railway.

On the Pacific lay the vast Montelimar hacienda, apple of Tacho's eye. The state railway had built a wharf for it and provided the workers for maintenance and improvement. The government was building a concrete highway to Montelimar though there were no important population centers along the route. The cement for that came from a factory in which Somoza boasted a 50 percent interest. The finest full-blooded livestock were imported for Montelimar. It was without doubt the most modern, lavishly equipped estate in Nicaragua.

In Montelimar Somoza erected a large distillery to purvey rotgut to thirsty Nicaraguans. This interest in the liquor business was most baleful for the land. Formerly, no alcohol could be sold on the haciendas, but Somoza introduced a new type of liquor license—the *patente ambulante*—which authorized taverns on wheels. Instead of waiting for the peons to come to town to get drunk on holidays, the booze peddlers drove right into the haciendas to dispense their wares. Alcoholism gnawed at the nation's fibre.

Other businesses in which Somoza had a pudgy finger ran all the way from a tannery in León; a cut in the gambling ring run illegally by a Syrian in the capital; 41 percent of the stock of a cotton mill at Cahualiniac built by the Salvadoran textile magnate, Gadal María; 50 percent of the Compañía de Fósforos Nacional Momotombo, which produced the world's worst matches under the government monopoly (cigarette lighters were banned). He levied $20 per 1,000 board feet of mahogany and other precious woods embarked on the Atlantic coast. He owned the Managua newspaper *Novedades,* power plants at Chinandega, Tipitapa, Estelí, Jinotega, La Libertad; sawmills all over the place.

Somoza's brother-in-law, Colonel Luis Manuel Debayle, when minister of health, ran the government quinine monopoly to fine purpose; quinine generously mixed with flour sold at outrageous prices in a fever-ridden land. After Pearl Harbor, when Nicaragua blossomed forth as an important source of rubber, Somoza waded in and organized his take. He divided the rubber territory amongst a group of favorites, who, with money advanced by the National Bank, commenced buying up rubber from the gatherers at 60 cordobas and reselling it to the United States at 130. But toward the end of 1942 the Rubber Reserve Corporation warned him off and sent its own men into the rubber region to buy directly from the producers. Somoza, sensing that Washington had a vital concern here, did not persist in his attempt to "organize" the industry.

War scarcities to Somoza were what Prohibition had been to Al Capone. Nails, tires, machetes, were sold through friends at anywhere from 200 to 600 percent of cost. It was a field day, but the scandal grew to such proportions that he felt compelled to hand over price control to the U.S. subadministrator of customs, Major T. G. Downing. But Downing, an honest and energetic man, did not have a free hand.

Somoza's properties had long overflowed Nicaragua's frontiers. He had apartment houses in Miami; the buildings that housed the Nicaraguan legations in Mexico and San José de Costa Rica were his, rented at a handsome figure. When he purchased a cattle ranch in Costa Rica, new hope flooded the hearts of Central American unionists. Nicaragua, they mused, was no longer big enough to contain Somoza's businesses. To keep on expanding, he would perforce have to unite Central America.

On the streets of Managua you could see little pushcarts bearing the initials AVM. They were built in the National Guard barracks and rented to peddlers for one cordoba (20 cents) a day. Behind the sergeant who ostensibly carried on this business was the president of the Republic. There was nothing too small to engage Somoza's voracity.

But the game played with foreign exchange was for big stakes by any standards.

When the Marines were in Nicaragua, it was brutal imperialism and all that, but they helped keep the cordoba firm at parity with the dollar by spending a lot of Uncle Sam's money. There were many speeches and much rejoicing when they left; but before anybody realized it, the cordoba got the bends. It was not only that the blue-uniformed tourists had gone, but coffee prices tumbled, and disease put an end to banana exports. Budgetary inflation also played its part: in 1932 an earthquake flattened the capital, and the government overworked the printing presses to pay for the expenses incurred. Though officially parity with the dollar continued as a beloved and lingering fairy tale, cordobas were being offered for quarters and dimes. Somoza, born under a lucky star, reached the presidency when the world was pulling out of the depression. Gold mining boomed and put coffee in a back seat. In 1939 a Chilean economist was brought in to see about putting the cordoba into shape. It became a managed currency backed by a dollar and gold stabilization fund, and instead of maintaining the pretense of parity, it was allowed to drop to five to one.

Nevertheless, the black market in dollars still continued in 1945. Somoza's friends bought the dollars to pay for their imports at the National Bank at five to one, but most merchants had to get them on the black market for six or six and a fraction and sometimes for more than seven cordobas apiece. At the same time, they were required to surrender the dollar credits arising from their exports at the rate of five to one. By this process businessmen were mulcted some 20 percent on all their transactions with the outside world. You could not walk down the main street of Managua without merchants obstructing your passage and beseeching you to sell them dollars at one to six. Not even Pan American Airways would accept payment in cordobas for tickets sold in Managua. Dollars turned over to the Central Bank at 1:5 had been known to reappear on the black market.

The wonder of it all was that, from the official figures, there was apparently no technical reason for the cordoba sagging so. On March 31, 1945, the stabilization fund supporting the cordoba supposedly amounted to 33.8 million cordobas or 72 percent of the country's entire circulation. The budget was said to be balanced. The commercial balance was broadly favorable—$15,412,444 in exports for 1944 against $10,279,951 in imports—quite apart from the nonrecorded shipments of cattle. The balance of payments (that is, after profits of foreign firms, debt service, and other "invisible" items were allowed for) showed a three and a half million dollar margin in three years. By all known norms of economics the cordoba should have been sturdy.

The key to the mystery seemed to be the huge quantities of money that Somoza had been sending out of the country against a stormy day. Most of his properties were mortgaged with the National Bank at inflated figures, and the money sent abroad. He did not wish to be caught by a revolution with the bulk of his worldly goods in

Nicaragua. What might happen to the National Bank when Somoza fell and it was left holding the bag was any man's guess.

In May 1945, when the black market rate for cordobas was 7.2 to one, and business folk had murder in their glances, I revisited Managua and tried tracking down the explanation of the cordoba's strange behavior. An interview with the glossy-pated finance minister, Ramón Sevilla, was enjoyable but not enlightening. The minister admitted that they had been lenient with the black-market brokers (*coyotes*). Rather. In his very antechamber, on my way out, I felt a tug at my coat. It was a *coyote:* had I any dollars to sell for seven to one? I struck up a friendship with that *coyote*, who was not exactly bright. Yes, he was a good friend of minister Sevilla and had no fear of arrest because he paid for a monthly "license" which permitted him to deal in dollars. "And not only in dollars," said he, proudly flicking the ashes of his cigar, "but in black-market gasoline. Of course, I got to pay the National Guard their cut, but I still do very well."

Nicaraguan politics ran along strict family lines. When the Conservative party had its inning, Nicaraguan legations swarmed with Chamorro ministers, secretaries, consuls. On the Liberal side the names Sacasa, Debayle, Argüello, and others run through Nicaraguan history like the begats of the Old Testament. Somoza himself was an upstart: prior to his own spectacular ascent, his family had produced only a single bandit of note. But he married a Debayle Sacasa and thus moved into the mainstream of Nicaraguan life. The younger generation was again splicing it with the Sacasas. Somoza's daughter Lilian married the debonair Guillermo Sevilla Sacasa, who was immediately afterward rewarded with the Washington ambassadorship.* Sacasas, Debayles, and Somozas in all degrees of affinity and contiguity sprawl on soft upholstery all over the place. With such extensive inbreeding, it was remarkable that there should be so much talent to the fore.

It was not only a rich life, but a merry one. Wife Salvadorita's birthday had been proclaimed the Day of the Army; daughter Lilian's picture had been put on the one-cordoba bills. In 1942, Lilian was crowned Queen of the Army. For the occasion, part of the National Guard was garbed in Roman costumes, sandals and all. The poor old archbishop was induced to crown her with a diamond-studded crown. The fun was financed with a forced levy on the National Guardsmen's

---

*Sevilla Sacasa beat all Washington diplomatic records by serving for decades as dean of the diplomatic corps. He lasted till July 1979, when Anastasio Somoza, Jr., was overthrown.

pay. Lilian's wedding, coming shortly after, was so flashy that fork-tongued Nicaraguans dubbed it "Camacho's Nuptials" after the classic episode in Cervantes.

And the marriage was blessed with fruit. In the summer of 1944 four-month-old Guillermo Sevilla Somoza was appointed mascot of the National Guard with the rank of captain. The ceremony was conducted with full solemnity in the presence of the diplomatic corps. (Somoza realized that so much circus was a mistake and tried convincing me afterward that he didn't know that it was going to happen and that he was "ashamed before the diplomats.") The previous day, the baby and his daddy had been decorated with the wings of the Nicaraguan air force.

Somoza had everything arranged for foolproof permanence. The election staged in 1936 had assured him the presidency until 1941. But by the time 1939 rolled around he already had his gaze fixed on distant horizons. A constituent assembly was convoked from amongst his lackeys, with a few domesticated Conservatives thrown in for appearance's sake. The assembly suppressed municipal elections, prolonged the presidential term from four years to six, and picked Somoza to rule the land up to 1947. In 1943, looking still further ahead, he had the Congress insert the Atlantic Charter into the constitution, along with a clause making an exception to the anti-reelectionist principle in cases where Nicaragua is at war in alliance with two or more other Central American republics. The latter, of course, was tailored to Tacho's needs. He thus had everything readied to help himself to another six years and bring the count up to 1953. Nicaragua was to be vouchsafed a thick backlog of bliss.

Tacho was trying to give the Atlantic Charter a decent burial in the Nicaraguan Constitution, but the charter had churned Central America up wondrously.

There were grave portents in the skies. And on the waters. In 1942 the government had purchased a decrepit secondhand boat, christened it the *General Somoza,* and put it into service on Lake Nicaragua. The lake is huge, and the only other vessel that plowed its waters was the *Victoria* (Victory). Yet the Ripleyesque variant occurred. The *General Somoza* and the *Victory* collided, and the *General Somoza* went down. All Nicaragua read augury into the mishap. At once, Somoza ordered salvaging operations begun. When they made no visible progress, he himself went to the scene and directed the work. For almost a year the *General Somoza* nestled cozily on the lake bottom, while her frantic namesake imported salvaging equipment and concluded his political speeches with the rousing promise: "The *General Somoza* will sail again." The nation, however, looked forward to another collision between General Somoza and Victory.

Tacho's robust appetite had aroused the nation against him. Quiet businessmen who would normally stick close to their counting-houses wore the wild look of rebels because the president's enterprises had hit them where it hurts.

His closest friends were drawing away from him. A Liberal opposition took shape. It was headed by Carlos Pasos, who had seconded Somoza in the 1936 coup and had since become a textile and lumber magnate by virtue of Tacho's favors. Pasos reached an agreement for a united oppositionist effort with Emiliano Chamorro, the exiled Conservative chieftain in Mexico. For the Liberal Convention at León, Pasos, a heavy, dullish man, had prepared a speech in which Somoza's businesses were catalogued. In a frank discussion with some of the oppositionist leaders during the Congress, Somoza declared: "I must maintain myself in power. I have many enemies and must defend my life and properties. Moreover, I am the only person who knows how to administer this country well."

When asked ironically how many more years he expected to remain in the presidency he replied: "No less than forty. But if the United States were to give me the least hint about leaving, I would clear out at once, asking only complete guarantees for myself." "After all," he continued, "I have the 'hollow reeds' [Nicaraguan for guns]. Tell Carlos Pasos that I know he has a speech prepared for the convention. If he insists on delivering it at the convention, let him not forget to come armed. I am not a guy to be overthrown with speeches." There was no gunplay because Pasos was arrested beforehand.

During this trying period Somoza could console himself with the throaty devotion of the U.S. embassy.

Though the creature of United States intervention, Somoza early fixed an adoring eye on European totalitarianism. He recognized the Franco regime when the Caudillo was still camping outside Madrid, and at home gave his blessing to a group of young rowdies, the "Blue Shirts," who later became the Nicaraguan branch of the Spanish Falange. In his office, during this stirring period, he had a composite photo of himself with Adolf Hitler incorporeally in the background. When the European war broke out and the German ship *Stella* sought refuge from the British blockade in a Nicaraguan port, Somoza, always alert to a good bargain, bought her. The British threatened to sink the vessel if it ever put to sea. Notorious Naziphiles adorned key government posts, and the Germans for a while were not impeded in the operation of a clandestine radio station in Nicaragua.

Yet none of these details could sour the State Department's friendship. When Somoza traveled to Washington in 1939, he was received with such gala demonstrativeness that Mexico City café-

dwellers dubbed his triumphant tour a dress rehearsal for the imminent visit of George VI. His rejoinder was, "Dress rehoisal my eye.
We'll see if the king does as well." He also bragged that his pilgrimage
had cast a deep shadow over the other Central American presidents, a
boast that certainly did not improve his relations with the Guatemalan
Napoleon, Ubico. During that Washington visit, some inconclusive
agreement for the building of the Nicaraguan canal was reached, and
Tacho returned to buy up lands along the route.*

Not long afterward, Washington sent him as ambassador a pleas-
ant, mild-mannered person, James Bolton Stewart. Stewart, occupying his first diplomatic post, just hadn't the strength of character to
withstand the seductive Tacho. Before Stewart knew it, he was accompanying Somoza on his political jaunts and gracing the platform at
political rallies. To the State Department's regard for the dictator, he
added a starry-eyedness definitely his own. Somoza, who loved a pun,
would even present him to friends as "my steward." One Easter,
Stewart, along with most of the Nicaraguan cabinet, was Somoza's
guest at his Montelimar estate. A ship was at the wharf loading cement from Somoza's factory for Costa Rica. Because of the holiday
there were not enough longshoremen on hand, so Somoza had his
ministers help with the job. Ambassador Stewart, throwing the
niceties of protocol to the winds, also rolled up his sleeves and pitched
in. The newspapers carried the story most commendingly. An oppositionist journalist commented on such episodes: "Frankly, there are
moments when Somoza satisfies me completely—when he humiliates
the representatives of the country to which Nicaragua owes her
humiliation."

At the U.S. embassy in Managua one could hear the most amazing pleading on behalf of Somoza. In May 1944 the first secretary
clinched his arguments to me as follows: "Anyway, who are we to
complain of Somoza when we have the Roosevelts back home."

U.S. diplomats seemed to believe that their country owed Somoza
a debt of gratitude for having declared war against Germany rather
than against the United States. To visiting journalists, Ambassador
Stewart would recount the doings of Tacho like a doting aunt. He was
doing a magnificent job in developing the country economically,
above all in the matter of highway construction. Yet practically all of

*The old dream of a Nicaraguan canal goes back to the early nineteenth
century, but it faded when the United States opted for Panama in 1901.
However, the Bryan-Chamorro Treaty of 1916, giving Washington an option
to build this other canal, remained in force. In the 1950s the treaty was
rescinded by agreement of both parties.

Somoza's road program had been financed by the United States. Former Nicaraguan ambassador to Washington, León Debayle, in a lecture given in 1943, placed Washington's loans and contributions for highways, sanitation, etc., at $13,000,000. This included $4,100,000 for the road to the Atlantic coast and the outright payment of two thirds of the cost of the Pan-American Highway, which was diverted to pass through Somoza's La Fundadora farm.

To Nicaraguans the Good Neighbor policy during this period held little that was radically new. First there had been intervention to impose a puppet and then—in the name of nonintervention—propaganda, funds, and connivance to keep him in the saddle.

In May 1944 foul gales blew in from El Salvador. Martínez had fallen there, and Nicaraguans were quick to seize the cue. An anti-Somoza demonstration was broken up, but the students occupied the university, and were dislodged only after much menace and cajoling. Opposition papers, previously disciplined by periods of suspension, were now shut down permanently.

It was at this juncture that I interviewed Somoza.

At the foot of the hill stood a huge modernistic monument bearing the letters, big and succinct: SOMOZA. You passed peering sentries as you climbed to the Presidential Palace. A trim National Guard officer bowed you into a large salon, gaudy with tiles. Near the door an antiaircraft gun stood in drowsy readiness for who-knows-what emergency. At the other end a platform accommodated a grand piano and a jukebox. The salon was lined with patient clients wearing the unmistakable look of job-seekers.

Somoza's spacious office was littered with every variety of junk: sport trophies, bronze models of horses and elephants. No less than four photos of Roosevelt were on the walls, intended, I supposed, as rabbits' feet.

Behind it all in a khaki shirt open at the collar, a rock-sized diamond on his pudgy finger, a sagging paunch, an effusive manner, and thinning hair, sat Tacho. His English was fantastically incorrect and fluent—akin to that of an Italian-American mobster. "Godammits" erupted into his speech when he was making an effort at persuasiveness.

I began by asking whether he wasn't sore at *Time* for allusions recently published. No, it was still his favorite magazine. Only there were a lot of people going around Managua spreading slanders about him. I told him that I had three notebooks and a bellyful of Somoza's businesses, and I didn't wish to discuss them. But discuss them we somehow did. On cattle, he flushed a little when I mentioned the names of his chief purchasing agents. He finally suggested that I see

X, a leading cattleman who had been allowed to export to Casta Rica, as proof that he didn't hog the trade for himself. Since X had been my principal informant on cattle, I felt that I was on the right track.

I apologized for my frankness in treating of his businesses instead of the weather. That proved that there was a certain amount of freedom in Nicaragua after all. Why, I should never dare question Ubico about his properties. He concurred with a roar, and smacked me heartily on the thigh.

I tried lighting a cigarette with Nicaraguan matches, produced by Tacho's factory. Hurriedly he produced a lighter. I declined: "Weren't lighters illegal in Nicaragua?" He smiled sheepishly.

As we continued on his enterprises, his voice became plaintive. "Godammit, I wanta make sure my family has enough to live on when I die." He admitted that he obtained credits from the central bank that he could never hope to get if he were a private citizen. But he did it for the country's good. He had worked hard ever since he was a kid.

What he was most convincing about was how he had helped set up the oppositionist leader, Carlos Pasos, in the cotton business. "That guy Pasos wants to be president, and he is so dumb. He accuses me of stealing most of the 5 percent party levy on all Liberal public employees' salaries. But he takes 5 percent of the entire national budget, which ain't the same thing, and figures out it runs into millions. How can a guy like that be president?"

Pasos's arithmetic was deplorable. But as former Liberal party treasurer, his charge that no more than 90,000 cordobas of that 5 percent levy had been handed over to the party in seven years, could not be lightly dismissed.

"Godammit, I'm tired of the presidency. I woik like a dog." He wanted Chamorro and Sacasa to return to Nicaragua. I mentioned an ex-Sandinista friend of mine, the poet Salomón de la Selva. "I want Sal to come back too. I don't know why he attacks me in Mexico. I never done him no harm."

"Didn't you ever say his poetry was bad?"

"Honest, I didn't. I don't know nuttin' about poetry."

I enquired about the suppression of the opposition papers. He replied: "You gotta understand our people. Everything they see printed they believe. Well, I can't let the papers say everything or they would start a panic."

He ended on this note: "I wanta treat everybody good, see? But if they don't come across, well, let them remember that I got an iron fist under my silk glove. I know that they complain that the glove is too thin, but I pray God that it never rip."

When Ubico fell in Guatemala a few weeks later, the waves of revolt lapped Somoza's throne. On the anniversary of U.S. independence (which Tacho celebrates with a two-day holiday) he was shouted down when he attempted to speak in front of the U.S. embassy. But Somoza had a cunning scheme to foil the opposition. When the Managua society women organized an antigovernment demonstration, he mobilized the city's whores to attack the politicking ladies. In a resplendent limousine bearing an official license plate arrived Nicolasa Sevilla, working madame of one of Managua's cut-rate brothels. Flourishing a knife, she threatened the wives and daughters of the capital's fancier families and spewed spirited obscenities at them. Her eloquence was backed up by swarms of screeching strumpets, who jostled and insulted the demonstrators. The "loyal" forces carried the day by surprise. Afterward Somoza received La Nicolasa in the presidential palace and thanked "his good friend" in hearty language proper to her trade. Nicolasa, indeed, became quite a pillar of the regime, and even invaded the assembly to buffet oppositionist deputies. Several months later the cause was deprived of her services when she was wounded in a brothel brawl and confined to bed nonprofessionally.

Somoza deported a couple of hundred oppositionists to the Corn Islands in the Caribbean, and cast Carlos Pasos and other leaders out of the country.

But what really poured oil on these lashing waters was Somoza's decision to veto the constitutional amendment permitting him another term. He offered the Liberal opposition all key posts in his regime, with the exception of the command of the National Guard and the Washington ambassadorship. He even proposed reimbursing them for expenses incurred in organizing the campaign against him. In the past he had bought oppositionists by the dozen and counted on doing so now. But the opposition turned him down.

So, instead, he discovered his passionate love for labor.

During his eight years in power Somoza had met attempts at labor organization by deporting the leaders to Little Corn Island in the Atlantic to live on coconuts and bananas with no shelter against the tropical sun. But in the fall of 1943, when things were taking a critical turn, his eye was caught by the Mexican labor leader, Vicente Lombardo Toledano. At the time Lombardo, who cleaved to the Communist party line, was trying to obtain a toehold for his Latin American Confederation of Labor in the dictator-ridden countries with the kind permission of the dictators. Lombardo journeyed to Managua and was enthusiastically introduced by Somoza at a huge open-air meeting. For two and a half hours Lombardo spoke without once mentioning Somoza's name. In private Somoza complained of this deplorable lack of manners, but he conserved his beaming smile for the world at large.

The romance was troubled with spats, as the best of idylls is wont to be. Now and again the Lombardista leaders would revisit the prisons long familiar to them. But on their release Somoza received them and wept with emotion. He explained that he was a hard worker himself, slaving away at his estates; that it was necessary to consider labor as not merely a physical but a moral act, and other inexpensive doodles. To his intimates there were asides of a different color: "If they think I am going to give them a labor code, they are crazy. . . . They are my worst enemies."

The labor leaders scurried to profit by Somoza's fleeting libertarian mood and organized a few thousand artisans and workers. For his part, Lombardo Toledano, in kilometric speeches outside the country, called for the support of Somoza's "progressive tendencies" against the "reactionary opposition." In April 1945 a labor code was actually passed. Without a doubt it was the most extravagant in Latin America, and perhaps in the world. The workers were promised the moon . . . on paper: four weeks' paid vacation annually; six weeks' paid leave for pregnant women workers before delivery and six afterwards. But none of this was ever implemented. As the country's principal capitalist, passionately attached to pennies, Somoza's interests lay elsewhere. His foreign minister was attorney for La Luz Mining Company, which exploited the Mosquito Indians in iniquitous fashion. When a couple of gold mines were shut down by strikes in June 1945, the government was anything but encouraging to the unions, and Somoza's flirtation with labor came to an abrupt close. Shortly afterward, he expelled the chief Lombardista leaders from the country.

Somoza's vetoing of the reelectionist amendment to the constitution, and his pro-labor pose, had the effect of solidifying his position after the July 1944 crisis. But no sooner had Somoza the sorcerer laid the storm then Somoza the greedy apprentice threw open the floodgates once again. Nicaraguans have a quaint way of catching monkeys. They cut a small hole in a gourd, fasten it to a tree, and insert a corncob into it. The monkey squeezes in its paw, grabs the cob, and then finds that it is unable to withdraw his closed fist. It never occurs to the beastie to drop the corn and make a getaway. Somoza's predicament was quite similar.

In May 1945, while on a gala tour to Bluefields to unveil a life-sized statue of himself, he listened enthusiastically to a speech of his secretary urging another term for Tacho. The reelectionist campaign was on again.

The constitutional clause barring presidential reelection did not bother Somoza. He argued that since he had not been elected in 1939, but merely "appointed" for another term by the constitutional assembly, he would not be violating the ban on reelection. He pleaded that he wished only to remain at the helm until his cherished project for a highway to the Caribbean had been realized and that he would resign

as soon as it was. At once, two thousand workers of Corinto tele-
graphed their offer to work gratis to terminate the road before the
close of his current period. Summoning the press, he announced that
he could not be kicked out of the presidential palace: the wartime
housing law prohibited the eviction of tenants paying less than $20
rent monthly, and he paid less than that. When the rumor got around
that someone had offered to wager 200,000 cordobas that Somoza
would not be in the presidency after May 1947, Somoza, in fine gambling fettle, upped the ante to one million cordobas and offered to
take on all comers ("just bring your million to the presidential
palace"). From Mexico Carlos Pasos wired his acceptance of the bet.
Again Somoza raised the ante—to 3,000,000 with his friends taking a
2,000,000 cordoba cut. And the official paper *Novedades* suddenly
came to resemble a bookie's ledger: entire columns were filled with
the names of those backing Somoza's wager and the amounts.

At a student festival the outgoing King of Ugliness appeared with
his chest covered with pop-bottle tops and orated: "I bet a million that
I'll be reelected. There's not another candidate with enough brains."
The National Guard arrested him and walked him thirty kilometers
before throwing him into jail for several days. Somoza was losing his
grip.

On the diplomatic front there was plenty of reason why he
should. U.S. Ambassador Stewart had been replaced by Fletcher Warren, a capable, Nicaragua-wise diplomat. Warren immediately took
the embassy off the Somoza bandwagon. The vigorous stand in favor
of democracy of the new American undersecretary of state, Spruille
Braden, was causing Somoza sleepless nights. In the light of it, the
fact that Somoza's daughter Lilian had known Truman's daughter at
school—much publicised in Nicaragua after President Truman's inauguration—seemed to lose some of its immense importance. When
Chile's president visited Nicaragua in November, the National Guard
had to intervene with drawn bayonets against the oppositionist demonstration. A couple of months later, Somoza's cabinet resigned
under the impact of another popular show of force. There was nothing rosy about sunset for Central America's most jovial dictator.*

---

*In 1947 Somoza conceded more or less free elections and allowed
Leonardo Argüello's election, but a month later overthrew him and replaced
him with an uncle of Somoza's, Victor Román y Reyes, who governed until
1951, with Somoza retaining the National Guard command, i.e., the real
government. In 1951 Somoza had himself reelected president and was getting set for further reelection when, in September 1956, the young poet
Rigoberto López Pérez took several shots at him. He was taken to the Canal
Zone's Gorgas hospital, and President Eisenhower sent down his personal
physicians and surgeons to repair the dictator; he died a few days later.

8

Shangri-La

THE FIFTH MEMBER OF THE CENTRAL AMERICAN FAMILY was a happy accident: a tiny Shangri-La perched on a volcano-girt plateau where the isthmus slims off. Coffee bushes pressed into the backyards of four small cities, San José, Cartago, Heredia, and Alajuela. Fancifully painted ox-carts creaked over well-paved roads; neither beast nor driver wore a harrowed look. When it rained, the barefooted peasants toted umbrellas with a dignity that no Englishman could outdo. Rural schoolhouses, which elsewhere in Central America rarely occurred outside official reports, were trim and plentiful. There were more teachers than soldiers.

The sensation of rustic felicity did not leave you in the capital, San José. Flimsy houses of wood and corrugated sheeting huddled around the magnificence of its theater. When closing hour came, the stores did not pull down forbidding iron curtains as was the Latin custom: nothing more was left between the goods on display and the law-abiding citizenry than a frail pane of glass. The townsfolk wore shoes and were well-dressed. Costa Rica had little Indian blood: on the central plateau, where ninety percent of the population was crowded, the inhabitants were almost all white.

The women were amazingly beautiful, though few retained their looks through maturity. In San José a merely pretty girl did not draw a second glance. Four times a week, in accordance with the tradition of the Spanish *paseo,* the girls walked around the Central Square in a huge cartwheel, while the young bloods moved in the opposite direction, stretching their limbs and feasting their eyes. To compete with such glamor, the movie houses on the plaza announced their programs with sirens reserved elsewhere for air-raid alarms.

In the other isthmian republics, coffee had been a harsh god, prone to whet avarice and put a jagged edge on human relations. Here it was raised by free labor. Modern advertising has made milk-drinkers conscious of the contentment of cows; when coffee addicts learn to distinguish human anguish in their cups, Costa Rica will pull ahead of the few coffee-producers that can rival it today.

The treatment of animals is a ready index to the human lot. In Mexico and the rest of Central America, the peasant vents on his burro the bile in his soul. Costa Rica, on the other hand, had laws against beating dogs or maltreating horses. It was forbidden to use a sharp goad on oxen, to kill a cat, to carry a chicken through the streets with its legs bound. Some years ago a bill had even been brought before Congress for an eight-hour day for beasts of burden and "social guarantees" for animals.

This tender regard for beasts had altered bullfighting in a rare way. The tools of the *torero*'s trade—*banderillas,* swords, the picador's *pic*—were outlawed. Late December each year an amateur bullfight was organized in a huge, improvised ring. Those who could not afford the price of a seat were admitted free—into the ring with the bull. Hundreds of men and boys faced the snorting monster and went through the flourishes of the art, using hats, coats, bedsheets, or newspapers as capes. When the bull lapsed into too serious a mood, the *toreros* had but one refuge—the large fountain in the center of the ring. They jumped in and got a ducking. A greased pole had been set up in the water, and the attempts of the more panicky to climb it provided the paying customers with unfailing laughs. The bull, an amateur like the rest, intended by destiny for beefsteaks rather than the heroic sport, hoisted the occasional *torero* onto his horns and trampled others. But it was good small-town fun, and both bull and *toreros* survived it.

In Central America, where poverty and ignorance are the rule, Costa Rica was as a one-carat diamond set in pewter. The oddity had its roots in history.

Central America as a whole was the lame duck of Spain's American possessions. There was little gold to hold the adventurous. Its conqueror, Pedro de Alvarado, left the captaincy-general in the hands of his wife and headed first to Peru and then to the Philippines in quest of richer pastures. Only those who lacked initiative or the price of a return ticket stayed on in these parts; they set themselves to extracting slower wealth from the Indians in agriculture. But in Costa Rica the Indians were few and primitive, and some were disconcertingly warlike. In 1741 there were only eight hundred pure-blooded Indians in all Costa Rica. It was bitter enough that a Spaniard of the epoch could not find gold, but to have to do his own work . . .

Most of the 700,000-odd Costa Ricans of our time are descended from a mere fifty families stranded in the region in 1573. Spanish commercial policy hung around the colony's neck like a millstone. The settlers raised wheat and corn, swapped flour and biscuits with the occasional boat from Cartagena or Portobello; they exported to Panama the mules needed there to haul ships' cargoes across the isthmus. This trade, however, was soon taxed to a dribble by the Spanish authorities at Guatemala City. A little cocoa grown in the Caribbean lowlands went to Nicaragua, but the Mosquito Negro-Indian half-breeds, incited by the British, devastated the coastal plantations. On one occasion they even kidnapped and murdered the colony's governor.

British, French, and Dutch pirates preyed on the sickly rivulet of commerce with the other Spanish colonies, while Spanish fiscal officers suppressed the promising contraband trade with British Jamaica in turtle-shells, logwood, and sarsaparilla. The miserable settlement pleaded in vain to be separated from the Kingdom of Guatemala, whose agriculture was competitive, and annexed to Panama. After restricting Costa Rica's dealings with Panama for two centuries, the Guatemalan authorities banned them outright in 1811 on the very eve of independence.

The colonists' houses and churches often crumbled into ruin for lack of Indians to repair them; many of the settlers fashioned their clothes from grass and leaves. With practically no commerce, towns failed to develop. It required official compulsion to group the colonists into the towns of Heredia, San José and Alajuela. As late as 1719 there was still no barber, doctor, or pharmacist, and practically no stores, in Cartago, the colonial capital. Coco beans circulated as money right up to 1850. The colony's name (Rich Coast), given it by its discoverers because of the Indians' gold ornaments, had become a cruel mockery.

Yet such abandonment was not without its blessings. The life of the Costa Rican approximated to that of the New England settler, and the effects, to an extent, were similar. With no Indians to enslave, large feudal domains had no reason for appearing. The colonists, Andalusians and Extremeños for the most part, learned to do their own work. Class distinctions were feeble. The gay ox-carts, which are the country's outstanding bit of folk art, could perhaps only have arisen amongst free peasants taking joy in their work.

When independence from Spain was achieved, this society of needy peasants showed a stability and sanity that contrasted with the nightmare enveloping the other Central American states. A Guatemalan historian with an abacus took it upon himself to count the revolutions that shook the isthmus during the first twenty years of its independence: of the figure 140 that he arrived at, only five fell to Costa Rica. The Church created no great problems, for God's ministers were as poor as the rest.

In this forgotten nook all passions flickered low. The Scot Glasgow Dunlap, who visited Costa Rica in the 1840s, reported the absence of crimes against lives and property. Erring wives did not find it necessary to hide their faithlessness from their husbands. It was enough that they promised not to transgress again for the cuckolded burgher and the seducer to dismiss the incident with a hearty laugh.

Even Costa Rican speech bears the marks of centuries of seclusion. It is studded with quaint idioms and varies widely from that of the rest of the isthmus. Because of their use of the strange diminutive "tico," Costa Ricans are dubbed *Ticos* by other Central Americans.

Coffee reached Costa Rica earlier than the other Central American republics. For here there was a vacuum to fill, whereas it got a foothold in Guatemala and Salvador only as their exports of cochineal and indigo fell into decay. In the latter states the advent of coffee brought with it the despoliation of most of the lands that the Indians still retained. In Costa Rica it produced, at least in its early stages, the further democratization of agriculture. The municipalities and the central government distributed coffee seedlings and fallow lands to the poorer folk to encourage the spread of the new crop.

Coffee gave Costa Rica its first wide window to the outside world. At long last it had a serious export product.

What the *Mayflower* is to Americans, the brig *Monarch* is to *Ticos*. To be sure she did not bring in a supply of ancestors, but she took out Costa Rica's first coffee shipment to Britain. In 1845 Captain William Le Lacheur brought the *Monarch* into the Pacific port of Puntarenas and bought a lot of coffee for England. Or at least he attempted to *buy* the coffee, but found that the impoverished Ticos had no use for gold and were interested only in barter. He thereupon sailed to Panama, picked up a cargo of textiles, and took them back to the Costa Ricans for their coffee.

It was the tea-drinking British who were to gild the future of Costa Rican coffee. Right up to 1886, when the Costa Rican railway to the Altantic was completed, Le Lacheur's sailing vessels made their 140-day voyages from Puntarenas to London via Cape Horn. Costa Rican coffee caught on in England, and the conservatism of the British did the rest. Until the recent war, upper-class families insisted on their Costa Rican coffee because their grandfathers had done so before them. It was largely a private trade to old customers who for flavor and tradition's sake were willing to pay more than world prices. In return Britain became the source of Costa Rica's industrial goods and capital.

Money poured forth from the expanding coffee farms. Clodhoppers wrapped in rags and leaves gave way to opulent planters abreast of Europe's latest fashions. Italian opera companies began arriving. The National Theater of San José, built in the nineties in vague imitation of L'Opéra of Paris, is a monument to the epoch: overnourished angels cavort in stone and paints amidst ornate gold-leafed columns. Italian artists were imported to do the murals. Given this background, coffee in Costa Rica became a religion rather than a mere crop. It was identified with the good things of life, while the foodstuffs were associated with the period of bumpkin backwardness. Whether it paid or not, coffee was grown out of snobbery. For the coffee-planter looked down upon the wheat-farmer, as the horseman of feudal times upon the churl on foot or ass. Even paupers with but an acre of land of their own would devote half or all of it to coffee instead of corn. Staple food crops were neglected, and the country came to depend on imports for much of its provisions.

Alongside 102,800 acres producing coffee, there were only 18,000 sown to corn, 19,500 to sugar cane (though unrefined sugar mixed with water is a principal food of the *Tico* peasant). In 1943 imports included 47,348 hundredweights of rice, 21,120 of corn, 27,609 of beans, 250,050 of wheat flour. The republic had excellent lands for raising all these products in excess of its needs. The Pacific province of Guanacaste, geologically a continuation of Nicaragua (of which it was formerly a part), was excellent cattle country; but Costa Rica imported 10,000 head of cattle annually, and until a 40-colon import tax was imposed in 1934, the figure was 22,000. The coffee-planters preferred importing cheaper rice from the East Indies and corn and beans from other parts of the isthmus to cultivating them at home. They were thus able to pay their workers less and avoid accentuating the labor shortage on the coffee plantations. Food crops received no tariff protection, and the government had recently been authorized to import foodstuffs itself in the event of scarcities and sell them to the consumer. The British Anti-Corn Law League of a century ago could not hope to find truer disciples than the Costa Rican coffee-planters. Dominated by the coffee interests, the banks frowned on loans to other agriculturalists.

Though the initial effect of coffee was to broaden the distribution of land, a contrary trend soon set in. With the influx of money, a merchant-planter oligarchy arose and closed its grip on the country's economy. It bought up the coffee of the small producers for export, loaned them money at usurious rates, and took their farms when payments fell into arrears. The struggle against this plutocracy imparted an episodic storminess to Costa Rican politics for the eighty-odd years that followed the introduction of coffee. Child's play though it was alongside the upheavals in the other republics, it shed a revealing light on social relationships. Sometimes the dictator who violated the constitution was acting against the commercial oligarchy; on at least one occasion he was its agent.

President Braulio Carrillo (1835–37; 1838–42) was a power-loving eccentric who ran the affairs of state from a dingy little office adjoining his wife's modest store. He gave land to the poor, but those who failed to cultivate their plots were whipped. Anticipating the Roosevelt New Deal, he assigned each family quotas of the various crops to plant and had the state buy up any excess to prevent a slump in prices. All this was tolerated, but when he ventured to pass elementary laws for the protection of labor and tried freeing the state finances from the control of the coffee magnates, he drew their wrath. Though indifferent to the stormy politics of the other republics, the merchants invited Francisco Morazán, exiled champion of Central American liberalism, to overthrow Carrillo. But once installed as Costa Rican president, Morazán mobilized the state's resources to continue the struggle for Central American union. That enraged all Costa Ricans alike: Morazán was overthrown and executed under a wise old tree on San José's central square.*

General Tomás Guardia, who ruled the country with a heavy hand from 1870 to 1882, trimmed the power of the merchants and reasserted the relative independence of the treasury. It was Guardia who began the railway to the Atlantic and brought the American Minor Keith in to complete it. To provide the railway with traffic before it had climbed to the populated plateau, Keith started planting bananas along the line and thus began an enterprise that grew into the regal United Fruit Company. Eventually the tail came to wag the dog, and United Fruit controlled not only railways but Central American governments. But before that happened, Minor Keith, as usually befalls pioneers, had been eliminated from the company.

The next president to tangle with the plutocracy, Alfredo González Flores, came to power in 1914. To compensate for the wartime drop in import duty revenues, González introduced an income tax. Touched in their moneybags, the oligarchy threw overboard the proud democratic traditions of the land, and in 1917 backed a coup headed by González's war minister, General Federico A. Tinoco. Anticipating Gandhi, the people responded by refusing to buy matches and other articles on which the state depended for its income. What really ruined Tinoco, however, was oil. He had granted an oil exploration concession to a U.S. company, behind which the keen-scented

---

*Many historians maintain that what riled the privileged families to whom Krehm alludes was not Morazán's attempts to reunify Central America's five republics but his tax levies on their goods and properties (which they never paid) to finance the defense of Guanacaste province, then threatened by neighboring Nicaragua, and to cover the big treasury deficit. Morazán was shot on 15 September 1842.

State Department sniffed British capital. Tinoco's adversaries were given every facility for organizing an expedition from U.S.-dominated Nicaragua. Tinoco was overthrown, and his brother killed.* It is a gentle irony that no oil was ever struck in Costa Rica; but the local politics were able to resume their tranquil amble. By 1942 the tiny land could boast eight ex-presidents in the pink of health residing within its frontiers.

Traditionally, *Tico* politics had been as scrupulously honest as they had been serene. When Clete González Víquez, a venerable Latinist, completed his second term as president in 1932, he was so poor that he had to sell his home. Congress voted him a life pension, but he indignantly rejected it. To get around his qualms, the deputies thought up the special post of historical researcher for him. Only then did he consent to live off the public budget, but he rose at six A.M. each morning to toddle down to the archives.

Yet Costa Rican politics were a very human game. After each presidential election, the winning party covered the campaign expenses by a levy on the salaries of all public employees. And the institution of the brother is nothing in Mexico alongside what it has long been in Costa Rica. President León Cortés (1936–40) appointed his brother administrator of the state-owned Pacific Railway, his brother-in-law minister of the interior, and got his son made president of Congress. President Rafael Angel Calderón Guardia (1940–44) named his father "first designate" (vice-president), his brother Francisco minister of the interior, and so forth.

Parties meant little in Costa Rican politics. Everything revolved around personalities, as one would expect in a well-regulated village where everyone knows what is cooking on everybody else's stove, come dinner hour. The political pattern had long remained very simple. The outgoing president usually backed one of the presidential candidates, who, having more cash, came out on top. The defeated aspirant shouted about fraud. Just as surely the incoming president broke with his sponsor, and the ensuing debate made the barn-rafters ring. The press joined in the fray, and for months and years thereafter the air was filled with Homeric clatter.

From 1932 to 1936 the presidency was occupied for the third

---

*In fact, the Tinoco brothers toyed with U.S. and British interests, offering port, oil, and agricultural concessions. Since President Woodrow Wilson insisted on not recognizing their regime, the Tinocos started negotiating with the Amory oil firm, linked to the famous Royal Dutch Shell magnate Lord Deterding. According to some historians, it was this clash of interests that finally led to the fall of the Tinoco brothers and the assassination of one of them, Joaquín.

time* by Ricardo Jiménez, a grand old man with the beard and soul of a saint and a tongue like Lucifer's tail. An erudite lawyer and old-fashioned liberal, Jiménez in his prime had battled against the foreign monopolies and done much to implant democratic practices after the mild turbulence of the last century. In the forties his sardonic witticisms still went the rounds in Costa Rica, and constituted a distinct literary genre. When an opponent, seeking to wound him through his rather scarlet mistress, had proposed setting aside a special red-light district in the capital, Jiménez countered: "Heavens, it would cost too much to build a fence around San José."

When his third term drew to its close, Jiménez chose his minister of public works, León Cortés, as successor. Cortés, a bilious ex-schoolteacher, was no sooner elected than he was at war with Jiménez. Cortés felt drawn to Germany, not because he was crazy enough to dream of imitating the Nazis in Costa Rica, but because their harsh efficiency appealed to his temperament. Besides, they bought a lot of good *Tico* coffee, even though in return they flooded the country with Aski marks. Cortés sent his son, Otto, to Berlin on a mission, and the boy sent back photos of Hitler and lyrics on the brown-shirted regime. Cortés had a puritanical streak: he would not permit his ministers or friends to take a drink in his presence. If it were feasible he would cheerfully have passed a law tucking the nation into bed at eight P.M. His one soft spot was for his wastrel son Otto.

A country may be known by its scandals. When Cortés left the presidency in 1940, a deputy accused him of having taken along a lamp from the presidential palace. Cortés sued for libel, and waved a receipt from the Finance Ministry to show that he had paid for the lamp. But his adversary pressed his attack: he brought up the matter of two hens and two roosters that Cortés had received from the National Agricultural School. His back to the wall, Cortés admitted that he had done wrong in accepting the fowl, but argued that the fault rested with the school director in making the gifts.

Cortés's wife had prevailed on him to pick as official candidate Dr. Rafael Angel Calderón Guardia, a personable, backslapping doctor. Old Ricardo Jiménez withdrew from the race, alleging favoritism. With only a Communist candidate to oppose him, Calderón chalked up over 100,000 votes, the largest in the country's history.

No sooner was Calderón properly installed than his relations with Cortés began to chill. But when son Otto's private life developed into a public scandal and Calderón decided to drop him as president of Congress, the break between Cortés and his successor became final.

---

*Nonconsecutive. The constitution bars immediate reelection—W.K.

All this was sufficiently true to the pattern of past decades. But the world conflagration began casting shadows of novel, tortured forms. Prices shot up; millions of dollars foolishly spent by U.S. army engineers on the emergency Pan-American Highway in Costa Rica, brought on a condition of economic dropsy. Wartime scarcities and priorities dangled cruel temptation before politicians' noses. John Maynard Keynes held that periods of rising prices produced great literature; he even related Shakespeare to the influx of American gold into Elizabethan England. Throughout Latin America the war's dizzy inflation brought on artistry of a different sort. Political morality scraped the bottom.

Before assuming the presidency, Dr. Calderón owned a fifteen-acre farm near Turrialba in partnership with his brother and his uncle; they sold it for $1,500. His brother Francisco worked as teller in a local bank. Dr. Calderón's salary as president was $68 a week; as minister of the interior Francisco earned $45. Yet on relinquishing the presidency in 1944, the brothers were the happy owners of a 4,000-acre farm "Tapanti" near Cartago, and a 24,000-acre cattle ranch "Chomes" in Guanacaste Province. In the swank new suburb Barrio Escalante, developed on land handsomely purchased from Calderón's finance minister, Manuel Escalante, Dr. Calderón had built a luxurious home. Alongside, Francisco had installed himself in an equally commodious dwelling, flashy with *nouveau riche* gadgets. As a filial gesture, they built their mother a house to match their own, next door. It was too bewildering a success story for the liking of the *Ticos,* who had always taken pride in the poverty of their retiring presidents.

Nicaraguans, who had seen acquisition on a really big scale, found it hard to understand why the *Ticos* were so volubly shocked. For the Calderóns' business triumphs had been of a relatively discreet sort. There was close contact with Victor Wolf, whose boats plied the Caribbean, who exported wood, imported cattle, and supplied the government with all manner of merchandise. He openly backed the Calderóns with funds for their politics and their enterprises. In return he received contracts for the construction of roads, schools, and other public works. Nobody in Costa Rica believed that much higgling took place when Wolf's contracts were drawn up.

When his affluence had lost President Calderón much popularity, he resorted to a shrewd political maneuver. He went left.

Calderón's background was fairly conventional. While a student in Belgium, he had become interested in the Church's social program as expounded by Cardinal Mercier. His father, a distinguished doctor, was known for his charities, and his son, too, had his feelings for the poor. But, devoutly Catholic, he had a dread of communism; and because Franco was playing St. George to that particular dragon,

Calderón had been anti-Loyalist during the Spanish Civil War. His wits, however, were nimble, and his nostrils keen to the trend of the times.

Headed by Manuel Mora, a brilliant and smooth apostle, the Communist party had pilloried Calderón and his corruption. But in 1941, when Russia suddenly found herself in the war, Communists started behaving strangely the world over. The Communist party reorganized itself and put out a new shingle: Vanguardia Popular, dedicated to upholding democracy, religion, and a lot of other mellow things. Mora extended a hand to the government, and Calderón seized it. Then the two started touring the country preaching the redemption of the downtrodden. In 1942 Calderón had already instituted a social insurance system; now he promised a labor code.

A weird alliance had come into being between grasping politicos and the nation's lower strata. It brought to mind Renaissance Italy, where merchant princes courted the *popolo minuto* as a means to absolute power in the age of Machiavelli.

The unorthodox mating bore fruit. The labor code provided an eight-hour day, time-and-a-half for overtime, two weeks' annual paid vacations, collective bargaining. The Communist-controlled unions, the Confederación de Trabajo de Costa Rica, were injected with new life.

Money wages doubled, not only because of the code, but because of the absorption of workers by the U.S. highway construction. Accustomed to running the country their way from behind the bland democratic facade, the coffee barons were up in arms. During the previous war they had overthrown a government because of income tax—the merest pecadillo alongside what Calderón had contrived. *Tico* politics had never been short on sound effects; but with a president who had both forsaken poverty and kicked privilege in the crotch, the air was shattered with din.

The immediate advantages of Calderón's social reforms were dissipated by soaring prices; higher wages lent further momentum to the inflationary spiral that the extravagances of the road-builders had set spinning. Between January 1941 and December 1944 Costa Rican statistics recorded a rise in living costs from 104.82 to 189.29. That swallowed up the wage increases and even bit into labor's living standard. One of Roosevelt's signal merits was his choice of a period of deflation to launch a program of social reform: all the money spent by the New Deal agencies helped lift the country out of the depression. In most Latin American countries social legislation got under way only during the war, when political upheavals made it unpostponable. Because of the timing, it caused violent economic dislocations. Had social-minded visionaries had more say in its governments a decade earlier, Latin America would certainly have come through the war in fitter shape.

Calderón decided upon Teodoro Picado Michalsky, president of Congress, as a successor, while the opposition's ranks closed around León Cortés. Had the labor code netted Calderón a more unequivocal popularity, he might have allowed himself the luxury of fair elections. But things had not worked out so simply. Moreover, lend-lease armament, sent into Costa Rica for no very clear purpose, provided too handy an instrument for intimidation. Not that the arms amounted to much. The U.S. War Department had pressed for the organization of a modern army in Costa Rica, but the State Department, happily inspired for once, overrode the project. The armament that went to Costa Rica consisted of fourteen jeeps, twenty-four tommy guns, six mortars, two field guns, six tripod machine guns, a couple of armored trucks, and 200 tear-gas grenades. Yet in pacific Costa Rica the moral effect was shattering. Soldiers riding around in jeeps seemed like Ghengis Khan's boys out of their century. Costa Ricans began referring to the jeep as *el jeep fatídico,* "the fateful jeep."

The elections inevitably took place in an atmosphere of violence. At San Francisco de Heredia stones were thrown, guns popped, heads were battered. An oppositionist demonstration in the capital was fired upon, while Vanguardia Popular headquarters were assaulted by the Cortesistas. The burghers of Arcadia found the ugly forces of the contemporary world closing in on them.

Nobody was surprised when Picado came out on top. A year later Francisco Calderón admitted to me that there had been plenty of irregularities. But he argued that the resuscitated dead had not altered their political opinions since their earthly sojourn: in the Cortesista strongholds they had voted for Cortés, and in the Picado centers for Picado.

The rest of the isthmus rocked with the repercussions of the Costa Rican elections. Ubico's press in Guatemala emptied its chamber pots on Calderón's head and raged against Costa Rica as a focus of communism. On the other hand, Calderón's friendship with Nicaraguan dictator Somoza grew like a cancer. Somoza had long sought to bring the little land into line with the four dictatorships to protect his southern flank. At a ball given him on his visit to San José in 1939, he had urged President Cortés's wife during waltzes: "Tell León not to be a fool, and to reelect himself like the rest of us."

Cortés, however, was not fool enough to try.

Paradoxically enough, it was under Calderón's leftist regime that Somoza got his foothold in Costa Rica. Most of the cattle he exported there went to Victor Wolf, the Calderóns' associate; many of the animals were fattened on the Calderóns' own Chomes ranch. There can be no doubt, too, that Somoza encouraged the Calderóns' appetites. They were as inspired by his example as a corner grocer might be by Rockefeller's record in oil.

On the other hand, it was from Costa Rica that Somoza got the idea for his own affair with the Communists. His chief of staff, Camilo González, had come to San José in 1942 with his boss's warning that playing around with the reds was dangerous stuff. In reply Calderón took him along when he toured the country expounding the social evangel. Astounded by the popular enthusiasm, González cried: *"Caramba,* it's sure the way to get them and hold them." Immediately after his return to Managua, Somoza, too, discovered his love for labor. Backing both regimes, the Communists helped cement the alliance and did not neglect their propaganda abroad.

Cortesistas, who in their fervor were given to visions, would swear that hundreds of Nicaraguan Guards were sent to Costa Rica during the 1943 elections to browbeat the citizenry and cast their votes for Picado. What is more certain is that when a handful of Nicaraguan revolutionaries set out from Costa Rica to invade Nicaragua in November 1944, Picado allowed the Nicaraguan Guard to enter Costa Rica and cut the expedition to pieces before it reached the frontier. Costa Rica had been led into an unbecoming concubinage with the Nicaraguan tyrant; *Ticos* whose political passions did not deaden their sense of decency walked around with queasy stomachs.

The Communist-Calderón pact wrenched politics out of their placid rut. For the first time a cohesive machine made its appearance. The *Tico* politico was transformed from an individualist into a gregarious animal, with, of course, a permanent leader of the pack. In 1943, in the first flush of their leftist successes, Calderón's followers even toyed with the idea of giving him a second term. But the trial balloon sent up burst with a loud bang. When a reelectionist amendment to the constitution was proposed, lawyers closed their offices, citizens put on black ties in mourning, women and children invaded Congress to voice their protest. The matter was quietly dropped.

Yet, significantly enough, when Picado took over, neither his kid brother nor his granddam was named first *designado* (vice-president), but Francisco Calderón. Nor did a break occur between Picado and his predecessor, according to the time-honored pattern.

The opposition dismissed Picado as a fly in the spider's web. He himself had no personal enemies; nobody questioned his absolute honesty. What they reproached him with was the philosophical resignation with which he accepted his position. When a visiting journalist mentioned the roomful of pet canaries that Honduran dictator Carías had shown him, Picado remarked: "Here, you know, I am the only caged bird."

From Calderón, Picado inherited an empty treasury and some six million dollars of floating debt. That was enough to paralyze his administration. It lived from hand to mouth, on a current account extended by the United Fruit Company against future taxes, loans by Victor Wolf, and by similar devices. In 1945 there was almost three million dollars of deficit. The public works program had been slashed; even work on the half-finished Presidential Palace had been suspended.

Though the men on the street did not see it that way, the financial mess did not necessarily mean that dishonest politicians had picked the treasury clean. It had its roots in the fantastic tax system. Even in 1943, when imports had dwindled because of the war, import duties alone accounted for 39 percent of the state's income. Taxes on alcohol made up another 21.19 percent. On the other hand, the highest bracket of corporation and income taxes amounted to merely 6 percent, and the large foreign corporations, like the United Fruit Company, were exempted. When the war shriveled imports, the bottom automatically fell out of the government's cashbox.

The Central American countries hurl themselves upon each passing tourist as though he were a major national resource. After paying something like seven dollars for a Costa Rican tourist visa (including a "tourist tax"), I found it necessary to pay one colon for a "medical stamp" on the way in, another colon for a "medical stamp" going out, and a further colon for a "sports stamp" when registering with the police. On the other hand, practically the total taxation paid by the United Fruit Company was fixed at two cents per bunch of bananas exported, or well less than two percent of its value, for the next thirty years. Touring United States Congressmen have returned from Central America with scare stories about the inroads of communism. The sad truth, however, is that even the "leftist" governments there have not always had the courage to distribute the tax burden more justly and put the curbs on privilege that the Anglo-Saxon countries had long come to accept as a matter of course.

You sent a telegram to President Picado requesting an interview, and awaited a reply from his secretary. The telephone rang. There was a warm, low voice at the other end: "This is Teodoro Picado. How are you? When can you come over?"

At the wooden, two-story Presidential Palace you were ushered into Picado's office with less ceremony than when a minor official received you in other lands. During your stay in Costa Rica such details gladdened your heart at every turn.

You didn't seem to have interrupted the president at anything momentous. No secretaries dashed in and out; the telephone complained only once in a half hour. You had the impression of chatting with a country doctor in his cozy office. When you left, the president saw you to the sidewalk.

Picado was a big, forthright man in his mid-forties with a daub of goatee beneath his lower lip. He was a man of broad culture. His Polish mother had sent him to Poland for his secondary schooling, and he startled visiting Poles by his fluent mastery of their tongue along with several other foreign languages. An outdoors man, he had visited every last nook of the country. He had been known to stay on horseback for twenty hours on end; when the U.S. military attaché accompanied him on one of his jaunts, he couldn't sit down for days afterward. Evil tongues suggested that the president's marathon riding was intended to prove that he could stay in the saddle.

I brought up the unseemly collaboration between his government and the Nicaraguan dictator, and the deplorable impression that it had created throughout Central America. He made no attempt to defend it on ethical grounds. But Nicaragua had a strong army, Costa Rica virtually none. With fifty thousand Nicaraguans resident in Costa Rica, Somoza was understandably concerned lest it become a base for revolutionary action against his regime. To avoid being transformed into the battlefield of Nicaragua's civil war, Costa Rica had to take certain precautionary measures. Not altogether convincingly, Picado denied that Somoza's National Guard had defeated the Nicaraguan revolutionaries on Costa Rican soil in November 1944. The forces were merely Costa Ricans of the frontier zone whose dark complexions had caused them to be mistaken for Nicaraguans. When I mentioned that Somoza, after all, had decorated Nicaraguan officers for the exploit, Picado had something to say about people being too ready to snatch glory not rightfully theirs.

Picado knew the outside world well enough to see Costa Rica in perspective, and he was not blind to its lighter side. "We were, you know, the first American country to declare war against Germany. We came through almost three and a half years of war without a single military casualty—until V-E Day. And then, during the victory celebrations, a rusty cannon exploded and wounded five of our soldiers."

President Picado urged me not to leave Costa Rica without seeing the archbishop. "There is a man with a real sense of humor. But be careful what you say to him. He is the most astute politico we have."

Monseñor Victor Sanabria leaped into international prominence in 1943, when Manuel Mora, the Communist chieftain, sent him the program of his new Vanguardia Popular and asked whether he saw any obstacle in the way of good Catholics joining that organization. Monseñor replied that there was none, and that the Church could not remain indifferent to the need for social reform. Nothing in Central

American ecclesiastic history had raised such a furor since 1545, when Father Bartolomé de las Casas was almost killed by the Spaniards of Chiapas for upholding the cause of their Indian slaves. The rightist press of Costa Rica and the dictator-ridden republics sputtered denunciations of the "Communist Archbishop." When Monseñor applied for a visa to attend a eucharistic congress in Guatemala a few months later, he was turned down. Heads were wagged over the pickle into which the "mitred fellow-traveler" had gotten himself. But there were greater surprises in store.

Monseñor was quite copper-colored, rare enough for a Costa Rican. But his fine face, certainly one of the most interesting in the isthmus, belied the nickname *El cholito* that his opponents had given him. He came from humble peasant stock in Cartago province. By his toil his father had become rich in lands, and did well growing potatoes on them. From earliest childhood Victor had pondered whether God really intended the peons to bear their cross far beyond the biblical seventh generation. He himself had every educational advantage: a brilliant student, he was sent to Rome to finish his schooling. On his return he did not have to devote himself to parochial duties long, but was assigned to teaching at the seminary. From there he passed to Alajuela as bishop. Meanwhile he produced volume after volume of an erudite and elegant history of the Costa Rican Church. Then, in 1940, at the age of thirty-six, he became the youngest archbishop in the annals of the Costa Rican Church and turned from writing history to making it.

Soon Manuel Mora came knocking at his door, and the two embarked on a series of informal chats that led to Mora's sensational letter and Monseñor's still more sensational reply. To those who called Communists the enemies of the Church, Sanabria had a serene reply: "If the devil himself were to come with propositions of social betterment, I would accept the offer. If he broke his word later on, it would merely redound to God's advantage. . . . In the struggle between mind and stomach, the stomach is bound to win in the long run. That is why the Communists have had such an easy time of it. Christ's doctrine has been gravely misinterpreted. Didn't He take the trouble to increase the loaves and fishes, so that there would be more to eat?"

Communist *Realpolitik* did not frighten Monseñor. As a wise cleric with a long view of history, he dismissed all politics, from San Francisco to Moscow, as *Realpolitik,* with a bored "Of course." You felt that he had a passion for the same game and was confident of outsmarting Mora. "If the Church, instead of defending privilege as it has in Mexico, took a hand in organizing genuine trade unions, the Communists would not have their present grip on Latin American labor."

On my way out, he remarked in jest that *Time* would be printing that "Costa Rica's archbishop talks too much."

But Monseñor not only talked divinely; he had already done something about putting his opinions into effect, with the help of a close associate.

If you had shut your eyes and listened to the youthful voice, brimming with conviction and denouncing the rival union for having "sold out" to the United Fruit Company, you would have taken the speaker for a Communist organizer of a decade ago flaying a conservative union. But it was Father Benjamín Núñez, twenty-nine-year-old head of the Rerum Novarum unions, having his say about the Communist-dominated Confederación de Trabajo de Costa Rica (CTCR). The Communists tried brushing Núñez aside as a young, unworldly idealist; but most Costa Ricans had the impression that they were worried. For while the Communists had got themselves entangled in the skein of practical politics, Núñez and his unions pranced about untrammeled and harassed them on their vulnerable left flank.

Boyish and effervescent, Núñez was the instrument of Archbishop Sanabria's labor policy, fashioned by him with love and care over a number of years. Both came from the same village of Cartago Province, San Rafael de Oreamuno. But whereas the archbishop was of a properous family, Núñez's father was a poor peasant. Núñez had not learned about social injustice from fat books of theory. When he was eight, his father had rented some additional land so that he and his six sons might grow corn. "After we brought in the harvest," recounted Núñez, "I was happy thinking that at last we should have some money. But to my dismay, on selling the corn father hadn't enough to pay the rent of the land. He pleaded with the landowner to take the price of the corn, and forget the rest, but the latter insisted on payment in full. The work of seven of us over a stretch of months, had only got us deeper in debt."

By dint of sacrifices the family had put Benjamín through school, and he was ordained at San José in 1938. One of his secondary teachers had been Father Sanabria; while at the seminary, Benjamín would sneak out at night to get to Sanabria's home for intoxicating discussions of social problems. In 1940, on the very day that he became archbishop, Monseñor had taken Núñez away from Heredia, where he was assistant pastor, and packed him off to study in the United States. The money for Núñez's tuition and upkeep Monseñor paid out of his own pocket.

After a year at Niagara University, Núñez went on to the Catholic University of America at Washington. There he became the favorite pupil of Father (later Bishop) Francis Haas, who had made a specialty of labor problems. During his two and a half years at C.U.A., Núñez obtained his master's degree and was working on his doctor's thesis when an urgent summons came. The archbishop called him back to organize Catholic unions in Costa Rica. That was immediately after Monseñor's epoch-making reply to Mora.

Núñez returned, his handsome head bulging with booklore. But could he bring trade unions forth from the void? Monseñor and his disciple had faith. In August 1943 Núñez opened his campaign with a speech at Cartago. Before long he had fifteen craft unions functioning. By 1945 there were at least ten thousand of his Rerum Novarum unions, probably more numerous though less disciplined than the rival CTCR.

Núñez insisted that his unions were not "anti" anything, neither anti-Communist nor anti-atheist. " 'Anti' attitudes engender fanaticism, hence we merely wish to be 'pro' certain things—pro-progress, pro-health, pro-welfare, etc."

Communism he saw not as a cause, but as an effect. It was necessary to grapple with the real cause, human misery: "As on the eve of the French Revolution, the people are fed up with the corruption and ineptitude of their rulers, and are willing to accept any social doctrine that promises a way out."

Rerum Novarum unions did not ask candidates for membership whether they were atheists, Protestants, or Catholics. All were welcome. "The unions," said Núñez, "include under their goal of 'welfare,' the implanting of these ethical and moral standards that are common to all religions and the monopoly of none."

Rare words on the lips of a Latin American priest. It was significant, too, that Núñez was the first member of the Costa Rican clergy trained in the United States. "What we consider fundamental is the human person and his sense of dignity. We are therefore neither Communists nor Socialists, but—if I may coin a term—'personists.' "

The unions' relation with the Church was by no means formal. The statutes read: "The Rerum Novarum Confederation professes respect for the Catholic Church as the defender of the workers. Although sponsored by the Church, the Confederation is in no way subordinated to Ecclesiastic authority. . . . The Confederation promises the Church to keep within the framework of Catholic social doctrine, and recognize an adviser named by the church to see that this promise is fulfilled."

From such a hat, of course, you could pull out almost any rabbit.

"Religion," said Núñez, "has two fundamental aspects: the vertical, involving the nexus between God and man, and the horizontal, concerning the relationship between man and man. The latter has largely been neglected up to now. That is why the Catholic Church in Latin America fears the inroads of Protestant missionaries. We haven't dared draw conclusions from the social doctrine of Christ. Every attempt to reform the status quo has been opposed."

These were revolutionary ideas in the Latin American Church. Getting them across to the clergy required considerable effort. Núñez conducted a course on social science at the seminary for higher-year students: a new generation of priests with well-ventilated minds was being formed. But it was also necessary to reshape the mentality of the older priests. For this purpose a Study Circle for Priests had been organized, to which only the most promising clergy were invited. Monseñor himself took his place as a humble student on a back bench, while the Benjamín of the priesthood, Núñez, led the discussion of such things as the constitutions of the Spanish Republic and of Soviet Russia in the light of Christian doctrine. Monseñor was much given to asking stooge questions to steer the debate along useful lines.

In 1945 the Rerum Novarum unions had a quaint reputation of being more "radical" than the Communist-headed CTCR. Cynics considered this natural for a newer organization that must win members from its rival. At first the United Fruit Company was seriously alarmed by the labor code, but as usual it found the means of making friends and influencing people. For reasons of political strategy, the Communists were in no belligerent mood. The regime, which they supported, was in financial straits and lived on advances from United Fruit. The percentage increase in wages had been lower in the banana industry than in other lines.

When the Rerum Noverum unions were started, the United Fruit Company invited Núñez to organize the banana workers. Still fearing the Communists, the company offered him every facility. Now the situation was reversed. In the fall of 1944, the company's top executive in Central America, Walter Turnbull, called on Manuel Mora; after their chat Vanguardia Popular and the CTCR issued statements declaring that the conditions on the banana plantations were basically fine.

Rerum Novarum disagreed. The workers of the Quepos and Parrita plantations, as a result of CTCR's stand, began flocking into Rerum Novarum. When Núñez went down to the Pacific coast to organize them, United Fruit offered him a plane for the trip. He declined. They pressed lodgings on him, but he begged off and lived in the homes of humble peons. He fell ill with fever during his stay, but built a union that could look the banana trust in the eye and talk working conditions without worrying about the political effect.

Rerum Novarum was making headway. Many reactionaries, who had denounced the archbishop as a communist agent, perked up their ears and began musing how splendid it would be if Rerum could be lined up against the government and its Communist allies. Núñez was offered 100,000 colones on condition that he attack the Communists. He replied that he would gladly accept the money if it were contributed to help improve labor conditions, but his unions could not be drawn into politics.

Núñez and Sanabria hoped that their experiment in Costa Rica might convince the Church throughout Latin America to revise its stand on social problems. The Mexican Church they definitely considered antiquated. They deplored that so many of Latin America's priests were being supplied by the fascist-minded Spanish Church; they looked forward to the day when enough priests would be trained in the United States and other democratic lands to fill Latin America's needs. Though the Vatican had apparently given its approval to Sanabria's experiment, it made no visible move to imitate it elsewhere.

While devoting himself to the uplift of labor, Monseñor had not lost sight of the Church's secular goals. Without undue fuss, Calderón scratched off the books an 1884 law preventing priests from teaching in schools of official academic standing. Calderón likewise gave his permission for the return of the Jesuits to Costa Rica after the war. Thus, while shocking old-fashioned clericals, Sanabria had been scoring victories for the Church where the diehards failed. Many anticlerical intellectuals were alarmed by the long-term implications of Monseñor's leftism.

Postscript. In March 1948 Costa Rica, which had once lived in happy mountain-locked obscurity, swept into the world's headlines. León Cortés had died two years before, and Otilio Ulate, publisher of the *Diario de Costa Rica,* who had begun life peddling tortillas, came to head the crusade against the Calderón-Communist alliance. Something went wrong with the government's plan in the March 1948 elections, and Ulate received a majority running against Rafael Angel Calderón. Calderón and Vanguardia shouted fraud, a charge that was not lacking in its picturesque aspect in view of the notorious official backing enjoyed by Calderón. The Tribunal Nacional Electoral upheld the election, but Congress, which Calderón held on his leash, declared the voting void. Ulate forces commanded by José Figueres took to the field, and a month of murderous warfare ensued.

Planes flew over the uninhabited cloud forest of the Cerro de la Muerte in the south and dropped homemade bombs; machine guns rattled in virgin thickets; Vanguardia organized a labor militia to defend the indefensible. In Costa Rica the forces of democracy and tyranny of the entire Caribbean faced each other. Somoza took time off from his current crusade against "communism" at home to dispatch men and arms in support of the Communist-backed Costa Rican regime. To counterbalance Nicaragua's brazen intervention, Figueres obtained arms from Guatemala. Even the Dominican dictator Trujillo, whose dread of the example of democratic Guatemala had caused him to take a growing interest in the affairs of the isthmus, contributed arms and aviators to the government. The Caribbean had become a mediterranean sea in the battle between democracy and tyranny. When Figueres captured Cartago, a truce was negotiated and Picado left for exile.*

New hope swelled the breasts of the Nicaraguan opposition. Feeling his Costa Rican flank exposed, Somoza moved his National Guard into Costa Rican territory to occupy strategic positions. The United States expressed its displeasure, and the National Guard withdrew into its own territory, but within a few weeks came United States recognition for Somoza's puppet regime in Nicaragua to reassure *Tacho* that his National Guard was not the only or even the most important factor in his defenses.

The responsibility for the wrecking of an idyll rested on strangely contrasted shoulders. The guilt was shared by Washington, which had imposed a military machine on a little land that had need of none; by Somoza, who had made of Costa Rica a province of his appetites; by the Communists, who had dragged the popular aspirations for social betterment through the mud by hitching them to the chariot of corrupt politicians.

Such paradoxes might at least have one positive result: they could convince the traditionally isolationist *Ticos*, perhaps, that there was no way of escaping the larger issues of Central American politics. Costa Rica's liberties could best be restored as part of a united Central American democracy erected on the bones of the last dictator.

---

*José Figueres governed until the following year, when a new constitution was drawn up. Under it, among other things, Costa Rica would in future have no professional army—a unique development in Hispanic American history, still in force today. Figueres was constitutional president from 1953 to 1958 and again from 1970 to 1974.

9

Road to Union

In springtime the thoughts of Central Americans turn to union. Spring had come.

For the Central American, the merger of the five states is a traditional anchor of forlorn hopes. It is a revolt against the nullity to which division has reduced his fatherland, healing balm for his lacerated self-respect as a citizen, and a promise that his country, which has had resources for little but presidents, armies, and jails, will afford his children the advantages of modern civilization. For a century after the dissolution of the short-lived Central American Federation (1821–39), the ghost of union has stalked the politics of the isthmus. Whenever a movement has arisen to challenge tyranny, it has espoused the cause of union. But the oppressors, too, have draped themselves in its banner. The restored Republic of Central America is a goal inscribed in the constitutions of four of the five states. Nowhere has union lain at once on so many tongues and under so many feet.

While the world was bursting its national integuments, Central America awaited integration from a handful of fiefs into a modern nation. The unity of the region is deeply imbedded in geography: from Tehuantepec to Darien the isthmus is a natural whole. Excluding Panama and southern Mexico from this extension, the remaining 7,500,000 people would constitute the fifth largest Latin American nation, amply endowed with natural resources. For the greater part of the colonial period the territories were administered jointly as the Kingdom of Guatemala. Even the wars with which their subsequent history has bled were of a special sort. Territorial changes have almost never followed the defeat of one state by another, nor was burdensome tribute exacted. The victor has been content to install rulers of his confidence in the vanquished capital. For if the economy and administration of the region have been broken into fragments, politics have continued spilling over frontiers. Local hatreds, where they exist, have been of the intimate sort generated in maladjusted families.

146

Under Spain the unity of the isthmus was administrative and nothing more; commerce that might have knitted its parts into an economic unit was absent. When independence from Spain was achieved, the Liberals rejected all centralization as a legacy of the colonial regime. Had they adopted centralism as basting to hold the region together until some future economic progress could provide tougher, flexible threads, they might have saved the Central American Republic as they desired. But they grasped blindly at the federalist example of the United States and unleashed a babel of localist furies.

The United States had chosen federalism as the only means of associating the former thirteen colonies with their background of separate administration under the British Crown. The burgeoning of trade and manufactures made for a unitary development far beyond the provisions of the constitution. In Central America the abolition of the Spanish centralization left nothing to hold province and province together. Every hitching post became a scepter of sovereignty.

The colonial aristocracy and the upper church hierarchy, centering in Guatemala and organized into the Conservative party, defended their privileges against the pretensions of the feeble middle class, the bookish professionals, and the urban population. The language and gestures of the Liberals were those of the French Revolution, but the social forces that uprooted feudalism in Europe were lacking. The rights of man in Central America were not intended to affect the bondage of Guatemala's Indians; for the mestizo peasants of the other provinces they made little economic sense. At best it was an affair of the towns, and the towns were mere clots in the nation's sluggish bloodstream.

In time the Guatemalan Conservatives learned to exploit the fanaticism of the Indians for their own ends. The priests had only to accuse the Liberals of urinating on prints of the Virgin and plotting to fill the country with godless foreigners in order to hurl the benighted Indians against the democratic aspirations of the towns. In 1837 the illiterate swineherd Rafael Carrera entered the capital with thousands of looting Indians. Over his frieze trousers he wore a gold-embroidered coat filched from the baggage of a defeated Liberal general; his chest was heavy with religious medallions. On his head sat a feathered woman's hat with a green veil. It was pageantry befitting a great occasion: the Guatemalan Conservatives had stumbled upon the means of harnessing the savagery of the land to uphold religion and order. For almost thirty years Carrera, mentored by the priests, was to guide the destinies of Guatemala. It was a feat that could not be duplicated in the other states. And because of that the Guatemalan Conservatives, who had at the beginning fought for the continued centralization of the isthmus under Guatemala City, now dissolved the federation to withdraw their happy state from the subversive influence of its mestizo neighbors. At the other extremity, white, democratic Costa Rica, alarmed by the turmoil of federal politics, likewise turned its back on the union. The Liberal champion of the federation, Francisco Morazán, was expelled from Central America by Carrera's hordes, and on his return shot by the Costa Ricans.

The Central Americans were not left to work their own ruin. Engaged in laying out and cutting up the world like so many bales of Manchester cotton, the British early grasped the importance of the interoceanic canal route. They intrigued and bullied to break up the Central American Federation so that the choicest morsels might fit inside the British maw. In Guatemala and Costa Rica they found willing allies. To Carrera, Queen Victoria became something of a fairy godmother across the seas—he called her *La Niña Toya* and she even sent him a diamond-studded sword. Once the federation lay in ruins, Whitehall claimed a protectorate over the fictitious "Kingdom of the Mosquito Indians," consisting of much of the Honduran north coast, the entire Caribbean coast of Nicaragua and Costa Rica, and a portion of present-day Panama. The British occupied the Bay Islands off the Honduran shore, blockaded Liberal El Salvador, and landed troops on Amapala Island in Gulf of Fonseca.

During this period the United States won Central American gratitude for its support against British aggression; U.S. diplomatic representatives had standing instructions to encourage the rebirth of the federation. After the Mexican war of 1847 had given fangs to U.S. Caribbean policy, war with Britain became an imminent danger. It was finally conjured away by the Clayton-Bulwer Treaty of 1850: Britain agreed to withdraw from Central America and accepted the principle of condominium with the United States over the future interoceanic canal. By the 1940s the only relic of British imperial ambitions in Central America was Belize (British Honduras), originally a pirates' lair tolerated by Spain.* Whitehall extracted recognition of its feeble claim to Belize from the servile Carrera government in return for a road connecting Guatemala City to the Caribbean, which the British, however, never troubled to build.

From the Clayton-Bulwer Treaty to the close of the century British and United States influences held each other at bay, and Central America enjoyed the greatest measure of autonomy in its history. Attempts to restore the federation recurred at least once every decade. But by that time vested bureaucratic interests had jelled; the

---

*Bear in mind that the author is writing about the situation in the 1940s. Belize became an independent state on 21 September 1981.

armies, presidents, and state employees had every reason to resist a measure that would create acute unemployment in their ranks. Moreover, the economic development attendant upon the introduction of coffee strengthened the ties of the five states with Europe, but not amongst themselves.

In 1885 the Guatemalan dictator Justo Rufino Barrios, having assured himself of the platonic goodwill of the United States and installed a puppet in the Honduran presidency, proclaimed the Central American Republic with himself as Supreme Chief. He invaded El Salvador in its name. But his atrocious despotism aroused no enthusiasm in the isthmus. When he fell in battle, Barrios in his own way demonstrated that union and democracy would have to go hand in hand.

The presidents of El Salvador, Honduras, and Nicaragua met on Amapala Island in 1895 and signed a pact for establishment of the Greater Republic of Central America within three years. Two years later Guatemala and Costa Rica decided to adhere to the Greater Republic. At long last Humpty-Dumpty seemed pieced together again. Yet neither the nursery rhyme nor the pattern of Central American politics was to be gainsaid. Because a few instruments of the Salvadoran military band were sent to Nicaragua, the Salvadoran militarists felt that their interests were being sacrificed and overthrew their government. The Greater Republic of Central America went to join its ancestors.

While the Boers were pressing Britain hard, Washington wrested from her the final renunciation of her Caribbean ambitions. The Hay-Pauncefote Treaty of 1901 put an end to the principle of joint British-American control over the future canal. Whereas coffee in the previous period had turned Central America's face toward Europe, the banana plantations that now began growing rank on the Caribbean littoral pulled north. Central America became the avowed backyard of the United States.

During the first decade of the century the politics of the isthmus were dominated by the rivalry of two perennial despots, José Santos Zelaya in Nicaragua and Manuel Estrada Cabrera in Guatemala. From time to time Zelaya sounded the call to Central American union, but merely in order to herd the other states into a common front against Cabrera. The student unionist movement, which took its unionism seriously, was hounded with like fervor by Zelaya and Cabrera. Cabrera was highly esteemed in Washington circles, and in its interventions in isthmus diplomacy the State Department was much given to seconding his intrigues.

After a Salvadoran-Guatemalan war in 1906, a final and durable peace had been negotiated aboard the U.S. battleship *Marblehead* with the generous help of Teddy Roosevelt's diplomats. Nevertheless, 1907 proved a lucky year for Zelaya. He stood his ground in the field against the martial alliances of Guatemala, Salvador, and Honduras, and even imposed his man Miguel Dávila in the Honduran presidency. Again Roosevelt intervened along with President Porfirio Díaz of Mexico. The Central American governments accepted his invitation to send delegates to a conference in Washington during November 1907.

At the conference the resolution of Honduras and Nicaragua for immediate Central American union was defeated on the grounds that union, an excellent thing in itself, had to be prepared by coordination of the laws and economies of the republics. That question having been decently buried, with the undertakers enacting the roles of principal mourners, a General Treaty of Peace and Friendship was signed. The governments were thereby forbidden to foment revolutions against neighboring regimes; the neutrality of Honduras was proclaimed. Schools of mining, mechanics, agriculture, trade, and pedagogy were to be established to serve all the republics. A railway was to be built to join the five states. It was decided to open a Central American Office in Guatemala to work for peaceful reconstruction of the Central American fatherland. These fine resolutions, which cropped up with melancholy regularity at subsequent conferences, led to exactly nothing. The elephantiasis of the state bureaucracy in the isthmus devoured the public treasuries and prevented any serious cultural or material progress.

Recently thwarted in his effort to sell Europe the compulsory arbitration of international disputes, Roosevelt turned to Central America, where he could apply his cure-all without obstruction. A Court of Central American Justice was set up with one member chosen by each government.

The State Department followed up this high-minded diplomacy by stirring up a revolution against Zelaya in Nicaragua, and permitting Samuel Zemurray, the American banana baron, to overthrow the Dávila regime in Honduras.* No sooner was the American puppet Adolfo Díaz seated in the Nicaraguan presidency than he negotiated the Bryan-Chamorro Treaty, giving the United States an option on the building of a canal through Nicaragua and the right to construct naval bases in the Gulf of Fonseca and on the Corn Islands in the

---

*Dávila was overthrown by his rival, Manuel Bonilla, in a revolt financed and armed by Sam Zemurray, an immigrant to the United States from Bessarabia who was forging the banana empire of Cuyamel Fruit. The U.S. government, under President William H. Taft, was looking the other way when the "banana fleet" of the Caribbean backed Zemurray and Bonilla.

Atlantic.* Costa Rica and El Salvador, alleging that the treaty violated their respective rights on the San Juan River and the Gulf of Fonseca, brought suit against Nicaragua in the Court of Central American Justice. They were awarded the decision by four votes to one. In protest Nicaragua withdrew from the court, while Washington loftily ignored the ruling of the tribunal that it had sponsored.

By this time Washington found itself in the position of Britain seventy years before: it saw in Central American federation a barrier to its appetites and did everything in its power to prevent it.

In 1920 the fall of the Cabrera dictatorship opened new vistas for union. The repercussions of the European war and the uneasiness aroused by United States expansion had produced a widespread ferment in favor of federation. At a conference in San José on December 1, 1920, Honduras again took the initiative, and all the states but Nicaragua agreed to it. They even accepted Nicaragua's ultimatum that they recognize the Bryan-Chamorro Treaty as the price of its adherence to the union. Yet Nicaragua, obviously executing instructions, still refused to sign the federation pact and withdrew.

The attitude of Nicaragua's U.S.-imposed government was ominous. Traditionally, Nicaragua had been one of the two states favoring union most. With its spacious fertile lowlands, it could become the granary of the isthmus if tariff walls were levelled. Only Honduras, the eternal battlefield of its neighbors' strife, had had a stauncher interest in merger.

The federation pact was signed by four states and ratified by the legislatures of Guatemala, El Salvador, and Honduras. When the separatists cited Nicaragua's stand as an indication of Washington's pleasure, the Costa Rican Congress rejected it by a scant majority. A federal constitution was adopted on September 9, 1921, by the National Constituent Assembly at Tegucigalpa. A Federal Council and members of the Federal Congress were elected. Washington promised its recognition as soon as the federal executive was installed in February.

But the inevitable struck again. The weak Unionist regime in Guatemala had incurred the wrath of two U.S. concerns, the International Railway of Central America and Electric Bond and Share, by

---

*The treaty was signed in 1914, but because of strong opposition in the U.S. Senate, it was ratified only in 1916, thanks to Secretary of State Lansing's warning that his approval was necessary in face of the possibility of war with the Kaiser's Germany. But neither in those years nor later did the United States actually contemplate building a canal in Nicaragua parallel to the Panama Canal.

cancelling the extravagant concessions granted them by dictator Cabrera.* On December fifth a military coup overthrew the democratic government, and took Guatemala out of the federation. The concessions to the American firms were restored. At once the State Department issued a warning to the rest of the federation to refrain from intervening on behalf of the legal regime in Guatemala. That was the death warrant of the federation.

Revived to celebrate the centenary of Central America's independence from Spain, the federation had lasted no longer than centenary celebrations should. After contributing to the disruption of the federation, the State Department reverted to its old game of tinkering with the dictatorships "to ensure peace." The five states were invited to send plenipotentiaries to Washington to negotiate a new treaty to replace that of 1907, to limit armaments, and to establish nonpermanent tribunals of investigation that would handle conflicts. The third point fell significantly short of the 1907 Court of Central American Justice. Washington had unpleasant memories of the tribunal that handed down a decision against the Bryan-Chamorro Treaty. Besides, since the United States had turned its back on the League of Nations, any similar scheme in Central America became undesirable. Just as missionaries decide matters of style for the pantless natives they clothe, so fad and whim in Washington governed Central American politics.

Once assembled in Washington, the delegates buried the business of political union with the dispatch that comes from much practice. But not before Carlos Ucles, one of the Honduran delegates, uttered some rasping truths: "The union is written into all the constitutions of Central America. . . . Why has it not been realized? The people want union; it is the rulers who do not want it. . . . All postponements only tend to make union more difficult. . . . The German union has been achieved, the Italian union, even that of Australia . . . but we cannot carry out ours because we are lacking in patriotism. We ought to be frank. If we are unionists, let us proceed to unite our countries; if we are not unionists, we must state so openly. . . . We ought not to deceive our people by telling them that we are unionists, and then instead of union giving them an international office or a pedagogic institute. . . . Union can be achieved even if there are different systems of weights and measures, even if there are different religions, and different forms of government. . . . Union exists even in countries of different

---

*The International Railway of Central America was one of the many properties of the United Fruit Co., a banana corporation which installed itself in Guatemala in 1898 and, at least until 1944, was the real government of the country.

languages. Take Switzerland. The secret is that those of us who are in power do not want to step down, and those who hope to rise to power wish to find it whole and undiminished. . . . It is feudalism pure and simple. . . . Instead of writing a document like that of independence consisting of only two lines, we present more and more projects. Today it is weights and measures, tomorrow it will be head-shawls."

The conference adopted the usual set of treaties, providing for the nonrecognition of regimes arising from violence even when legitimised by subsequent elections, nonintervention in the affairs of other republics, the reduction of armaments, extradition, experimental farms, and many other things that were to remain dead letters. The 1923 conference differed from that of 1907 primarily in that Mexico was not invited. For in Mexico there was no longer the Díaz dictatorship, inflexibly hostile to Central American union, but a revolutionary government that favored the union of the isthmus states as a barricade against United States encroachment.

After 1923 revolutions continued with their old rhythm, some backed by United States business and favored by the State Department, others frowned upon according to the dictates of caprice and interest. It was only in the thirties that Central American politics finally became "stabilized." Four dictatorships, all duly blessed by Washington, boasted the solidity of dungeon walls and the certainty of shackles.*

And the comedy of union continued apace. In 1934 dictator Ubico of Guatemala invited the other four states to a union conference in Guatemala. Political federation was soon disposed of: the dictators had long ago come to regard their posts as part of their anatomy, and they would as soon slice off one of their buttocks as step down from power. Behind closed doors measures were concerted for coordination of the police of the republics, extradition of political exiles (Costa Rica dissenting), and the gagging of the press.

With the coming of the Good Neighbor policy† and the advent of

---

*The four dictatorships were: that of Jorge Ubico in Guatemala, imposed in 1931; that of Maximiliano Hernández Martínez in El Salvador, in 1931; that of Tiburcio Carías Andino in Honduras, in 1933; and that of Anastasio Somoza García in Nicaragua, in 1937. From this and other like circumstances arose the popular description of Franklin Roosevelt's "Good Neighbor Policy" as "Good Neighborliness with Dictators."

†The policy to which we refer in the previous note. Roosevelt proclaimed it a few weeks after his first inauguration in 1933. In synthesis, it consisted of cancelling "Gunboat Diplomacy" in Central American and the Caribbean and installing a diplomacy of nonintervention in those countries' internal affairs, a promise not always strictly fulfilled, or if it was, with ambivalent and selective applications.

World War II, the State Department gradually underwent a change of heart on the subject of union. It had abandoned the armed intervention in the isthmus that a united Central America might resist. Besides, Central America had become so indisputably part of the U.S. sphere of influence that no sane local politician, no matter what his outlook, cared to challenge the fact. And negotiating the necessary agreements for highway construction, raw material purchases, and strategic bases with five Lilliputian republics was senselessly complex. When in 1939 Central American unionists went exploring to Washington, they found a sympathetic if detached interest.

With their fine eye for anniversaries, Central Americans could not overlook the centenary of the execution of Francisco Morazán, champion of the federation, in 1942. A conference of unionists from all five republics was convoked to meet at San José on September 15. Ostensibly, the prime mover was Salvador Mendieta, sexagenarian rector of the Universidad Central de Managua. Behind the scenes was Nicaraguan dictator Somoza.

A legendary figure, Mendieta had for over forty years ridden the ideal of union as a sort of private hobbyhorse. Time was when it was a spirited steed. During the first two decades of this century Mendieta's Unionist party had kept proudly aloof from Liberal and Conservative political jobbers and directed its bolts at the mighty. Though the party could never count on a mass following, it kindled the imagination of a whole generation of Central American students. Quixote Mendieta learned to know intimately the jails of most of the republics, and even carried his message of isthmus unity to the indifferent ears of Europe. In four bulky, rambling volumes he diagnosed the "Diseases of Central America" and prescribed a list of remedies varying from a national diet with fewer beans to union amongst the states. His central thesis was that union could come only through a popular democratic movement: counting on the existing governments for its realization was "like entrusting an antimalaria campaign to the mosquitoes."

Yet in 1942 Mendieta was doing precisely that. Quixote had not only come to recognize windmills as windmills, but set himself to milling corn.

The San José Conference did not take place. In 1934 when Ubico had tried his hand at unifying the republics, he had even expressed his willingness to leave the Guatemalan presidency if the cause of union required it. But now he was incensed that Somoza, who had an annoying way of bragging that he was Washington's favorite Central American dictator, should be trying to outdo him in pomp and selflessness. Mendieta published a letter in the Nicaraguan press denouncing Ubico's persecution of Guatemalan unionists who were working for the San José Conference. Ubico protested to Somoza, and permitted a press campaign on the deplorable internal conditions of Nicaragua. Relations between the two regimes were strained almost to the point of rupture. Finally Somoza saw fit to dismiss Mendieta from his university post and call off the San José Conference. Central America's tragedy has always been tinctured with farce.

And then came the spring floods that washed away most of the stage props and some of the principal actors. Politics, so long frozen into gargoylelike forms, became fluid once more. Withered hopes acquired bowels, flesh, and coursing blood. In the summer of 1944, with dictators Martínez and Ubico prostrate, the Unionist party met at Santa Ana in El Salvador and proposed the immediate merger of El Salvador and Guatemala under a provisional government consisting of representatives of each state . . . and one of the Unionist party. Only by a narrow margin did the Congress defeat a motion that it declare itself in permanent session until such fusion were achieved.

Weightier than the self-importance of the Unionist party was the confidence of the people. Nothing seemed beyond their reach. The front in the war between dictatorship and democracy extended unbroken from Nicaragua to Guatemala; exiles flowed back and forth across the frontiers. An intimate comradeship sprang up between nation and nation.

The Arévalo government came to power in Guatemala lyric with ideals and noble intentions. Had the Romerista party* triumphed in El Salvador shortly afterward, it is highly probable that the union of the two states would have been consummated at once. But the military coup in El Salvador in October 1944 and its subsequent recognition by the State Department stifled and demoralized the democratic movement throughout the isthmus: an unstable equilibrium ensued between the militarist reaction and the revolutionary forces. And as the months slipped by, the Guatemalan regime became set in its ways, enmeshed in routine and caution, and progressively less likely to embark on any venture that required vision and daring. Central American union will be achieved by the fresh momentum of popular revolutions or not at all. It is likely that the Osmín Aguirre coup in Salvador and the accolade bestowed on it by Washington ruined the prospects for a united Central America in the present generation.

Nevertheless, federation remained a favorite topic for official conversations. On May 17, 1945, President Arévalo of Guatemala met President Castañeda of El Salvador at San Cristóbal and signed a pact for eventual union by the classic stages: coordination of the armies,

---

*The Romerista party of Pío Romero Bosque, president of El Salvador from 1927 to 1931.

education, partial free trade, fewer immigration formalities, and other fine things that in the past had led nowhere over mountains of red tape. During the discussions Arévalo inspected the San Cristóbal prison and found an Indian serving a term for smuggling. Paternally he patted him on the head and admonished him: "Don't be so impatient, my son. Soon there will be no need for smuggling."

He was too optimistic. In reality the San Cristóbal discussions had little enough to do with federation. For Arévalo it was a device for drawing El Salvador away from its friendship with the Honduran and Nicaraguan dictatorships. Castañeda had agreed to it in the hope of winning popular support at home. But the military caste, on whose lap Castañeda was seated, loathed everything connected with the new Guatemala, and was more than ever hostile to the fusion of the two republics.

And yet as the immediate political probability of merger dwindled, long-term forces were at work leveling the hurdles on its path.

The abysmal living standard of Guatemala's Indians aroused apprehension in the other states. It made Guatemala particularly unsuited for any commercial give-and-take, and was at the bottom of its deceptively strong trading position. For while producing coffee for export, its Indians consume practically no imported merchandise. That made even a free-trade treaty with Guatemala—much more so political union—a very unappetizing proposition for the neighboring states. Thus El Salvador, which in the fall of 1941 signed a partial free trade treaty with Guatemala, made haste to denounce it two years later. Guatemala unloaded cheese, vegetables, dairy products, and textiles on El Salvador and bought little in return. The recent revolution in Guatemala had improved the condition of its Indians somewhat, and began to make possible a more balanced trade.

The sadism of the classic Guatemalan dictatorships had operated as a repellent on the peoples of the other republics, where tyranny had never been known to assume such crushing form. Should the democratic regime in Guatemala survive, union would lose, for other Central Americans, its aspect of admission into a medieval torture chamber.

Though the *mystique* of union was potent, there had been only feeble economic sinews drawing the republics together. The economies of the five states, competitive rather than complementary, were tilted toward the United States and Europe. Coffee, bananas, and cocoa made up nine tenths of Costa Rican exports; gold and coffee were Nicaragua's mainstays; bananas alone accounted for eighty percent of Honduran shipments; coffee for almost ninety percent of El Salvador's; coffee and bananas for ninety percent of Guatemala's.*

Communications within the isthmus reflected this situation. Its railways were interoceanic lines or fragments of such, built to haul coffee and bananas to tidewater rather than to serve trade amongst the states. Yet in this respect World War II had labored more mightily than a century of poetry and rhetoric on behalf of union. The Inter-American Highway, initiated to give the United States land access to the Panama Canal, cut boldly across frontiers and mountains; it bade fair to become the suture for the eventual unification of Central America.

Its cost was staggering. Few of the republics could have undertaken their share alone. That is why the Nicaraguans in banter call it the Hirohito Road: but for the Japanese it might never have been built.

As an early echo of Pearl Harbor, the U.S. Congress voted $20,000,000 to be used by the Public Roads Administration in building the Inter-American Highway in Central America. Local governments were to match the sums spent by the United States in their countries with half as much money of their own. As the Pacific situation grew grimmer, the U.S. Army decided that the work on the road had to be stepped up. It therefore authorized the United States Army Corps of Engineers to construct an emergency road in Central America to fill in the uncompleted stretches of the Inter-American Highway.

Speed was the goal, and money no consideration. With little road-building background, it was perhaps inevitable that the engineers should have left a trail of bacchanalian waste. The cost-plus-fixed-fee basis on which its contracts were let did not enjoin economy. It was hamstrung by transport difficulties. An entire town of engineers and mechanics was brought down from the United States to Costa Rica and lolled about for a year, while the U.S.E.D. had all available transport for its equipment snatched out from under its nose by other government agencies operating on higher priorities. Its contractors never bargained with local merchants, and before anyone knew it, the prices of everything in Costa Rica, from tinned milk to

---

*Production figures, like the percentages of the export market, have continued to change to this day, as new products for the region have been added, such as sugar, cotton, and meat (Honduras, Nicaragua). Furthermore, the creation in the fifties and sixties of the Central American Common Market spurred the rise of industrial products (El Salvador, Guatemala), which diversified and speeded up the regional economy.

arteriosclerotic whores, had shot skyward. The economy of the little land was sorely dislocated. Originally, the Corps of Engineers had estimated that it would cost some $14,700,000 to drive the emergency road through the isthmus to the Panama Canal. When its work was abandoned in October 1943, it had spent almost $40,000,000 and had relatively little to show for it. Construction had barely been begun in Costa Rica and Panama; the work in Guatemala was far from its goal. Transitable stretches from border to border existed only in Nicaragua, Honduras, and El Salvador.

The Public Roads Administration, which continued the work, fared much better. In 1946 Congress voted a new $5,000,000 appropriation for the Inter-American Highway, and P.R.A. was able to predict cautiously that the road would be completed to Panama in 1949 with a further $20,000,000 expenditure.

The Inter-American was transforming some of the countries through which it passed. It had given Costa Rica a frontier of expansion relatively as important as the American Midwest a century ago. For the first time it had opened up the General Valley in the South with an area of some 600 fertile square miles, almost as large as the Central Plateau where Costa Rican agriculture and settlement had hitherto been concentrated. On its own, Costa Rica could never have dreamed of undertaking the fabulous mountain surgery involved: some of the construction between Cartago and the General Valley ranked with the heaviest carried out anywhere in the world. From Cartago south the road clings to the continental divide; at least at one point on clear days you can see both oceans. It reaches for heaven—almost 11,000 feet—threads its way through cloud forest, and then glides into the sweltering tropics. Here and there, crossing the new road, you can find the Indian trial that served without improvement from pre-Conquest days, when Aztec merchants traveled on foot over it to Panama, right up to 1941. In addition to the money voted for the work in Central America in general, a special grant of $12,000,000 was made by the U.S. Congress in 1943 to cope with the wild Costa Rican terrain.

In Nicaragua and Panama, too, the road brought abundant good lands within reach of markets. But outweighing these local benefits was the promise of the road to Central America as a whole. For the first time it would acquire an artery running down its length. Bus and trucking lines had already begun joining capitals that previously had no contact except by air and sea. Provincial battlements were crumbling; the outlines of a Central American nation were beginning to appear.

With improved communications, a middle class could be expected to form and dispute the economic and political power of the feudal planters. In the past, intellectuals had sighed for a greater fatherland, but for the reactionary landowner the midget Central American republics were ideal. It mattered nothing that industries could find no breathing space within their borders; he could import his industrial goods more cheaply. Or that the cost of maintaining a full-blown state, and army, a diplomatic service and all, left scant money for popular education and social services; ignorant peons work for less wages. And when he tired of the sordid setting, he could always spend half his year in the United States or Europe.

On the other hand, if a middle class took shape, it would be able to find elbowroom only through fusion of the states. United, Central America would provide a sizable market for secondary industries. Diverted from bureaucratic to productive ends, the national income would raise the masses from their harrowing misery. The economic forces upon which any democracy rests would be released from the straitjacket of the old boundaries.

For forty years United States diplomacy in Central America had propped up the feudal forces that blocked the way to union. Now the United States was making handsome amends. Whatever the uncertainties of the political future, the Inter-American Highway is here to stay. And along it the people of the isthmus would mature to democracy and unification. Once again U.S. technology was compensating for the brief vision of U.S. statesmanship.*

---

*The later history of the isthmus shows that there were no subsequent achievements toward "democracy and unification," only a few flashes of liberalization, promptly rectified in the linked interests of the local ruling classes and the foreign policy of the United States.

10

Bimetallism in the Canal Zone

Y<small>OU ARRIVED AT THE</small> B<small>ALBOA</small> <small>AIRPORT</small> in the Canal Zone hot and thirsty and cast around for a water fountain. When you had drunk the edge off your thirst, you raised your eyes and saw stenciled on the wall: Gold only.

"My, what a strange error," you mused. "Surely they mean 'cold only.'" Then it occurred to you that no water fountain is equipped with hot water. Your mind chewed on the riddle.

As you come across the women's and men's rooms on the way out, you encountered the same ominous Gold only. Midas, surely, had been left far behind. Later you discovered two sets of wickets in Canal Zone Post Offices, Gold and Silver. You awakened to the fact that it was Jim Crow in the tropics, glazed over with a thin hypocrisy that if anything made it more revolting. Below the Mason-Dixon Line it had the merit of being forthright.

Alongside the canal, a monument to his capacity for wrestling with material obstacles, man had created a snarl of social problems. We join oceans and set up barriers between man and man.

The North Americans, like the French before them, found that British West Indian Negroes were indispensable for the building of the canal. They had tried Chinese, Irish, and Panamanian Negroes, but these either fell victim to disease or were lazy or undisciplined. From Jamaica came tractable blacks, hardworking and relatively immune to the deadly germs that infested the canal route. Under the French no racial problem had arisen from the immigration of tens of thousands of Jamaicans: they tended to assimilate with the Panamanians who, having much Negro blood themselves, were not bitten by racial prejudice.

But then the French went bankrupt and the United States took over. For some obscure reason most of the straw bosses sent down were Southerners, perhaps because they were more inured to hot climate; possibly, as in the case of Haiti, because they were felt to have

160

experience in "handling" Negroes. Or it may simply have been the working of that unwritten social law that prompts every nation to step outside its own frontiers with its worse foot. In any case the Southern straw bosses brought with them their peculiar convictions as to how society ought to be run.

It was quite out of the question to introduce an open system of Jim Crow in Panama, where so much black blood is mingled with even the bluest streams. So they took a page from William Jennings Bryan, and resorted to bimetallism.* The laborers, accustomed to silver currencies, were paid in silver; the United States technicians and straw bosses received greenbacks, that is, gold. The knavery of the human heart appealed to the resourceful cowardice of the mind, and the unspeakable thing was covered up with a new set of words—the "gold and silver rolls." Gold and silver commissaries, toilets, dispensaries, schools, Post Office wickets, and other novel things—some even unknown in the U.S. South—came into existence.

Of course, a good many Northerners also came to the canal in those early rough-and-tumble days. But most of these fell in with the gold-and-silver plan with sufficient enthusiasm to make the Civil War seem an unfortunate misunderstanding. Human frailties are the same the world over: for many folks who had to come all the way to Panama to find a job as a foreman, having fellow-humans to step on provided a consoling sense of their own importance.

The reaction of most Northerners who came to the Canal Zone with the Army and Navy during the war years was very different. In 1945 a white army doctor from New York remarked to me, "And here we had been of the opinion that the canal was being operated by the United States of America, and not the State of Alabama. There is so much that one doesn't learn in the geography books."

In 1913, the year of peak employment during the canal construction, there were 44,711 men on the silver roll. Most were British West Indians. They had not foisted themselves upon the Canal Zone authorities. So active were the recruiting agents in Jamaica that the British government tried discouraging the drain on the island's labor force by imposing a one-pound tax on each emigrant. Though Negroes enjoyed relative freedom from racial discrimination in Jamaica, they were drawn to Panama by the big silver dollars which were later to become so sinister.

Practically all who came in the early years were humble peasants who raised no protest against the unaccustomed Jim Crow into which

---

*The same Bryan who as Woodrow Wilson's first Secretary of State gave his name to the treaty signed with Nicaragua's Emiliano Chamorro.

they were cast. Later, however, schoolmasters were brought in from Jamaica for the laborers' children, and discontent became vocal. By 1945 there did not seem to be a Jamaican in the Canal Zone who was not outraged. The chauffeurs of the ramshackle taxis that carried you from the airport to your hotel needed no great encouragement to spill their sorrow. "God," one told me, "must have made an awful mistake. He created men black and white instead of just white."

Gold and silver in the Canal Zone created complexities unknown to the currency experts. Gold, of course, was not merely run-of-the-mine gold but specifically white gold, once so popular with jewelers. Theoretically, a silver-roll employee was one earning up to a maximum of $80 per month. But a few special silver roll posts had been created paying $100 and providing two-month paid vacations annually and other privileges proper to the gold roll. The purpose was to attract cultured Negroes by the economic lure, while leaving them subject to Jim Crow. The heads of the silver schools in the Canal Zone, for example, were on this special silver roll.

The overwhelming majority of the silver-rollers were West Indian Negroes and their Panama-born children (criollos). North American Negroes were not imported in quantity, partly because they did not get along well with the Jamaicans. Nonetheless, there were about a dozen continental U.S. Negroes on the gold roll, in addition to the forty-odd Virgin Island Negroes on the special silver roll. In theory they were pure gold, enjoying the full accolade of the Zone's accounting department. Yet they never dared enter a gold toilet; their children were relegated to the limited facilities of the silver schools. They did use gold commissaries. Naturally they were not eligible for the gold clubs and had to queue up before the silver wicket at the Post Office. At best, they were silver with imperfect, blotchy gold plating.

On the other hand, sons of gold employees working at silver jobs during their holidays used all gold conveniences. For Canal Zoners had an old-fashioned disbelief in the transmutation of metals.

Poor, white Yugoslavs and other Eastern European navvies on the silver roll were obliged to stick to silver toilets. In this the Zone was broader-minded than the Southern Motherland, where the dignity of a white skin must be upheld regardless of what was stuffed into it.

On certain occasions the silver roller actually came out ahead. Anyone with a black epidermis must line up on the silver side of the dispensary. There he paid a mere ten cents for medicaments that cost twenty-five for those in the gold queue. *Noblesse oblige.*

Wedged into the very groin of the hemisphere, the Canal Zone put the United States on display to Latin Americans. The effect was neither fair nor flattering. Black, Indian, and white blood were mixed in every proportion in most Latin American nations. Though it had become fashionable amongst upper-crust snobs to imitate the Good Neighbor's racial prejudice, the ordinary Latin considered racial tolerance an earmark of culture.

On Panama itself the influence of the Zone's Jim Crow has been still more deplorable. The canal had brought prosperity and sanitation to Panama, but at a heavy price. The little country was a head without a body, its skull trepanned and fitted with an alien gold plate. There was no populated hinterland where Panamanians could escape the bruising social impact of the Zone and nurture their self-respect. Panamanians suffered cruelly from a "spick" complex:* they were the only Latin American nation amongst whom could be found people ashamed of talking Spanish in the presence of North Americans. Inevitably the Zone's set of values had imposed themselves, and Spanish rated as an inferior tongue, not unlike Otomí in Mexico or Cakchiquel in Guatemala. This lent a morbid note to Panamanian-United States relations, and made it possible for the worst type of nationalistic charlatan to flourish in Panamanian politics. But it also led some Panamanians to indulge their inferiority neurosis toward North Americans, by copying their prejudices. Impotent against the insulting ways of the Zone, these Panamanians asserted themselves by stepping on the Jamaicans.

The inelegant truth was that Panama, where kinky hair, flat noses, and protuberant lips were likely to crop up in the very best families, had gone race-conscious. Negroes had been refused admission into Panama City beer gardens. When accompanied by whites this was scarcely possible, but I witnessed how uncomfortable their stay could be made. With the editor of the local Jamaican newspaper and his friend I visited the Balboa Beer Garden. The drinks were slung at us. No sooner had we finished them than the glasses were snatched away. We ordered a second round and sipped it soulfully. One beer garden had been transformed into a private club as a means of keeping Negroes out. Even Panamanian youngsters of rich chocolate complexion were given increasingly to barring children a shade darker from their circle of playmates and trying to strike up a friendship with those a mite paler. There was an unsuccessful attempt to eliminate blacks from the Panamanian ball-teams going abroad to represent the country in international games. When a middle-class Panamanian octoroon was ill and his color somewhat wan, it was customary for his friends to congratulate him on how *well* he looked.

Not only the Panamanians were affected. Jamaicans were often

---

*This derogatory name for Latin Americans, popular at the time, referred to their difficulties in speaking the English language.

sentimental about their British tie, because of the absence of official race prejudice in the British West Indies. Yet, shameful to relate, these last few years the British legation in Panama had been organizing two receptions on the King's Birthday: one for blacks in the morning and the other for whites in the afternoon. The crushing majority of His Majesty's subjects resident in Panama, who were of an ebony hue, had been greatly saddened by this. Jim Crow seemed to follow thick on the heels of lend-lease.

Panama needed some scholar to do a *Middletown* on it. Undoubtedly, it was one of the most intricate, artificial communities in the world: national groups had been imported from across the seas and were not allowed to strike root in their new habitat; there were endless stratifications, interpenetrations of culture, borrowed values. Even the dominant mores of the American South could not be imported unchanged in this setting. It was impossible to treat the more influential Panamanians like Southern Negroes, whatever their color. Weird anomalies sprang up.

When they could afford it, many Panamanians preferred sending their children to gold schools in the Canal Zone, for educational standards were higher there than in Panama. Some of these tots were quite dusky, more so perhaps than the child of a North American gold-roll Negro who had to attend a silver school. The routine nitric acid test to distinguish gold from silver was scarcely feasible. Hence the practice was for the Panamanian child to appear in person when the application was made, so that the principal could look him over discreetly and judge whether he was not too negroid for the lily-white school. The Ku Klux Klan would have been unhappy about this relaxation of standards.

And then there were pious fictions, and more than the usual ingredient of protocollary cant. Señor X, owner of one of the two large bilingual papers, was a wealthy man of social pretensions. He was blacker than many a mulatto, but the official myth was that he was white. Goering, too, had his Aryan Jews. Though Señor X had access to the most exigent circles, I did not discover whether he had ever tried entering a gold toilet.

The Canal Zone provided the last glimpse of the American continent for many black soldiers and sailors headed for the Pacific war. Some carried away wormwood memories. Though not in the employ of the Zone, and hence neither gold nor silver, they were made to toe the silver line. A week before I visited there in May 1945, four sailors had come into the dining room of the well-run Tivoli Hotel, owned by the U.S. government. Three were white; the fourth, a Percy Anderson Moore, was black. Genuinely embarrassed, the manager offered to fix up a table in a private room where no one would see them. "Mister, there aren't any gold or silver bullets in this war," one of the white lads blurted out, and the four left indignant.

The position of the West Indian was precarious as well as humiliating. He had been brought there to dig a ditch, and stayed on to maintain it. He lived in Panama, yet was not of it. His language was approximately that of his white Canal Zone masters. He knew little Spanish, and often his Panama-born children grew up without a complete knowledge of it. He was clannish, as any oppressed minority is wont to be. The Panamanians resented him. Originally it was not because of his color, but because he did not speak their language. He had at times a manner of waving his loyalty to the British Crown.

That made him particularly vulnerable to the rapacious Panamanian politico. Panama was a strange place. There was little agriculture, due to the wretched communications with the interior (something that the Inter-American Highway will eventually do much to remedy). Essentially, Panama was a bazaar alongside a ditch. The Panamanians had little to do with the ditch: that was the business of the North Americans and the West Indians. They also had not much to do with the bazaar, for business had been run largely by foreigners: Chinese, Syrians, East Indians, and European Jews. Some of these grew rich, and the Panamanian politicos were tempted by the inviting kill. Early in the war Arnulfo Arias, a profascist demagogue, dominated the scene as president of the republic. He could not beard the North Americans as he had led his electorate to expect; instead, he resorted to less risky substitutes. He decreed that all bootblacks must wear uniforms and have telephones installed at their stands. He "nationalized" commerce, meaning that the Chinese and East Indian merchants were expropriated. They had to sell their businesses for what politicos were willing to offer, frequently less than ten percent of their value. Or they were compelled to accept a politico as partner to serve as a front.

The West Indians played no part in commerce, but Arnulfo could hardly overlook them as a national resource. As early as 1926 Panama had banned all immigration of West Indian or Guiana Indians whose language was not Spanish. Arnulfo carried matters farther. He prohibited East and West Indians from occupying any but menial jobs. That is why you saw so many former East Indian merchants driving taxis. Because of their humbler economic category, this law meant less to the West Indians. For them the Denationalization Law of 1941 was the big blow.

At one stroke all naturalized Jamaicans and even the *criollos* were deprived of their Panamanian citizenship. Even the children of one Panamanian and one West Indian parent were thus cast into the void. And they had no other passport, since the British allegiance of

Jamaicans had only rarely been maintained by their sons. Thirty thousand Negroes found themselves without a country. It was the Wandering Jew presented with an all-black cast. Their fathers had done the bulk of the dirty work building the canal to which Panama owed its prosperity. They had dark thoughts.

The law permitted the president to bestow citizenship on individual criollos. Three thousand of the homeless thirty thousand applied to the Arnulfo Arias government to have their citizenship restored to them. Such applications cost from $25 to $100 in lawyers' fees, and it was obviously wise to choose a lawyer among Arias's friends. Seven hundred of these applications were granted. The British government stepped in and permitted those deprived of their Panamanian nationality, even when born in Panama, to become British subjects.

Arias's interior minister, Ernesto de la Guardia, was responsible for the execution of the Denationalization Law. In September 1941, when the North Americans unseated Arnulfo, de la Guardia became president.* To bolster his dictatorial regime, he gave citizenship to all children born in Panama. In gratitude the Jamaicans were supposed to vote for de la Guardia in the May 1945 elections for a constituent assembly. Instead, they voted for the democratic opposition. De la Guardia cursed them as ingrates, and for a while their nationality seemed suspended by a hair again. But de la Guardia ensnared himself in the intricacy of his own maneuvers, and was succeeded by a democratic government. The *criollos* continued as Panamanians, but exposed to the vicissitudes of Panama's hectic politics.

The younger leaders of the West Indian community regarded assimilation to Spanish culture as a partial solution to the problem of their people. In 1940 the census showed a higher literacy rate among West Indian Negroes (86.9 percent) than for whites (77.1 percent) or mestizos (55.7 percent). A Panamanian, Gil Blas Tejeira, wrote: "With a deeper sense of culture than exists among Panamanians of other races and mixtures, these West Indians have been able to rise to such a degree that illiteracy among them is almost unknown. In their little English schools, where the Royal Reader still does duty as text, almost all have been able to decipher the mysteries of the alphabet."

This remarkable effort, however, gave them only an English edu-

---

*Arnulfo Arias Madrid was ousted from the presidency of Panama in 1941, 1951, and again in 1968. The first time was by direct pressure from President Roosevelt, because of Arias's notorious flirtations with the Nazi-Fascist Axis. He again presented himself as a candidate in 1984 at the age of almost eighty-five, now much more friendly with the U.S. President, Ronald Reagan.

cation. And the resentment of Panamanians rested in part on the fact that they did not learn Spanish as their native tongue.

The remedy was in the hands of the Canal Zone educational authorities. True, only forty percent of the West Indians actually resided in the Zone, for housing there was chronically inadequate. High officials who had to serve twenty years before being promoted to occupancy of a comfortable bungalow were not too eager to push the building program even in normal times: the social distinction connected with ample quarters would vanish if all had them. And in the allotment of houses, the silver laborers naturally fared worst. Sixty percent of the latter had to live in crowded rat-infested tenements in Panama City, and be bled by unscrupulous landlords who were often prominent Panamanian statesmen. But few Jamaicans living in Panama City would enroll their children in the overpacked Panamanian schools.

Until recently the Canal Zone schools, gold and silver, had taught no Spanish at all. Now it was taught badly in the secondary schools . . . by teachers imported from the United States! Few of the graduates learned to speak it. Good-neighborliness had brought compulsory Spanish to Texan primary schools, but the Canal Zone had eschewed such sentimentality. In 1943 the West Indian youth organization petitioned the Zone authorities to have Spanish put on the curriculum of primary silver schools. They were refused on the ground that the basic subjects were still handled inadequately. Rightly or wrongly, some Jamaicans felt that the Canal Zone was not eager for the Jamaican children to learn Spanish too well, lest they wander off and find jobs in Panama.

Born and living under a North American administration on what was technically Panamanian soil, the *criollo* could neither acquire U.S. citizenship nor equip himself for life as a Panamanian. In recent years, his lot had improved minutely. The first silver junior high schools were established in 1932, and a couple of silver vocational schools were decided upon in 1944. But these did not touch the root of his problem. For decades smug prejudice, the set rut, inertia, and red tape had prevented the Canal Zone authorities from recognizing that a problem existed at all. Gold was regally indifferent to silver's tarnish.

Serious economic disadvantages accompanied racial discrimination. It mattered little how skilled a Jamaican or *criollo* artisan might be: he was almost invariably rated semiskilled and paid accordingly. A colored clerical worker was listed as an office helper even though he might shoulder the real responsibility of running the office, while his white superior, serving a purely decorative function, collected several times his salary. This, however, was not a purely racial situation: as

168 DEMOCRACIES AND TYRANNIES OF THE CARIBBEAN

non-North Americans, Jamaicans and *criollos* could not enter the civil service to become clerks.

The gold workers had long had unions grouped together in the Central Labor Union and affiliated with the American Federation of Labor. These organizations had never felt kindly toward colored workers. Repeatedly they had campaigned to have silver workers dismissed from responsible posts. Formerly Jamaicans and *criollos* used to hold jobs as telephone wiremen and railway engineers. Due to the pressure of the A.F. of L. unions, they did not anymore. At the outbreak of the war the gold Metal Trades Council tried to get all aliens—primarily Jamaicans and *criollos*—eliminated from the Zone "for defense reasons." Washington refused to comply. But Washington likewise failed to strengthen the Canal's defenses by removing the weighty grievances of the thirty thousand black workers that made it function.

The Atlantic Charter and the high ideals of the United Nations left no mark on the gold and silver system in the Zone. In April 1946 the Panamanian labor delegation to the International Labor Organization, meeting in Mexico, demanded an investigation of racial discrimination in the Canal Zone. The C.I.O. followed this up by launching a strikeless drive to organize all Zone workers irrespective of race, nationality, or metal. In no time at all eleven thousand silver laborers had signed up. When last heard from, the Canal Zone military authorities, jolted by the prospects of a gold-and-silver alloy, were running slivers in their hands ripping off the gold and silver signs.

Yet it would have been so much prettier if the initiative had come voluntarily from Washington.*

---

*The discrimination persisted on general lines until 7 September 1977, when the Carter-Torrijos treaty was signed. The Hay-Bunau Varilla treaty, in force from 18 November 1903, made seventy years of Canal Zone discrimination possible by placing in U.S. hands total power over Canal ownership and use. On 1 October 1979 the United States began to yield part of that power. Panama will gain full ownership of the Canal and its environs by 31 December 1999.

II

Era of a Good Neighbor

A ROSE IS A ROSE, but some roses are rosier than others. And occasionally nature exerts herself to produce a rose that is the perfect embodiment of roselike properties, all velvety fragrance set in thorns. Similarly, the grotesque dictatorlets that have stalked through the earlier chapters of this book were summed up and outdone in the person of the Dominican Republic president, doctor, and generalisimo Rafael Leonidas Trujillo. There the racketeering of the Nicaraguan Somoza cohabited with the sadism of the Guatemalan Ubico under a crazy quilt of exhibitionism; in fiction such a character would be torn apart by the critics for its slapdash improbability.

The correct way to date a public document in the Dominican Republic was the 121th year of the Independence, the 104th of the Renovation, and the 18th of the Era of Trujillo. In this, Trujillo was one up on Christ, whose notes for the Sermon on the Mount were not dated A.D. In marble, bronze, cement, and paint you constantly met the words "Era de Trujillo." And an era it was.

The Generalisimo collected monuments as others do stamps. Whenever he went abroad and saw an impressive monument, he had a replica built to himself. He visited France and saw the eternal flame to the Unknown Soldier: on his return he installed an eternal flame to himself under a reconstructed colonial wall. He visited Washington and the obelisk to George Washington caught his eye; immediately he erected one to himself on the George Washington driveway in Ciudad Trujillo by the sea. Dominicans shuddered at the thought that it might occur to him to go sightseeing in Egypt.

The people called the obelisk to Trujillo "the male monument"; a few blocks away there was another monument to him of more complex form, which they called "the female monument." Their litters had overrun the country like Australian rabbits. White plaster busts of the Generalisimo, mass-produced from moulds, were everywhere—an estimated 1,800 in the capital alone. You entered a

169

government office and it was the first thing that you ran into; you
turned a corner into the adjoining office and there was another one.
Towns were constantly petitioning the Congress to have another bust
of the Generalisimo set up in a naked corner of another square. And,
according to the official paper, *La Nación,* Congress "debated" the
point before granting the request.

Unless I am mistaken, Trujillo was the first five-star general in the
world, and five stars had been elevated to his coat-of-arms. They were
all over the Jaragua Hotel, the luxurious hostelry built with an Export-Import Bank loan. Five stars graced the fronts of the
magnificent headquarters of the Dominican party. The license plate
of his car was a solid gold plaque with five stars on it and the words
below: "Benefactor de la Patria." When the Generalisimo appeared in
public, etiquette required that his fellow citizens place their hats over
their hearts and bow their heads. For not even the Mikado in his
period of divinity could be allowed to steal a trick on the G'isimo.

During my trip through the country in 1945 I took some random
notes on some of the inscriptions. On a home for the aged: "Trujillo is
the only one who gives us shelter." On the most insignificant village
pumps: "Trujillo alone gives us water to drink." On a hospital: "Only
Trujillo cures you." On a very ordinary town market in Santiago:
"This structure will bear witness through the centuries of the grandeur of the Era of Trujillo." On the fortress near the new harbor in
the capital, where a small area was reclaimed from the river: "Trujillo,
Hacedor de esta Tierra" (Creator of this land)—the ambiguity of the
phrase was, of course, perfectly deliberate. The Dominicans prepare
a delicious dessert from pineapples and eggs which they call "Love
with Jealousy." Trujillo had a bad case of that with respect to himself.

He had bestowed the title *Benefactor de la Patria,* and *Libertador
Financiero,* on himself, and was continually splitting up provinces so
that he could name the fragments after himself and his relatives.
There was a Trujillo province in honor of himself, a Trujillo Valdez
province in honor of his father; Libertador and Benefactor provinces
named with his titles, and a San Rafael province after his saint. The
main street in every town was called Trujillo and the next important
bore the name of his father or mother. Teams and clubs bore the
name of his eighteen-year-old son Ramfis (Rafael Leónidas).
Bridges—including those ordered and paid for by the previous regime—were called Julia Molina for his mother, María Martínez for his
wife, or carried the names of his maternal and paternal grandparents.
When his mother's birthday rolled around, the Supreme Court and
the University paraded in honor of *la Matrona Excelsa y la Primera
Dama de la República.*

Poets and orators were a bit of a bore throughout Latin America, but in the Dominican Republic the menace had assumed fabulous forms. Every occupant of a post, to say nothing of the candidates for it, had to rhyme and discourse to Trujillo's greater glory. Since their livelihoods depended upon their overtopping other poetasters and rhetors, their metaphors became hopelessly scrambled and their similes positively surrealistic. The G'isimo started out being a flower's fragrance and a lion's claws, and before you knew it he was a flower's claws and a lion's fragrance. I heard him sung as "una flor exquisitamente exquisita."

Periodically, a contest was announced for the best biography of Trujillo. In 1938 Gilberto Sánchez Lustrino carried off the laurel with his "Trujillo, Constructor de una Nacionalidad." A passage from this gem explained the cyclone that flattened out Santo Domingo in 1930: "The cyclone had no other origin than the rivalry of the gods. Neptune was afraid that the golden-maned horses of his chariot would kidnap Aphrodite and offer her to the new Latin God, to whom under the cupola of Quisqueya [the legendary name for Santo Domingo] glory was being rendered in an ecstasy of adoration. Hence he filled his lungs and blew the surf high in a haughty, provocative gesture. But seeing his rival challenging his anger amidst the infernal destruction, he took fright."

Several years previously Trujillo, itching for recognition as an international statesman, had advanced the idea of an American League of Nations. By virtue of this slightly threadbare proposal, he had modestly placed himself alongside Christ and Bolívar. I quote from one of the several biographies of him by A. R. Nanita, whom the Dominican official press likened to Stefan Zweig. "Two thousand years ago Jesus preached his doctrine of Justice and Peace, . . . over a century ago Bolívar projected his Federation of American Nations; ten years ago Trujillo submitted his luminous project creating the League of American Nations." From the same biography, which visitors found on their night tables at the Hotel Jaragua: "Trujillo has no manias. He doesn't collect stamps like Franklin Delano Roosevelt, nor ancient coins like the misanthrope King Victor Emmanuel, nor lions and tigers like Goering and the Venezuelan Gómez. . . ."

And the G'isimo sits back and sips it all in. Occasionally he pens a note to the author of such an atrocity congratulating him on his "interesting contribution to literature."

The best monument to the Era of Trujillo that I found was neither a mound, a monolith, a slab, nor a statue, but a private home. It was in the capital near the U.S. embassy and belonged to Henri Garçon, a building contractor who has made a lot of money working for the government. The house was built in the shape of a ship with a waterline, a funnel, portholes, and all. On it was painted the name *still there 1984*

Vitalicio. It was intended as an architectural plea to Trujillo to assume the presidency for life. A period that could inspire that was truly an era apart—the Era of Trujillo.

Streams of blue blood coursed through Trujillo's official biographies. The Nanita opus informed us: "His is an illustrious pedigree. Of pure Spanish stock and conquering adventurous spirit, the Trujillos brought their blood to America in the glorious days of the colonization and conquest of the new world." The truth is that a Spanish sergeant, José Trujillo Monagas, came to Santo Domingo during its temporary reannexation to Spain in the 1860s, and begat an illegitimate child on a humble mulatto girl of Bani, Silveria Valdez. The sergeant went on to Cuba shortly afterward and took a hand in hounding the Cuban revolutionaries. Eventually he became police chief of Havana. The child that he left abandoned in Santo Domingo became the Generalisimo's father, a perfectly inoffensive person who engaged now and again in horse theft. When he died in 1937, he was buried in the Cathedral of Ciudad Trujillo, and the then puppet-president Jacinto Peynado orated: "Never have such honorable remains been deposited in this Cathedral." That is the same Cathedral, of course, where lie the bones of Christopher Columbus.

But back to Nanita for more family tree. "The Chevaliers [the G'ismo's maternal family] come from that Napoleonic France that astounded the world with the feats of its captains. They descend from Joseph Chevalier, Marquis de Philbourou." When I was in Ciudad Trujillo, I had the excellent fortune to meet another descendant of the Marquis de Philbourou. He was the Haitian minister, a fantastic old mulatto called Chevalier, who was also in his relative Trujillo's pay. A grand cynic with a belly laugh that came straight from the jungle, Chevalier had been one of the servitors of the United States occupation in Haiti and boasted of having been F. D. Roosevelt's bootlegger during Prohibition. Chevalier was Trujillo's distant cousin: the gay Marquis de Philborou had fathered their common ancestor on a Haitian slave. ("C'est mon cousin, et je l'aime bien, quoi," Chevalier would roar.) Given Trujillo's rabid anti-Haitian campaign, bringing up his own Haitian descent was very much like finding the late Hitler a Jewish grandmother. With malice aforethought, I mentioned casually to several high government officials that I had met a charming relation of the G'isimo, the Haitian minister. Invariably the answer came with a thin, nervous laugh: "Nonsense, how could the Haitian minister be a relative of the Generalisimo!"

But when I returned to Chevalier and told him that he was being repudiated, he reached for a couple of photos of Trujillo autographed with the dedication "A mi querido pariente, Chevalier" (To my dear relative, Chevalier).

Rafael Leonidas Trujillo was born in 1891 at San Cristóbal, some thirty kilometers to the west of the capital, a circumstance that was to cause grave architectonic eruptions in the region forty years later. The family was mouse-poor, and a large one—four daughters and seven sons (popularly known as "the seven plagues of Egypt"). Rafael received only the most rudimentary schooling. He helped his father rustle cattle and horses, and worked in turn as store clerk, telegraphist, and forest guard. The mother was an ignorant but kindly mulatto. Under her son's presidency, she lived in a heavily guarded mansion next to the Haitian legation and was somewhat dazed by all the rumpus raised in her honor.

Given this background, Trujillo in normal times might have ended up dangling from the end of a rope, or as an obscure village bully.

It was the occupation of the Dominican Republic that started Under Secretary of State Sumner Welles on the gloomy train of reflections that ultimately led to the formulation of the Good Neighbor policy.* There was nothing of the revolutionary thinker or iconoclast about Sumner Welles; but because of that, the understatement of his book *Naboth's Vineyard* was more damning of the United States busybodying in the Caribbean during the Big Stick period than ten times its weight in anti-imperialist tracts.†

The U.S. customs collectorship that was foisted on the Dominican Republic in 1907 proved the wedge for outright occupation. The half-fatuous, half-Machiavellian meddling of the Department of State contributed to keeping the land in a constant state of civil strife. To meet this, the government perforce had to run up a considerable floating debt. This, Washington alleged, violated the terms of the customs receivership convention that forbade the government to contract new debts. On these grounds the Marines moved in.

The purpose of the occupation was supposedly to teach the Dominicans new standards of honesty and patriotism. Yet the U.S. minister, James Mark Sullivan, who prepared the ground for the occupation, was an unsavory ward heeler who after a U.S. Senate

---

*Benjamin Sumner Welles was named by President Woodrow Wilson U.S. minister-commissioner to the Dominican Republic during the occupation, which lasted from 1916 to 1924. Subsequently, he continued in the State Department till the end of the forties as Under Secretary of State for Inter-American Affairs and adviser to President Roosevelt on Western Hemisphere problems.

†*Naboth's Vineyard*, subtitled *The Dominican Republic, 1844–1924*, was published in 1928. In it Welles explains, partially at least, the history of U.S. policy toward that country during that period.

enquiry was graciously permitted to resign his Dominican post. Sociologist as well as uplifter, Sullivan gravely prophesied in his dispatches to Secretary of State William Jennings Bryan that baseball, then becoming popular for the first time in the Dominican Republic, would unquestionably prove "a real substitute for the excitement of revolutions." For his part Bryan asked Sullivan for a list of jobs and salaries in the customs administration so that "deserving Democrats might be appointed." The efficiency of the receivership suffered woefully.

In Haiti and Nicaragua the North Americans found natives willing to form puppet regimes under the occupation. But in the Dominican Republic, where political morality had not dipped so low, a point was reached where no Dominicans would lend themselves to the farce. It was therefore necessary to set up a "Dominican government" consisting wholly of United States naval officers. Most of these lacked even a knowledge of Spanish; their grasp of politics was of the same order. Bumblingly, they sent a note to their "great and good friend" dictator Federico Tinoco of Costa Rica, whom the State Department was boycotting, proposing that relations be established between the two regimes. An urgent corrective came from Washington. This "government" contracted and squandered loans in the name of the Dominican Republic. Finally, when the U.S. Navy and State Department fell out on Dominican policy, the State Department refused to authorize further loans, and the naval government simply faded away.

So much from Sumner Welles, but there are significant aspects of the occupation that are ignored in his book. The Land Courts set up by the North Americans to regularize the titles of holdings used their powers to deprive many peasants of their plots for the benefit of the U.S. sugar interests. The occupation authorities manipulated the Dominican tariff to favor U.S. imports. As a result, the local shoe and tanning industries disappeared entirely and others declined.

But the greatest defect of Welles's account is that it was written too early, before the full effects of the intervention could be assessed. On the whole, Dominican politics had been fairly honest: there were presidents who stepped from the presidential palace into the very shadow of the poorhouse. Even the caudillos who dominated the country's public life seasoned their ambitions with a pinch of patriotism; they risked their lives and fortunes and underwent years of exile for their dim principles. On the other hand, the occupation brought to the fore the completely mercenary adventurer, who served the North Americans when few self-respecting Dominicans would and then availed himself of the efficient military machine they left behind to install himself in power. The disarming of the nation effected by the Marines delivered it to the tyrant's mercies.

Trujillo had an uncle, Teodolo Pina Chevalier, a gambler by profession, who worked for a while as an interpreter for the occupation Intelligence Service. Uncle Teodolo managed to get Rafael a job in the National Guard that the North Americans were organizing.* He was a tough, smart lad with a flair for leadership; before a year had passed he was taking part as second lieutenant in persecution of the guerrillas who resisted the occupation in the east. There he learned useful lessons about subduing a people, which would stand him in excellent stead in later years. When the North Americans withdrew in 1924, he was recommended for promotion to a colonelcy, and became head of the spry new army shortly afterward. He was a model army chief: his troops were respectful of civilians and committed few abuses.

While thus nursing his prestige with the public, he was quietly at work weeding out officers whose loyalty to himself was doubtful and replacing them with unconditional henchmen. And he had already begun accumulating wealth. In 1929 a financial mission under General Charles Dawes came to the Dominican Republic to recommend financial and administrative reforms. They found that expenditures of $529,875 by the National Guard had not been satisfactorily accounted for, and there were murmurs for Trujillo's dismissal. But President Horacio Vázquez, the legendary chieftain of the long fight against foreign domination, had become fatuous with age and was preparing his own reelection. Vázquez retained Trujillo at the head of the army because he believed that he had in him a staunch supporter against those of his old comrades who frowned on his second term.

Trujillo played both ends against the middle. When the oppositionist leader, Rafael Estrella Urena, captured the fortress at Santiago, Trujillo refused to send the army in the government's defense. Arms sent to Vázquez by President Gerardo Machado of Cuba were intercepted by the U.S. occupation authorities in Haiti. Vázquez fell, and Estrella Urena was sworn in as provisional president.

Estrella Urena was soon cured of any notions that he might have had of hanging on to the presidency. He was induced to run for vice-president on Trujillo's ticket. Vázquez had respected the liberty of press and assembly, but Trujillo decided that his countrymen required a little softening up. His gunmen known as *La 42* got busy, assaulting opposition meetings with machine guns. His opponents could pit nothing against these weapons but chalk: the town walls appeared covered with the phrase: *"No puede ser."* The sentence was completed by word of mouth—"por ladron de caballos."† For the whole first

---

*The "Constabulary" or "National Guard" was a recipe used by the United States in Haiti, the Dominican Republic, Nicaragua, and Panama, in all cases with supervision and training by U.S. troops. It was one of the worst of all legacies to the peoples of Central America and the Caribbean.

†"It cannot be—not by a horse thief."—W.K.

decade of the Era of Trujillo, Dominicans found it sagacious to avoid the word combination of *no puede ser,* even in parlor gossip. Trujillo's terror was such that the opposition candidates withdrew from the race. On May 16, 1930, Trujillo was "elected" president.

When the legality of the election came before the Supreme Court, Trujillo's gunmen invaded the courtroom and dispersed the judges. The ensuing weeks were sticky with the blood of opposi- tionists. On June 1, for example, *La 42* broke into the home of the poet Virgilio Martínez Reyna and killed both him and his pregnant wife, who tried to shield her husband.

Trujillo was the creature of the U.S. Marine Corps rather than of the State Department. There was a long-standing enmity between him and Welles, who during his residence in the republic as U.S. commissioner had formed an intimate friendship with Horacio Váz- quez. During the long years when he guided the State Department's Latin American policy Welles kept his dislike of Trujillo very much to himself; but Trujillo lost no occasion for calumniating Welles to visit- ing journalists.* On the other hand, General H. Russel, the American high commissioner to Haiti, offered Trujillo every encouragement in his conspiracy against Dominican liberties. And no sooner was Trujillo inaugurated on August 16 than United States recognition came.

Trujillo made an art of murder, planning and savoring every bloody work with Florentine finesse. In September 1930 the G'isimo released General Alberto Larancuent from prison, received him in his office, embraced him with affection, and promised to let bygones be bygones. That same evening Larancuent was summoned to a rendez- vous in the Parque Colón. While waiting for his man, the lights on the square went out, and he was fired upon and killed.

When his gunmen brought him the head of Desiderio Arias, he rewarded them with promotions. Then he paid a call on Arias's widow to express his condolences.† Indeed, visiting his victims' families to declare his grief in velvety tones was one of the Generalisimo's favorite amusements. And the bereaved, scared out of their wits, had to lend themselves to the farce. Scant wonder that one of Trujillo's nicknames in the Republic was "Beautiful Murder."

The technique of Trujillo's slayings had evolved in a manner

---

*From this period comes the famous anecdote that remains part of the history and political science of Hispanic America. When Welles told Roosevelt that Trujillo was a "son of a bitch," the President replied: "I know he's an S.O.B., but he's *our* S.O.B." With time this dialogue came to be transferred to Somoza and Ubico.

†Desiderio Arias, a general opposed to Trujillo, had been president fleet- ingly in 1916.

worthy of a progressive age. In the early years his triggermen would cruise into a town, spot their victim, and mow him down. Their automobile was known as *la carreta de la muerte** and gave several hundred malcontents a lift to a better life. The defect of this routine was that there was too much gunplay: innocent bystanders were often hurt. Trujillo therefore abandoned it for the more refined *paseo*. A couple of Cuban assassins, formerly members of Machado's death squad, were enlisted. These "invited" their victims to accompany them in their car and left the bodies in some isolated spot.

More recently, perhaps because of the wartime gasoline shortage, Trujillo had again reverted to doing some of his butchering on the main streets of the capital. But there was nothing untidy about his methods. When Servio Fuentes was assassinated on a downtown street in 1946, his grave had already been dug and an ambulance was standing at the curb ready to pick up the body.

Trujillo's wrath pursued his opponents across the seas. In April 1935 a Dominican exile, Sergio Bencosme, was killed in his New York boardinghouse by a gunman who came asking for him and the oppositionist leader Angel Morales. A grand jury in New York indicted Luis Fuentes Rubirosa, cousin of Trujillo's son-in-law (who later married the heiress Doris Duke and represented Trujillo in Buenos Aires). Fuentes left for the Dominican Republic by the first plane after the murder and was made an officer of the Dominican army. When the U.S. government pressed for his extradition, he simply disappeared.†

These energetic methods served to cow the country into a calm so petrified that, if you cast a pebble into a pond you half expected that there would be no ripples. Members of the symphony orchestra—along with others in the government's employ—got used to filling out questionnaires containing such questions as the following: "Does anybody in your family correspond with anyone outside the country?" "With whom?" "Is any member of your family opposed to the regime of Generalisimo Trujillo?"

This salutary terror was directed against friends as well as foes.

---

*The death cart.—W.K.

†The most famous internationally of Trujillo's assassinations was that of the Basque professor Jesús de Galíndez, kidnapped in New York City on 12 March 1956 by the dictator's gunmen and clandestinely flown back to the Dominican Republic in a private plane piloted by the North American Murphy. Back in Santo Domingo, Galíndez was *personally* tortured and killed by Trujillo, while pilot Murphy was "disappeared" forever. Galíndez had committed the crime of writing, as a Columbia University doctoral thesis, *The Era of Trujillo*—one of the most accurate descriptions of that despot's regime.

On assuming office every deputy, senator, and minister was obliged to hand in his resignation to Trujillo with the date left blank. And every morning Trujillo's paper, *La Nación,* appeared with a list of resignations and new appointments. Those who resigned did not know about it until they read *La Nación.* That is why *La Nación* was read so frantically. There had been cases of ministers failing to read *La Nación* one morning and turning up at their offices only to find a successor already installed. There was a constant rotation of deputies, senators, ministers, and sundry officials; literally thousands of people had been named and renamed members of Congress in the era of Trujillo. It served to keep them on their toes. They worked away at their jobs sometimes as much as twelve hours a day. And in their spare moments they composed articles, speeches, and poems in honor of Trujillo.

The strange custom obtained in the Dominican Republic for the newspapers to blow a siren whenever a substantial bit of news came in: one toot for international news and two for local news. Local news was reduced largely to some important public figure's having "resigned." Hence, whenever the siren sounded twice, official sent to the newspaper offices to see whose number was up. An embittered officeholder coined the bon mot: "Occupying a post in the Dominican Republican is a period of anguish between two siren blasts."

When Trujillo completed his second term, he "retired" to his old post as head of the National Guard. In the presidency he left a fat, bald old cynic, Jacinto "Mozo" Peynado.* One of Peynado's first official acts was to raise Trujillo's nine-year-old son Ramfis's rank from colonel to brigadier general. A minor social complication arose from Peynado's appointment. According to the letter of the law, Mrs. Peynado would have been First Lady of the Land, with precedence over Trujillo's mother and wife. But Trujillo at once passed a law establishing that there would henceforth be three first ladies—his mother, his wife, and, as a poor third, Mrs. Peynado.

It was Peynado who while president erected a sign in electric bulbs before his home reading "Dios y Trujillo" (God and Trujillo). Shortly afterward Trujillo ran into a bad squall when world opinion became exercised over his mass assassination of Haitians.† When

---

*Of President Peynado it was said: "He cannot be Peynado [combed] because he is bald; he cannot be Mozo [a young lad] because he is old; nor Jacinto [hyacinth] because he smells bad."—W.K.

†On 2, 3, and 4 October 1937 there was a colossal massacre of Haitian residents of the Dominican Republic, especially in the border area between the two countries. The estimated death toll—men, women, and children—fluctuated between twelve and twenty-five thousand, and the international protest and scandal forced Trujillo to commit himself to paying a $750,000 indemnity to the Haitian government. He never completed the payment.

someone mentioned the gravity of the situation to Peynado, he was perfectly unruffled: "I don't give a damn if anything happens. All I have to do is add an 'a' before the Dios of my sign and strike out the 'y.' Then it will read 'Adios Trujillo.'"* Peynado died of his exertions in the presidency, and was succeeded by another puppet before Trujillo in 1941 again put on the presidential sash.†

Trujillo treated his ministers like domestics. Throughout my interview with him, his secretary, Vega, whose status was that of cabinet minister, stood at stiff attention alongside the desk before which the G'isimo and I were seated. When Trujillo wished to dismiss a minister, he often had recourse to a little ruse that also served to emphasize his own omniscience at the same time. A file was quietly taken from the given ministry and Trujillo pored over it. When he was ready, he leaned on a button and the unfortunate minister arrived. Then Trujillo began shooting at him detailed questions related to that file, and the minister, of course, could not hold his own. That served as justification for the minister's resignation appearing in *La Nación* the following morning. Or a cross-examination of the minister on the contents of that morning's *La Nación* would serve the same purpose. (Trujillo amongst other things liked to be called "the Nation's First Journalist.")

The efficiency resulting from this system went far to explain the achievements of the Trujillo regime. For achievements there undeniably were.

The Dominican Republic is a land of broad plains and a relatively sparse, hard-working population. During the colonial period it was devoted primarily to grazing, and the richness of its soil was still unmined: on the vast Cibao plain in the center of the island it was possible to raise three and even four crops of corn each year. It had a healthily varied economy; in addition to sugar, grown primarily by U.S. concerns for the British market, there were coffee, cacao, precious woods, rice, and fruits for export. In many respects Trujillo had pushed the economic development of these resources begun by previous regimes.

Along with Peru, the Dominican Republic was the only large

---

*This same sign inspired a Spanish refugee to exclaim: "Caramba, one can't even piss on God anymore without splashing his *compadre*." Trujillo's police, who naturally overheard, proposed expelling the Spaniard for irreverence (to Trujillo of course, not God), but Trujillo found the remark amusing.—W.K.

†Peynado was replaced by Manuel J. Troncoso (1940–42), and subsequently Trujillo had himself elected three more times. In 1952 he yielded the presidency to his brother Héctor Bienvenido Trujillo (1952–60), and after that to one of his most faithful henchmen, Joaquín Balaguer (1960–62). In 1961, still the strongman of the country, Trujillo was assassinated.

American sugar producer that, for lack of British or U.S. tariff pref-
erence, had to sell its sugar on the open world market. In years of glut
this meant ruinously low prices, but in times of sugar scarcity Peruvian and Dominican sugar fetched far more than the British or U.S.
ceiling prices. In 1947, when the Cubans were delivering sugar to the
United States for about four cents a pound, the open world price had
soared to as much as ten cents. Dominican sugar exports rose from
433,023,225 kilos, worth $8,509,177, in 1936 to 749,462,051 kilos,
worth $43,451,604, in 1944. And even then the most sensational rise
in sugar prices took place in the three subsequent years. As a result,
the government coffers had been overflowing. In 1948 Trujillo was
able to pay off the country's entire foreign debt.

He had also had plentiful money for public works. Most of these
were located where the tourist was sure to see them. The best building
in almost any town was the majestic concrete structure that housed
the official Dominican party. San Cristóbal, the Generalisimo's birth-
place, had been transformed from an obscure unkempt town to a
cluster of lavish marble halls that would do for any World's Fair. The
lovely boulevard along the capital's seafront, the model market, the
Jaragua Hotel—the most luxurious, and one of the worst run, in the
Caribbean—are so many further medals that the G'isimo wore on his
chest.

Perhaps the most solid of the G'isimo's achievements was his irrigation program. Between 1931 and 1941, 23,000-odd acres were irrigated, and almost 40,000 between 1942 and 1944. Yet in 1930—the
reader will remember that Trujillo reached the presidency only in the
middle of that year—over 6,000 acres were irrigated: a clear indication that Dominican irrigation had been but a continuation of work
begun by the previous democratic government rather than an epoch-
making innovation. The owner of the land benefiting from such irrigation was obliged to cede to the state one quarter of his acreage. This
in turn was used for the settling of agricultural colonies. Poor Dominican peasants were given land, tools, seed, and the occasional loan of
tractors. After five years they received a title to the *use* of this land.
They could not alienate it, and they were indefinitely subject to state
regimentation. The Ministry of Agriculture told them what to sow on
90 percent of their land; they could not absent themselves from the
colony, even in the evenings, without written permission from the
supervisor. Because of this lack of freedom, the turnover of personnel
in these colonies was considerable.

I visited the colony "Rafael de El Llano" near San Juan. It consisted of 5,700 acres, 2,500 of which were already under cultivation,
for the most part smiling fields of rice where before there had been
desert. There 368 peasant families had settled. The peasants them-

selves had built 138 primitive shacks, and the government had contributed 25. A tenth of these colonists owned a bit of their own land elsewhere, and many were leaving the colony because they preferred cultivating their own wretched lands. On a hillside, set out in stones, were the inevitable five stars and the words *Rafael el Grande—Una Prueba Mas* (Rafael the Great—one more proof). It shed some light on the contemporary world that power-drunk Trujillo, with neither understanding of nor sympathy for socialism, should have hit upon state colonies as a means of buttressing his regime.

Trujillo had imported Alfonso Rochac, the exiled Salvadoran democratic leader and banking specialist, to help organize an Agrarian Bank to provide credit for small farmers. The modern system of land registry introduced by the U.S. occupation made it possible to establish a smoothly functioning farm credit system. Here, as in many instances, the G'isimo had given foreign technicians a relatively free hand in their work.

While providing many peasants with water for their crops, the government was careful to skim off the cream. The official craze for monuments and circuses had made necessary a brutally heavy taxation, imposed irrationally according to the dictator's caprice. There was a $2 per hundredweight tax on all rice grown, a tax on tobacco cultivation, on sugar milling. A 4 percent tax on merchants' stocks that had to be paid each six months, even on items that for lack of customers had already paid the tax once or several times before. Living costs had rocketed because of Trujillo's excessive exportation of foodstuffs. Amidst all the glories of the era the poor stuffed themselves with raw mangoes as never before.

According to official figures, which were offered the visitor with the aggressiveness of a punch in the eye, under Trujillo schools had been increased from 525 to 2,223, including 1,133 emergency primary schools giving two-year courses; the number of pupils had risen from 50,360 to 220,299. The educational budget had gone up from $716,103 to $2,307,759 in 1945. The most casual trip through the country would convince one that new schools had indeed been built— something unheard of under the Central American dictatorships— but that the increase indicated by the official statistics was highly improbable.

Random sampling in Bani, an important town in the south, revealed a more moderate measure of progress. The primary school that I visited there was called Trujillo Valdez, after the G'isimo's father, but it had been built by the government of Horacio Vázquez that Trujillo overthrew. It had 475 pupils, all boys, and eleven teachers. In addition there was a girls' primary school called Escuela Duarte with 500 pupils, likewise built under Vázquez. Four months before my visit, a new mixed coeducational primary school had been completed. Thus two of the three existing primary schools had been built by Vázquez, who had been in power six years, and one by the G'isimo who amongst his many titles cherished that of "First School-teacher." There was no lack but an excess of diplomaed school-teachers, and there was considerable unemployment amongst them. That did not suggest a 300 percent increase in students enrolled in fifteen years. The Bani teachers whom I interviewed had holes at the elbows of their jackets.

My investigations in a couple of other towns produced results very parallel to those in Bani.

Trujillo was completing a flashy University City, designed by a Spanish refugee, on the outskirts of the capital at a cost of two million dollars. It was one of his most impressive window displays. Benefits to the students were unlikely to outweigh the moral hurt done by dressing them in uniforms and forcing them to parade as the University Guard on the birthdays of the G'isimo and his favorite relatives.

In 1930 the capital was flattened by a cyclone, with a toll of 3,000 dead and 12,000 wounded. This had provided rapid-transit sociologists with a false point of reference for judging the G'isimo's feats of construction. Obviously it was necessary to rebuild the city, and naturally it was modernized as it was rebuilt. On the strength of that Trujillo came to consider himself a modern Romulus and changed the name of the city from Santo Domingo to Ciudad Trujillo. Though money poured in from all over the world to aid the victims, and though he levied a forced contribution on all bank deposits, no accounting for the money was ever made public.

Primarily, Trujillo was no thieving politician, but big business incarnate. Unlike Carías in Honduras, he was not reduced to picking the treasury clean so that nothing remained for roads and schools. His commercial enterprises were of such inordinate magnitude that the government dwindled in importance to a sideline. He had as little temptation to steal directly from the treasury as the president of a steel trust would have to rifle the firm's petty cash box. One diplomat in Ciudad Trujillo summed up to me his observations over several years: "If you try interpreting the setup here in terms of politics, you will get nowhere. It is not a country but a feudal domain. Trujillo is lord of everybody's life and chattels. He is a progressive overlord, concerned about drainage and plumbing. But he is annoyed at having to waste energy putting on an act to convince the imbeciles of the outside world that his feud is a democracy, or for that matter a country at all."

Trujillo had a passion for land, particularly other people's land. By a variety of methods, he had long since accumulated enough to make him the country's greatest landowner, not excepting the U.S. sugar estates. First in the list of his properties was the vast La Fundación hacienda which had its center on the outskirts of his home town of San Cristóbal. By 1945 it stretched practically from Bani to the capital and measured some 200,000 acres.

Trujillo began by supporting the claims of squatters on a neglected farm owned by a couple of aged Frenchwomen. Then he bought those lands from the squatters. When the French minister protested, he compensated the women by giving them lands belonging to Sumner Welles near the capital at La Francia. When he offered Welles compensation elsewhere, Welles declined. It was thus that he began realizing his dream of owning a big estate outside the town that had known him as a penniless boy. Then he commenced absorbing neighbors. "If he could not buy from the proprietors, he bought from their widows," is the way one of his victims put it to me.

Neighbors who were reluctant to sell had their irrigation ditches destroyed by the government on the pretext that they bred mosquitoes. Sometimes they were arrested on charges of horse theft; or they were forced to sell their produce to La Fundación at impossible prices.

The G'isimo's estates extended all over the country at the time of my visit. His most recent acquisition was 12,000 acres near Yamasa in Trujillo province. It was hard to estimate the total acreage of his holdings because they were in a constant state of flux. He was always selling lands to the government and buying them back. A recent sample: a few years ago he sold the finca Altagracia-Julia (at Kilometer 10 of the Mella road) to the state as an experimental station for $80,000. In 1945 one of his agents, a certain Isidro Fromenta, bought it back for $20,000.

Like so many Latin American dictators, Trujillo had a weakness for cattle. He had the state bring in blooded bulls to service the peasants' cows at remount stations throughout the country. Like so much in the Dominican Republic, it was not too clear just to whom the bulls belonged, the state or Trujillo. You asked the attendants at the remount station and they replied: "Es del Jefe" ("It's the chief's"). Such a distinction appeared irrelevant to most Dominicans.

I visited La Fundación and admired the splendid cows milked mechanically to radio music (Trujillo was convinced that they gave more milk that way). The men who supervised the hacienda were privates of the National Guard who wore their uniforms. In addition to milk, La Fundación produced copra for the G'isimo's soap factory in the capital, coffee, and field crops.

La Fundación was the basis of the G'isimo's dairy business. His dairy was known as La Central Lechera and had a charming feature:

every other dairy selling milk in the capital had to pay it one centavo per liter. In the Dominican Republic a centavo is known as a "chele." That prompted a Spanish refugee radio announcer to refer to the Central Lechera as the Central Chelera. Soon he was not announcing any longer.

The most effective way of dominating the cattle business was to control the slaughterhouses. In 1942 the Dominican government built a modern slaughterhouse and refrigeration plant at Cami with the aid of a loan from the Export-Import Bank. The Cami slaughterhouse was now Trujillo's property and was of immense aid to him in buying cattle cheap and selling them dear. He likewise had a corner on cattle exports to the other West Indies; such cattle as others managed to sell to Curaçao were heavily taxed by one of his brothers. His brother Petán and a few privileged army officers shared the business of supplying the other towns with meat.

Before the Era of Trujillo salt was obtained from many mines and from the sea. In 1930 Congress prohibited its extraction from the sea and gave a monopoly for its manufacture to a company organized by Trujillo—La Salinera C por A. It took the peasants a long time to grow accustomed to the new system, and the National Guard found it necessary to kill a good many who were surprised *in flagrante* lifting a gourdful of water from the sea to season their food. In the first fifteen years of La Salinera's existence the price of salt jumped 500 percent.

Around 1932 Trujillo introduced advanced legislation requiring the state and all employers to insure the lives and limbs of their employees against accidents. Workers and employers both paid premiums. At the same moment Trujillo set up La Compañía de Seguros San Rafael, which had the business all to itself. Premiums were high; indemnities were low, and often not paid at all.

The G'isimo's Compañía Anónima Tabacalera was the only tobacco manufacturing company in the republic. An Italian competitor was eliminated by being placed on the blacklist. U.S. cigarettes cost sixty-five cents a package, and the Dominican brands thirty-five cents.

In 1938 Trujillo decided from his reading of history that a nation's sinews were in its merchant marine, and at once passed legislation to provide state aid to shipping companies. More than any other Dominican he had suffered humiliation from the lack of a Dominican fleet. Shortly before, when he had had a gorgeous admiral's uniform made for himself and wanted to give his fellow citizens the treat of seeing him in it, he had been reduced to hiring a foreign ship in which to sail along the coast, calling at every port. Now he organized the Compañía Naviera and bought two old ships, renaming them *San Rafael* and *El Presidente Trujillo.* Heavily backed by the state, the company did well and put a lot of sailboats trading with the other islands out of business. During the war, submarines sank the ships, but the company had a brilliant postwar future.

The huge U.S. sugar estates which produced for the export market were practically the only enterprises that Trujillo respected. But he did enjoy a monopoly of the domestic sugar trade in partnership with the firm Armenteros & Cía. He was also major shareholder of the only beer factory, the domestic aviation line, a shoe factory, a peanut oil and a henequen sack factory, a truck line, the race track, and other miscellaneities.

In addition to the official customs of the Dominican state, there was Trujillo's private customs office known as *Las Aduanitas.* After paying the government duties, merchants must pay the *aduanitas,* a second levy that varied from 80 cents per pair of shoes exported to 10 cents per sack of cement imported.

The G'isimo's third wife, María de los Angeles Martínez de Trujillo, daughter of an Andalucian milk-peddler, operated the Compañía Bancaria Nacional, popularly known as *El Banquito.* El Banquito advanced money to government employees on their next month's play for a mere 4 percent monthly. Its monopoly in this line was protected by a law passed by Trujillo against usury. Mrs. Trujillo's brother Paquito managed for her the Ferretería Read C por A, which got all the government hardware orders, and the Caribbean Motors, which had various automobile agencies. Trujillo's eldest brother, Virgilio, used to be minister to France. When Trujillo in 1936 had "retired" from the presidency, he decided to visit France, all a-tinkle with medals and with a full wardrobe of uniforms. Virgilio cautioned a little discretion, since to the French government the Generalisimo was not even head of a peanut republic, but merely head of its army. Though Trujillo brought along an iron lung as a gift to a Parisian hospital, the French press was ribald in its commentary. Subsequently, the two brothers had been on frigid terms. Fortunately, Virgilio had put aside a little money from his profits on armament sales to the Spanish Republic and his business in visas to the refugees. He now lived in ample retirement, the least hated of the clan.

Brother Arismendi is better known as Petán. Petán liked fruit and had a monopoly exporting it to Puerto Rico and other islands. At Bánao, eighty-seven miles from the capital on the Santiago Road, he also had his private internal customs: all corn passing the spot had to pay him one dollar per hundred pounds, and other products correspondingly. He also owned a radio station.

Romeo Trujillo, known as "Pipi," had never quite grown up. Yet he earned a handsome living from the country's prostitutes, who had to pay him a certain quota or go to jail for immorality. Dominicans told an anecdote connected with this. The Dominican for prostitute is "*cuero*" (literally, a hide or skin). When brother Petán imposed a levy on hides, he provoked a heated discussion with the other brothers, whose empires continually impinged on one another. As usual, it was the old mother who intervened to restore peace. When she heard that Petán was muscling in on the *cueros*, she reproached him: "Now Petan. None of that. You know that the *cueros* are Pipi's."

Pipi had organized the bootblacks into a "union," and collected part of their earnings. He also had his own private toll on the Santiago Road. Every week his agents brought him in the take—bagfuls of coins. Then Pipi, a harmless fellow, liked to stuff his pockets with coins and jingle them before his friends.

Pedro, a major in the Guard, did a modest business in lands (mostly other people's).

General Haníbal Trujillo accumulated rackets and wealth like the rest, but his prosperity went to his head. After a little shooting affray in which he killed a couple of people, Trujillo decided to liquidate him. Only the tearful intervention of the mother saved Haníbal's life. But he spent several years in exile in Puerto Rico. Around 1943 he returned, but it was a subdued Haníbal. No longer did he ride down the main street in a Mexican charro costume as of old or talk of becoming president.

Héctor, the blackest member of the family, was known as El Negro, and was closest to Trujillo. He was head of the army and sold lands to the government.

So much for the brothers. There were four sisters. Nieves Luisa used to be a prostitute, and under the Vázquez regime Trujillo, embarrassed by her occupation, had Vázquez expel her to Cuba. In 1945 she was respectably married to an army major, and could be seen having a merry time in the capital's night clubs almost any evening. Sister Marina was the wife of a General García, once head of the army, last reported to be a senator. Sister Japonesa had the deputy Luis Monteagudo for spouse. But it was Julieta who had married most brilliantly—to Ramón Savinón Lluberes, who had the national lottery concession and collected real estate as a hobby.

War scarcities added materially to the prosperity of this happy, bustling brood. Pipi was good-naturedly engaged in selling fistfuls of coupons for black-market gasoline at $1.50 a gallon. The tire business was in the hands of the G'isimo himself, and was run for him by his then Secretary of State Vega. When I lunched with Vega, we were constantly interrupted by people who came up and openly discussed their tire needs. As early as 1939 the G'isimo was reputed worth as much as $25,000,000, with much of it invested abroad. But that was before the war and its golden opportunities.

Trujillo was a fond father to his two children. Flor de Oro, his daughter by the first of his three wives, was given to marrying with the frequency proper to an heiress of such proportions. When she took a Brazilian as her fourth husband, G'isimo made Portuguese a compulsory language in Dominican schools.

His favorite child, Rafael Leónidas (or Ramfis), had grown up a pampered weakling, not interested in a military career. This had been a blow to Trujillo, who had his heart set on a dynasty—hence the slogan "Trujillo Eternamente" (not only for 653 light-years). Parks, schools, clubs galore had been named after Ramfis. His tutor was the Spanish Republican refugee José Almoina, a smart Gallego who held six official posts—Trujillo's private secretary, Portuguese professor at the University, professor at the School of Fine Arts, director of intellectual relations at the Foreign Office, professor at the diplomatic school, and Ramfis's tutor. In Spain he had been a minor post office employee in Zamora province.

Trujillo's private life was on a scale comparable to that of his businesses. In addition to a stately mansion in the capital and luxurious residences ever ready to receive him in each part of the country, he had built an especially comfortable retreat across the Ozuma River from Ciudad Trujillo and named it Sans Souci. After his trip to Paris he imported the most expensive French prostitutes and lodged them there. When he went on trips in his luxurious yacht, an entire deck was reserved for his harem. On the whole he enjoyed a reputation that did not lag behind that of his cherished bulls, and looked older than his years.

His biographer Nanita tells us that he had a great way with the ladies, and when that didn't work there were other expedients. Four years ago a man called Minino died a brusque death for refusing to turn over his niece for the G'isimo's pleasures. When a well-born lass caught his fancy, he began by asking her to pick herself a husband, and there was a command marriage as a preliminary. But affairs of state did not always allow him to look after the necessary exploration and arrangements in person.

He could count for assistance on the grand old lady of the frontier, Isabel Mayer, popularly known as "La Celestina." Sra. Mayer was a sparkling old octoroon in her late sixties, still handsome though gone to fat. With considerable wealth and charm, if slight schooling, she had lived in Paris, Berlin, and New York and could carry on a racy, witty conversation. She adored Trujillo with an intense disinterested passion, and was one of the most influential people in the land. She had recently been a senator, and was now the Comisionada de la Frontera, with several governors to jump at the crack of her whip. The United Fruit Company had named after her one of the banana farms on its immense new Dominican plantation; that was no more than justice, since she had helped get them the sweeping concession. One of the pleasantest memories of my stay in the republic was the evening spent at her home in Montecristi. A visit to Isabel Mayer's was almost obligatory for foreign journalists, statesmen, and diplomats. Her table creaked under its majestic spread, and her home resounded with the gay laughter of beautiful girls. "Life is a carnival," she mused with a heave of her matronly bosom, "and we have to play our part. But I have lived. Have some more seafood. It is awfully good for men."

Doña Isabel had extensive properties near the northern Haitian frontier, and did not like Haitians. "I am afraid of them," she told me. "They know a lot about herbs and botany, and practice sorcery. The local girls go absolutely mad about them."

An innocent little party was held for the G'isimo at Doña Isabel's home in 1937. The wine and women were particularly good, and the G'isimo was in no abstemious mood. When Doña Isabel complained to Trujillo that those blasted Haitians had stolen some of her cattle again, Trujillo pounded the table and said that he would put a stop to that once and for all. He gave orders there and then that every Haitian in the country be butchered. An order from the G'isimo was never questioned, whether he was in his cups or not. So while the revelry continued at Doña Isabel's, the National Guard hunted down Haitians on the frontier and in the cities of the interior and butchered at least ten thousand. Babies' heads were bashed against rocks; pregnant women were ripped open with bayonets. I met a Dominican near Monte Cristi who told me that he could not eat pork for a whole year afterward because he had seen the pigs gorging themselves on Haitian corpses. People in Santiago and the capital hid their Haitian servants from the soldiers; the sugar estates refused to surrender their Haitian workers. Army officers were given the lands of the deceased. When the news leaked out, indignation abroad flared high. A Mexican-Cuban-United States commission awarded the Haitian government $750,000 in reparations, to be used for looking after the many thousands of refugees who had escaped into Haiti. That was the beginning of Trujillo's proudest achievement—the Dominicanization of the frontier.

The historical background between Haiti and the Dominican Republic is a troubled one. For seventeen years after the Dominicans appealed to Haiti to help them expel the Spaniards, they were under Haitian misrule. When they achieved their independence in 1844, there were several Haitian invasions. Dominican politics in the ensuing two decades was reduced largely to seeking a great power willing to annex the republic and protect it against the Haitians. The population pressure in overcrowded Haiti, a mountainous, eroded land, brought tens of thousands of Haitian squatters into the spacious virgin plains on the Dominican side of the frontier. Haitian money circulated, and creole was spoken as much as Spanish at points forty kilometers within Dominican territory. The frontier itself was finally marked out only in 1939. At first Trujillo tried expelling the Haitians, but it is hard to deprive living peasants of their land. After the mass slaughter, he explained in a speech made in Santiago's town hall: "I came to the conclusion that there was only one way out—a general massacre."

Subsequently Trujillo had resorted to keeping the embers of hatred at white heat. The "reconquest of the frontier" was presented as a crusade for race, civilization, and religion. At an official banquet at Dajaboa that I attended, a sleazy politician leaned over my shoulder and purred: "You can eat heartily and without misgivings. This isn't Haiti, and the meat is not baby's flesh." In a country that was itself a happy example of tolerance, with blacks, mulattoes and relatively few whites living together on easy terms, this racist poison was particularly incongruous.

On the southern part of the frontier, the Dominican village Comendador had been renamed Elias Piña after a Dominican hero in the War of Independence against Haiti. It used to be a cluster of thatched huts behind a customhouse. Trujillo had rebuilt it along magnificent modern lines—with lavish barracks, post office, administrative buildings, and a school. The region was practically devoid of population on the Dominican side, and the imposing structures in Elias Piña served no other purpose than to set off Dominican civilization from Haitian barbarity. The comandante who showed me around belabored the point. When he reached the routine outbursts about Haitian paganism, the rhythms of voodoo drums became audible. But, oddly enough, they came from the Dominican side of the frontier.

As a reprisal against this campaign of hatred, Haitian President Lescot refused to allow Haitians to go to the Dominican Republic to harvest sugar on the large estates. The wartime sugar expansion was thus severely hampered by labor shortage, particularly since the British had refused to permit Jamaicans to leave for the Dominican Republic unless the sugar companies provided decent housing and paid the peons $1.50 daily. A Dominican rural proletariat did not exist in numbers adequate to the sugar industry's needs. Even the irrigation on colonies that Trujillo had strung out along the frontier suffered from the lack of labor, and would have been more flourishing if Haitian colonists were allowed.

I found the Haitian-Dominican frontier practically closed—both to people and to merchandise. Not a happy instance of Good Neighborliness.

It was partly the desire to increase the white blood in the country that induced Trujillo to grant visas to some four thousand Spanish Republicans after the Spanish Civil War. That also netted him some much-needed publicity abroad after the international scandal created by his assassination of Haitians. Some of these visas cost the Spaniards a mere $200 per head, others were extended completely free. Due to the backwardness of the country, and the unfitness of most of the immigrants for tropical agriculture, almost all of the Spaniards skipped off to Venezuela and Mexico after a few years of grueling hardships. Only two hundred remained at the time of my visit. But they left their mark on the country. Culture had profited vastly: many Spaniards were on the University staff; a well-known Catalan composer conducted the orchestra and taught composition for a while. And though discretion was imposed on them by their instinct for self-preservation, their presence had affected the political thinking of the country. In 1942, when a strike occurred amongst the workers of the Romana sugar plantation, the government arrested forty Spaniards as ringleaders and whisked them out to Mexico.

Trujillo handled his goodwill on a scale worthy of a mammoth international trust, rather than the government of an obscure Caribbean republic. Writers and politicians who signed one of the periodic protests against his regime were used to getting invitations to visit the Dominican Republic without expense to themselves. And if they were in a receptive mood, that was a mere beginning. Former U.S. Senator Hamilton Fish, after pillorying Trujillo for his Haitian massacre, traveled to Ciudad Trujillo and returned with both an eloquent regard for the Generalisimo's achievements and—as a Senate enquiry was later to establish—a $25,000 check. In his stable of "public relations counsellors"—duly registered with the State Department—Trujillo counted such eminences as Joseph E. Davies of *Mission to Moscow* fame.* It was enough for a Dominican refugee to address a letter trouncing Trujillo to a Mexican magazine for the dictator to buy up a dozen pages of the publication and fill them with photos of his bridges and irrigation ditches. Pamphlets on the glories of his regime had been distributed at the gates of U.S. Army camps.

Temptation was strewn in the path of visiting journalists in many Latin American lands, but nowhere on such a scale. They did not have to carry impressive credentials: Trujillo was unable to distinguish. In his domain they would find largesse, hospitality, and really

---

*Among others serving in this capacity were a son of Franklin D. Roosevelt and, after his term as Vice-President of the United States, lawyer Richard M. Nixon.

still a technique

high-class opportunities for exercising their prostate glands. Every-thing was offered on a platter with consummate elegance, if no great subtlety.

Yet heaven shield the journalist if he attacked Trujillo on leaving the country. When Mr. Branzell Brown gave an unflattering version of the Dominican situation in an interview in *El Universal* of Caracas in March 1946, *El Universal* received a wordy cable from Ciudad Trujillo, which it published on Mr. Brown's insistence. The cable ac-cused Brown of having "insulted" a young lady at the home of Isabel Mayer, of having been drunk throughout his stay, of borrowing $500, and leaving his hotel bill unpaid.

I had occasion to see how the thin edge of the wedge was applied. The evening before I left the country, Trujillo's secretary Vega phoned to ask me whether I could submit a memorandum on how the government might improve its press relations abroad.

"I am sorry, but my work for *Time* magazine does not permit me to act as public relations counsellor for any government."

"But you would not have to sign the memorandum. It would be enough to write just a few lines."

Couldn't I talk it over with him? No, I was busy that night. Finally I begged off, offering to give my views by word of mouth to a for-merly liberal journalist of note who had entered Trujillo's hire. The next morning I told my colleague what he already knew, that "the G'isimo had only to pull down the statues to himself, change the name of the capital back to Santo Domingo, and give the country free elec-tions, and there would be no reason for him to worry about his press abroad." Then I took the plane for Haiti.

The defeat of the Axis promised to bring the democratic millen-nium even to the Caribbean. For a while it seemed as though Trujillo really had cause to worry about his foreign relations.

In the U.S. State Department's attitude toward him, Trujillo had always missed the note of rapture that made life pleasing to the Cen-tral American dictators; for many years Sumner Welles lurked in the background with his unflattering mental reservations. Nonetheless, Good-Neighborliness was brought to a high measure of fulfillment in the early part of the war by U.S. Ambassador Avra Warren. Mr. War-ren identified himself utterly with the G'isimo's regime, and even enrolled his son as a cadet in the Dominican National Guard. But in 1944 Washington sent Warren to woo dictators elsewhere, and his place was taken by Ellis Briggs, an impossible young man with a vague resemblance to Groucho Marx and loathsome democratic convictions. So grievously was Briggs lacking in the ways of a courtier that he even insisted on looking into the G'isimo's tire racket. Trujillo complained bitterly about Briggs to Nelson Rockefeller, who shortly afterward became assistant secretary of state in charge of Latin American affairs. As a result, Briggs was whisked out of the Dominican Republic so fast that he had not even the time to take leave of his diplomatic colleagues. Chungking, China, is just about the remotest possible spot from Ciudad Trujillo; it was in Chungking that Briggs received his new appointment.

Trujillo had regained as much of his composure as the crash of dictatorships on the other side of the Caribbean permitted, when Spruille Braden displaced Nelson Rockefeller in Washington and brought Briggs back from China as his assistant. Avra Warren was banished from Latin America altogether and sent to New Zealand, where he could do no harm. Choking with rage, the G'isimo filled the columns of his press with the praises of Juan Domingo Perón, Braden's arch-foe.* A nigh-illiterate U.S. "journalist" was hired to write a widely distributed pamphlet entitled *I Accuse Braden.*

Naturally, these misadventures of the Generalisimo abroad gave new heart to his battered opponents at home. One fine morning in the spring of 1945 his statutes in Puerto Plata appeared smeared in excrement. Where the inscriptions on village pumps read: "Trujillo is the only one who gives you water," unknown hands scribbled "and takes away your bread." Mimeographed leaflets went the rounds. Suspects were imprisoned, tortured, assassinated. The more fortunate found their way to foreign legations.

In 1930, when Trujilllo had come to power, he had forced all other parties to dissolve into his Dominican party. This party, with a majority of the country's adult population, 669,735, on its rolls, was as personal an accessory of the G'isimo as his necktie or jockstrap. Its statutes "declare and recognize as its only Supreme Chief Generalisimo and Doctor R. Trujillo. . . . the funds of the party can be disbursed only by express order of the party chief." With the ten percent of all state employees' salaries that went to the party, it bought some milk from Trujillo's farm for distribution amongst schoolchildren, gave away some free breakfasts, ran the odd night school, and built itself gaudy headquarters.

Disquieted by the trend of the times, Trujillo decided to erect a democratic front for his place of business. In May 1945 *La Nación* called upon the former independent parties, peacefully interred since 1930, to bestir themselves, reorganize their ranks, and come out into

---

*Juan D. Perón, president of Argentina (1946–55 and 1973–74), was vigorously set upon by ambassador Spruille Braden for some months in 1945–46. Truman later named Braden Under Secretary of State for Inter-American Affairs, and in that capacity he continued to assail Perón, until the State Department retired him because his intemperance caused problems to United States relations with a large number of Hemisphere governments.

the open. Several onetime leaders of these defunct bodies declined, pretexting poor health. But *La Nación* persisted, publishing names of those who "unless we are mistaken" had belonged to the dissolved parties. Some denied that they had ever belonged to any but the great Dominican party; others moaned that they had publicly withdrawn from the said parties in 1930. Thereupon Trujillo issued a manifesto to members of the Dominican party "giving them the right" to withdraw from it and adhere to any other party of their choice within a three-month period. No one availed himself of this gracious privilege and *La Nación* cited the circumstance as further proof of the regime's eminently democratic character.

A few former oppositionist leaders, however, were pressed into service to reorganize their late parties. One was Rafael Estrella Urena, Trujillo's original vice-president, who died shortly afterward.

For a while the Communists offered themselves for the farce, and in May 1946 *La Nación* was able to publish a manifesto of the Dominican Communist party. The only refugees who accepted Trujillo's invitation to return to the republic were Communists. They had begun organizing legal trade unions the previous year and Mexico's Lombardo Toledano even received these into his C.TA.L.* With Trujillo's blessing, these dubious unions were even able to obtain certain wage raises in industries in which the Generalisimo was not too vitally interested. But by November 1946, Trujillo broke up a Communist meeting in Ciudad Trujillo, began persecuting the Communists once more, and of course tried to depict the entire refugee movement as Communist.

In May 1947 Trujillo held his "elections" and obtained 93 percent of the votes for another term as president. The two "opposition" candidates had not made a single speech during the campaign, and one had even issued a proclamation backing Trujillo for the presidency.

But the G'isimo's troubles continued and for a while it seemed as if the Era of Trujillo was drawing to a close. Braden, to be sure, had been forced out of the State Department for opposing the army's scheme to equip Latin America's dictators with the most up-to-date armament.† But with a degree of assistance from the more democratic regimes of Venezuela, Cuba, and Guatemala, the Dominican

---

*Lombardo's aborted effort to form an all-Latin American union.—W.K.

†This explanation is only partially correct. Another has to be added: Braden unnecessarily complicated inter-Hemisphere relations at a time when President Truman was modifying relations with the Soviet Union, the Cold War was under way, and the Inter-American Reciprocal Assistance Treaty— i.e., the continental military bloc, which still remains in force—was being urgently readied.

refugees had composed their differences and proceeded to organize a mighty expedition to liberate Trujilloland. For over a year the preparations went on. The expeditionary force, numbering about fifteen hundred men trained on the school grounds at Holguín in eastern Cuba. War-veteran pilots were recruited in the United States to fly sixteen planes. Cuban Education Minister José Alemán put many of the revolutionaries on his ministry's payroll.

Trujillo's fabulous luck still held. For one thing the revolutionaries were indiscreet; a friendly U.S. journalist broadcast from New York that the expedition was about to sail. Trujillo threatened to bring protest before the United Nations, and the State Department, which had tried looking the other way, seemed genuinely alarmed. Under the effects of U.S. pressure and Trujillo's cash, the Cuban government split on the issue and panicked. Army Chief Genoveno Pérez Damara raided the estate of Education Minister Alemán and captured some of the Dominicans' arms. President Grau San Martín reluctantly dispatched the Cuban navy to prevent the expedition from sailing. Its members were disarmed and arrested. Haggard and disillusioned, they were brought to Havana and released. Cuba simmered with indignation.

It mattered little that Trujillo was seated on the prostrate body of the Dominican people thanks only to United States intervention and United States arms; to have countenanced the revolutionary expedition would have been "intervention and a violation of Dominican sovereignty."

Recovered from his fright, Trujillo proceeded to purchase $4,000,000 worth of arms and munitions from Brazil. Venezuela protested to Brazil that the arms were intended by Trujillo to equip a counterrevolutionary expedition against the Caracas regime.* In vain. Washington did nothing to hinder a peaceful transaction between two sovereign states. The Era of Trujillo stretched joyously ahead, and democracy was on everyone's lips.†

---

*A reference to the government of writer-professor Rómulo Gallegos, which was finally overthrown by a military coup in 1948.

†Krehm's sarcasm is still valid today. Trujillo was shot to death on 31 May 1961, but his disappearance did not weaken the power of his henchmen. After U.S. troops invaded the Dominican Republic in April of 1965, by order of President Lyndon B. Johnson, the United States installed one of them, Joaquín Balaguer, and kept him in power for thirteen years (1966–78).

12

Dark Destiny

IN VAIN YOU SOUGHT IN PORT-AU-PRINCE traces of St. Domingue, most coveted of eighteenth-century colonies, whose riches went to raise chateaux on the Loire and mansions in Nantes and Bordeaux. There were names on the ramshackle stores that might come from any French town; but the malodorous trickle in the open drainage ditches, the swarming shanties, the open-air market where under a broiling sun trade proceeded langorously in flour-sack clothing, counted-out beans, corncobs, and peanuts, called to mind some overgrown African village. You came across some artisan's shop where a glistening Negro, bared to the waist, turned a huge wooden wheel the livelong day—the prime mover in lieu of a tiny electric motor or even the wheel horse that Europe's Middle Ages knew. In the Lower Town it was only rarely that you saw a new building; less frequent still was the sight of a fat or even well-nourished person. The city reeked of urine and decay.

As you made your way along the broken pavements, you tripped over stark-naked pickaninnies, their bellies bulging with hunger and hookworm. When political scandal ran low, *Le Nouvelliste,* the shrill organ of the mulatto ruling group, thundered at the police to impose fig leaves or decent confinement on these youngsters, lest the morals of little girls of good families chancing to pass by, be blasted. From their cooler comfortable residences up the hill the mulatto elite presided over the black country's destinies, and were much concerned with surface appearances. A decade ago a law had been passed imposing a month's imprisonment on anybody in the capital not wearing shoes. That is why you saw barefoot peasants on their way to town with sandals slung over their shoulders. Yet it would have taken more than a few fig leaves to cover up Haiti's abject poverty. After a spell of it, you turned eagerly to rest your eyes on the sail-flecked finger of sea that penetrated blue and serene to the heart of this distressing human anthill.

After intense exploitation by French sugar planters, this tiny mountainous land with over three million inhabitants and a weary soil was given over to destructive agriculture by the liberated slaves. In 1945 there was less than a hectare of arable land for each adult peasant. Plows were unknown: holes were poked in the ground with a stick and a handful of seeds was thrown in; corn, bananas, yucca, and beans grew promiscuously in one little plot. What coffee there was, was practically wild. It was never washed and little of it was treated after picking as the modern market demands. Deforestation had proceeded to dangerous degrees, and heavy downpours washed the hillsides away. Each year there was less soil left to feed the mounting population. Most of the peasants ate but a single meal a day—at night. In the morning they would swallow a cup of coffee, go into the fields to work, stop at noon to munch a mango or an orange, and eat nothing substantial until the evening repast of rice and beans with an occasional chunk of meat.

Malaria, yaws, hookworm, and other diseases infested the land. You found children with arms as thin as broomsticks. It spoke highly of the morale of the people that they maintained a remarkable cleanliness in the face of such conditions. Their little wooden shacks, with doors and windows quaintly avoiding anything resembling a right angle—the loose-limbedness of the Negro expressed architecturally—were often painted a trim blue. On Sundays, particularly in the banana and sisal regions where exports had brought some ready cash, the finery in which the peasants were decked out might deceive you. A disproportionate part of their income went for clothes. One peasant meeting another in his Sunday apparel would greet the clothes rather than the wearer, "*Bonjour rade*" (*rade* is creole for clothes).

Haiti stood at the bottom of the list of all Latin American nations with respect to the value of exports per capita ($2.86); budgetary revenue ($1.71); annual expenditure for public education ($0.23). And, of course, at the top of the list in population density—281 per square mile, over twice that of its runner-up, El Salvador.

While the misery accumulated within, Haiti had ever fewer outlets for emigration. Practically every Caribbean country had introduced bans on Haitian immigration, except for strictly seasonal immigrants. Your typical Haitian had even ceased trying to foretell what the future held in store.

His voodoo religion, compounded of Christianity and ancestral African rites, was the Haitian's one great emotional outlet. It had sustained him in the days of slavery, and continued to provide an escape from his wretchedness. When the drums started laying their contrapuntal spell in the burden of the hollow bamboo horns, he ceased being a hungry peasant and became the receptacle of a snake divinity, a *loa*. His voice wailed supplications, and his eyes glistened transfixed. Nature was provident when she bequeathed the blacks, most sorely tried of Adam's children, so rich a rhythmic sense. Visit any *bambouche*, or Saturday night fiesta, on the outskirts of Port-au-Prince, and you would see that as sorry as was the vessel he drank from, the poor Haitian quaffed life in deep draughts. But here again the elite, who furtively resorted to voodoo in its degenerate magic phases, had been preoccupied about the opinion of the outside world and had passed statutes outlawing voodoo rites.

How did Haiti, richest of eighteenth-century colonies, become the hemisphere's most pauperized country? First came the devastation of the War for Independence, which was in essence a slave revolt, the most destructive of civil wars. By one process or another most of the land eventually came to be partitioned amongst the ex-slaves, unprepared either culturally or economically to maintain the engineering works of the French. Throughout the land as I found it you came across abandoned colonial aqueducts; to find remnants of major irrigation works of the colony you had to dig as deep as for archeological ruins. In cold terms of economic efficiency, the slave revolution had become a major catastrophe. Yet in human values there could be no doubt about its "justification." The Haitian superstition of "zombies"—men killed by sorcerers and then revived only in body to serve them as soulless drudges—was at bottom an expressive bit of symbolism on the subject of slavery. And expressive, too, was the detail that when there was the least suspicion that a death had been due to sorcery, the deceased's relatives would run the corpse through with a knife to make sure that it could not be revived and enslaved as a zombie. Such folk customs were more important in striking the balance of the slave revolution than figures on the decline of production.

As the price of recognizing Haitian independence, France exacted a crushing indemnification for the former planters—160,000,000 francs, later reduced to 60,000,000. This stripped the republic of the little capital that might have been used to retrieve its agriculture. The reluctance of the white nations to accept anything so unpardonably insolent as a black republic enveloped the young state in a virtual international boycott. Haiti had been the first Latin American country to achieve independence; she lent Bolívar asylum, encouragement, and material aid for the liberation of the southern continent. Nevertheless, in 1826 the United States had Haiti barred from the Pan American Congress at Panama—which the North American delegates anyhow failed to attend. It was only after Lincoln abolished slavery that Washington deigned to establish relations with Haiti.

The development of a native bourgeoisie was aborted, and this accentuated the country's economic stagnation. It was not that the mulatto upper class was shiftless: French historians had left their tribute to the *affranchis,* the colored freedmen, as the most industrious and parsimonious agriculturalists of the colony. But friction between the mulatto elite and the ocean of poor blacks had been constant since independence. It reached a tragic climax in 1883 under the black president Louis Salomon, when the poor Negroes pillaged and set fire to the stores of the Port-au-Prince bourgeoisie and pretty well wiped them out. After that, only foreigners, operating under the protection of their legations, felt secure in commerce. Large-scale trade became the monopoly of Frenchmen, Italians, Germans, and Syrians. The energy of the elite was confined to usury (money was commonly lent at 12 percent monthly), to the professions, and, above all, to politics. This diverted Haiti from the highroad of economic development.

The parasitism of the elite added further to the hectic character of Haitian politics: for public office became the one great feeding trough available to it. From 1912 to 1915, when United States intervention came, no fewer than six presidents succeeded one another, and four of these were violently ejected. Finance for revolutions came liberally from the foreign merchants angling for special privileges. Haiti found her politics becoming uncontrollably turgid as the lusts of the great powers closed in on her.

Resenting French financial supremacy in Haiti, Washington had long set its heart on a customs receivership there, and advanced that as its price for the recognition of each successive revolutionary president. And whenever its proposal was rejected, it did not hide its eagerness in looking forward to the next president. In one instance the revolutionary army was practically escorted by a U.S. warship on its triumphant march down the coast.

We have already come to know the goal of U.S. diplomacy in the Caribbean during this period: a "Co-prosperity Sphere" to be achieved by imposing a customs receivership and a U.S. officered constabulary in each of the countries. Some of these republics, having defaulted on their debts, offered a convenient opening. But Haiti had religiously maintained the service on its debt, held entirely by Frenchmen, until the very day of the U.S. occupation.

On July 27, 1915, just as an enraged mob was tearing President Vilbrun Guillaume Sam to tatters as a reprisal for the mass execution of political prisoners, the U.S. cruiser *Washington* entered the harbor of Port-au-Prince and landed Marines. They were to stay in Haiti for twenty years.

Though President Sudre Dartiguenave was elected by the Haitian assembly with a little prodding from U.S. bayonets, he nevertheless refused to sign the 1915 treaty with the United States imposing a customs receivership, financial tutelage and a U.S.-commanded constabulary. Unruffled, the Marines merely seized the customhouse by force, and when Dartiguenave protested, the U.S. Navy assumed the powers and responsibilities of government under martial law.

To prevent the peasants from being deprived of their plots, Haiti had a traditional ban against foreigners' owning land. Now the North Americans demanded that this restriction be erased from the constitution and that the acts of the occupation be declared "approved by the free will of the Haitian people." Two successive congresses were sent home by the Marines when they refused to produce constitutional amendments in this sense. Instead, a plebiscite was held and yielded 67,337 votes favorable to the amendments and 335 against. Thirty years later, all this has a strangely familiar ring.

With supreme tact the North Americans introduced forced labor for road-building, the *corvée*, in the one country of the world that had known a successful slave revolution. Widespread uprisings resulted, especially in the north. In repressing these the Marines killed 3,500 Haitians according to Haitian sources, 1,500 according to the findings of the U.S. Senate inquiry of 1921–22.

The Marines acted as a goon squad for the National City Bank of New York. When the Haitian government hesitated to transform the National Bank of the Republic of Haiti (up to then controlled by French capitalists) into a subsidiary of the National City Bank of New York and give it a monopoly in the importation of gold money, the occupation authorities withheld the salaries of the Haitian president and other high authorities.

The Haitian government resisted the conversion of its 6 percent internal debt into a 7 percent external debt as a menace to its sovereignty. But naturally it had no say in the matter. In 1922 the first $16,000,000 of a $40,000,000 loan was floated by the National City Bank for the customary commission. The proceeds were used in part to pay interest on the bonds of the Haitian Railway guaranteed by the government. The president of the railway company was Roger Farnham, who was also vice-president of the National City Bank of New York, and vice-president of the National Bank of the Republic of Haiti. These railway bonds had been owned in France, and by 1922 had fallen steeply. They could have been bought on the French market for less than $800,000. Instead, the U.S. financial adviser allowed unpaid interest on them to accrue to $2,000,000, and then paid it. In the interim the National City Bank of New York had acquired at least seventy percent of the issue for the price of an unpopular song.

Originally, most of the occupation officers were chosen from the Southern states, because of their "experience in handling blacks." The president of Haiti, because of his color, was thus not permitted to set foot in the American Officers' Club in Port-au-Prince. The most damnable aspect of the occupation was that it outraged the soul of Haitians by teaching them for the first time that they were a nation of "niggers."

The occupation did undertake notable sanitation and built many rural hospitals. But of all its works these endured least. In 1945 the frames of the hospitals stood gaunt and empty; Haitian political doctors had long since relieved them of their equipment. The antimalarial drainage works had fallen into neglect.

In the closing years of the occupation, public opinion in the United States provided a decided corrective to the wisdom of the Marines. Methods became blander, and after the visit of the Forbes Commission of Enquiry, appointed by President Hoover, free elections were held in 1930 for the assembly and the senate. The outcome was a whopping victory for the Nationalists, who had opposed the occupation from the beginning. After much political jobbing, Congress chose Stenio Vincent as president. A mouse-poor mulatto teacher and lawyer, Vincent wore something of a halo because of his spirited opposition to the Marines. His coming to power seemed the final triumph of nationalism. On August 21, 1934, the day the last Marine left Haiti, Vincent was able to hoist over the Dessalines barracks the Haitian flag—red and blue, formed from the French tricolor by symbolically suppressing the white.

The millennium painted by Vincent on that occasion did not materialize. A pall of economic depression lay upon the land. Before 1935 Haitian trade had been oriented primarily toward France. The Haitian-U.S. trade treaty of that year was more effective in bringing on French reprisals than in opening the U.S. market to Haitian products. Exports dropped to half their former value. At bottom, more than a cyclic phenomenon, this derived from the death agonies of Haiti's basic export crops, cacao and coffee. Vincent managed to obtain a $5,500,000 loan from the U.S. Export-Import Bank to finance road construction by a North American contractor. Little positive came from that expenditure.

Vincent and his circle proceeded to enrich themselves by those sordid little devices that bespeak the poverty of a land. In 1934 the concession of the U.S. power company in the capital was on the verge of expiry, and the company's physical properties were to revert to the government. Instead, the government renewed the concession for fifty years, and there was an unseemly spat in Congress about distribution of the power company's bribes. In 1935, when the senate objected to the monopoly given to the Standard Fruit Company for the export of bananas, Vincent removed eleven senators to force the concession through. His old nationalist comrades accused him of having sold out. Visas were sold to European refugees at handsome prices, but many of these unfortunates found that the time limit on their validity had run out before they could arrange transportation to Haiti.

Vincent's most brilliant kill was in connection with the reparations paid by the Dominican government for the massacre of Haitians in 1934, described in the foregoing chapter. Originally the reparations were set at $750,000, of which $250,000 was paid at once, and the balance was to follow in annual $100,000 installments. Trujillo, however, reached an agreement whereby the debt would be cancelled by a lump sum of $300,000 instead of $500,000. The difference was split between Trujillo and Vincent's clique. The reparations were to have been used to establish cooperative settlements of the thousands of Haitian refugees. But the funds were badly mismanaged; only one of these repatriate colonies, at Morne du Commissaire, still existed in 1945.

In 1935 the National Bank of the Republic of Haiti was bought back from the National City Bank of New York. But the key posts of the national bank remained in the hands of North Americans—the bank president was a former mason in the Panama Canal Zone, and the manager an ex-Marine. Other Latin American countries had benefitted from the excellent technical advisers sent from Washington; Haiti, pariah among nations, was given less consideration. While the Haitian central bank had $8,000,000 on deposit in New York, the government of Haiti was reduced to seeking five percent loans where it could find them.

Faced with mounting discontent, Vincent curtailed civil liberties. When the Dominican massacre took place, and the press tried voicing the indignation of the Haitian nation, it was gagged. Journalists were condemned to hard labor. Some of Vincent's former nationalist comrades languished in his prisons.

Vincent had everything prepared in 1941 to help himself to a third term, when Washington blighted his game. It gave him to understand that if he reelected himself, economic reprisals would be forthcoming. Moodily, Vincent withdrew in favor of the Haitian minister in Washington, Elie Lescot.

Lescot, a charming *bon vivant*, had started life with only the scrappiest elementary education. In his youth he was appointed consul in Cuba, and accumulated a minor fortune exploiting the Haitian immigrants working on Cuban sugar estates. With these savings he took off for Paris, where he went through them in record time. Then he opened a little bookshop and finally ran a tie factory. But his destiny clearly lay in Haiti, where it was possible for a man of this talents to get by on less work. Under the occupation he got himself a job as *juge d'instruction,* though he had had absolutely no legal training, and was

later named the government's representative before the Supreme
Court. In these posts he excelled at persecuting President Vincent's
former nationalist comrades.

In 1934 Lescot was sent to Ciudad Trujillo as minister, and became indebted to Trujillo for multiple favors. Trujillo presented him
with a beautiful gold and mother-of-pearl revolver, and a luxurious
car, and was ever ready to help him out of the financial difficulties
arising from his epicurean ways. The receptions at the Haitian legation took on such splendor that no one could quite figure out how
Lescot managed on his meager official allowance.

Finally Vincent grew suspicious of the intimacy that had developed between his gifted minister at Ciudad Trujillo and his formidable neighbor and shipped Lescot to Washington as minister. He
could not have made a worse blunder. For Lescot applied his flair for
sinuous intrigue in that broader decisive arena and ruined Vincent.
He convinced the State Department that Vincent was a vulgar crook.
People warned Vincent against Lescot, but the latter seemed to exercise an occult dominion over the president. Some Haitians insisted
that this was because he had in his possession a photostat of Trujillo's
check to Vincent in connection with the massacre reparations. In any
case, when Washington blocked Vincent's plans for a third term, he
had Lescot to thank for it. Washington used its influence to put Lescot, unpopular in Haiti because of his collaboration with the occupation, in the saddle.

Not that the going was altogether smooth. While in Washington,
Lescot had received $60,000 from his government for the purchase of
arms. No arms were bought, but Lescot raced through $35,000 of the
money living in the style to which he had become accustomed. There
came a day when the financial adviser to the Haitian government
found that $35,000 had not been accounted for, and raised a big row.
Lescot thereupon sent a tearful plea to Trujillo complaining that his
unscrupulous opponents were trying to ruin him, and could his old
friend advance him $35,000 to permit him to balance his accounts.
Trujillo sent the $35,000. The one sour note in this tale is that Lescot
never troubled to reimburse Trujillo. In 1945, when relations between
the two became unfriendly, Trujillo was mean enough to publish his
correspondence with Lescot on the matter.

Once ensconced in the presidency, Lescot applied himself to re-
couping his family's fortunes. His eldest son, Gérard, who had
flunked in the first year of his medical studies, became foreign
minister at the age of twenty-eight. A younger son, Henri, blossomed
forth as the business genius of the family. He acquired a monopoly of
the domestic trade in sisal and straw products, took over a factory of
essential oils, and entered into an intimate business association with

the Jamaican magnate Oswald Brandt. The expropriation of enemy alien property offered handsome opportunities to the Lescots. In 1944 the Standard Fruit Company, which had enjoyed a monopoly of banana exports for the entire country, was relieved of the banana trade in the southern peninsula. Half of this territory was turned over for monopolist banana exports to a firm headed by one of Gérard Lescot's brothers-in-law.

The Lescots became closely linked to the powerful Syrian colony, which monopolized the trade in textiles and other branches of commerce. Vincent had banned them from retail commerce; under Lescot they regained their full ascendancy. The elite had always snubbed them because of their humble immigrant origins, but now it became quite the thing for Syrian weddings to be celebrated in the presidential palace. That did not improve Lescot's standing with the elite. On the other hand, his appointment of mulattoes to all important posts, particularly those abroad, offended the blacks. Vincent had taken care to maintain a balance between job-holders of the two color groups.

U.S. economic assistance was forthcoming for Lescot. In 1941 the Société Haitienne-Americaine de Développement Agricole (SHADA) was formed with a $5,000,000 loan from the Export-Import Bank as capital, and given a monopoly of rubber cultivation and export. The conditions attached to this loan were certainly unique in the annals of business: though the Haitian government assumed responsibility for its repayment, the management of SHADA was vested in the Export-Import Bank. As general manager of SHADA, the Export-Import Bank named Thomas A. Fennell, a lowly employee of the U.S. Department of Agriculture whose main experience was as an orchid collector. The board consisted of four North Americans and three Haitians. So powerless were the Haitians that they were unable even to get a grammatical error in the French version of the contract corrected.

Fennell became the economic dictator of Haiti. Notions of grandeur went to his head, and he had an unerring way of dismissing the criticism of competent Haitian and North American agronomists: "Don't you know that there is a war on? There is no time for discussion." For $250,000 of Haiti's money he bought a sisal plantation that had previously been offered for $40,000 by its North American owner. He acquired the branch of the National Railway from Cap Haitien to Grande Rivière and proceeded to replace the food farms along it with sisal. Now sisal has the strange property of growing best on arid, chalky soil that will serve for no other crop. Devoting good lands to it results only in an inferior fiber and higher costs for weeding. Though rubber experts had declared Haiti unsuitable for hevea rubber, Fennell convinced Lescot otherwise. To make room for sisal and hevea, squatters were paid ten dollars for their huts and given forty-eight hours to get off their lands. Even their pleas to be allowed to harvest their standing crops went unheeded. Those peasants who could produce a title to their farms were paid five dollars rent per carreau (3.2 acres).

So much destruction served little practical purpose. By the end of the war SHADA had shipped only 3,681,269 of the 25,000,000 pounds of sisal it had contracted to deliver to the U.S. government. Hevea, as the experts had foreseen, likewise proved a disaster: in 1945 the superintendents' residences at Bayeux, built by SHADA at $35,000 or so apiece, overlooked abandoned plantations. Almost everything else that it set its hand to resulted in similar failures— lemon grass, citronella, luffa sponges. Only its lumbering operations showed a mild profit, out of all proportion to either its capital or its losses in sisal and rubber.

So much for SHADA's performance with the five million dollars lent Haiti by the Export-Import Bank. But to make the havoc still greater it became the agent of the U.S. Rubber Development Corporation for its cryptostegia program. Cryptostegia is a vine that grows wild in the parched Gonaives section of Haiti. When you break a branch of it, you obtain a sticky sap with a high latex content. The U.S. government decided to gamble on it as a source of rubber in a big way. Given the acute wartime rubber shortage, that in itself was justifiable; but unfortunately for its gambling, it chose less than competent croupiers in SHADA and as overpopulated a land as Haiti.

For cryptostegia alone, SHADA acquired some 107,000 acres of land—almost a twentieth of the country's entire arable area. Fennell in Port-au-Prince would mark on a map with a pencil the areas needed by SHADA, and President Lescot would invariably agree to declare them strategic zones. Then the peasants would be cleared off the land to make room for cryptostegia. For the coffee, bananas, and cacao that it ripped up, SHADA paid the peasants a compensation of $25 per carreau—ridiculously low since the three plants are perennials. Mangoes, guavas, cashews, bitter orange trees, were hacked down in quantity with no indemnity whatsoever. At least a million trees were felled, with serious consequences in soil erosion, especially on the mountainsides of the north. The nation looked on in horror. Attila westward-bound could not have had a worse press.

At its peak 92,000 workers were on SHADA's payroll—all but 18,000 for cryptostegia. Money flowed fast and inflated prices, for the thirty cents daily that SHADA paid its laborers was more cash than they had seen before. In United States publications the project was hailed as the salvation of Haiti, but Haiti's most cherished patrimony, its independent peasantry, was fast disappearing down the jaws of the foreign monster.

Occasionally, the reaction of the peasants to their dispossession was violent. Negotiations were under way for the increase of the Garde Nationale at SHADA's expense to prevent the peasants from defending their land against SHADA with their machetes.

That proved unnecessary, for cryptostegia collapsed. The maroca bug and the drought killed the plants. By the middle of 1944 SHADA was paying laborers throughout Haiti to tear up the cryptostegia and hand the devastated lands back to the peasants. The $6,773,000 spent on the cryptostegia—this time U.S. money—did not yield a single pound of rubber. Fennell resigned as general manager of SHADA and left Haiti to occupy a well-upholstered post in Puerto Rico. Haiti was left with five million dollars more of debt—almost 60 percent of its annual budget—and with its food production seriously diminished. Washington launched a modest food production program in the island, jointly financed by the two governments, to repair some of the damage. The elite sputtered with indignation and hoped that somehow the five million dollars wasted by the Export-Import Bank's appointees would not have to be repaid to the bank. Of all the strange goodwill projects in Latin America, SHADA was certainly the most productive of ill will.

Lescot's prestige was linked with SHADA, and suffered seriously from its debacle. Nevertheless, he persuaded Congress, which in Haiti elects the president, to vote him another seven years in power upon the expiry of his first term. At the same time Congress decided to extend its own life "until the signing of the last peace treaty," which apparently could not be negotiated without its assistance. To support such ill-timed ambitions, Lescot inevitably felt the need to batter down his opposition: newspapers were shut down, and refractory members of Congress unseated.

Though Lescot had reached the presidency with Trujillo's backing, the Generalisimo's venomous anti-Haitian campaign soon ruffled relations between the two regimes. Not even Roosevelt's personal intervention was able to move Lescot to lift his ban on Haitian labor going to the Dominican Republic to harvest the sugar cane. In Ciudad Trujillo the Generalisimo supported a group of the more discredited Haitian refugees, whose job it was to fill the ears of visiting journalists with the villainies of Lescot. Yet Lescot never dared reply openly to Trujillo's provocations: on superior orders the Haitian press avoided even a mention of the Generalisimo's name.

Trujillo was no man to confine himself to the written or spoken word. In November 1944 a plot for the assassination of Lescot was unearthed in Port-au-Prince in which Trujillo's trigger finger was very evident. A couple of journalists long resident in the neighboring republic were arrested and eventually executed. The U.S. embassy was asked to help check the arms found in possession of the conspirators, and the F.B.I. through their serial numbers identified them as lend-lease material that had been shipped to the Dominican Republic. Yet Trujillo went his sinister way, and published the correspondence with Lescot of an earlier period showing that the Haitian president had been in his pay.

What proved fatal to Lescot, however, were not the daggers and arsenic of his next-door neighbor, but the glacial stare of the State Department. Washington made no secret of its displeasure over Lescot's reelection. Perennial dictatorships had its blessing in Central America at the time, but its inscrutable will ruled them out in Haiti. When Lescot pleaded for a new loan to salvage SHADA, he found the State Department stone-deaf. Lescot in despair scoured the United States and even Canada for private bankers who would provide the desperately needed loan. Contact was at length established with a syndicate of U.S. financiers who for sundry favors offered Haiti a loan permitting her to repay the debt to the National City Bank of New York that served as the pretext for the continued U.S. control of her finances. Lescot could not have made a crasser blunder.

On January 3, 1946, Lescot suppressed the paper of the university students, *La Ruche*, which had been permitted to appear for a couple of months. On the seventh the students left their classes and paraded to the American embassy to cries of *"Vive la Liberté!" "A bas le marché noir!" "A bas la misère!"* Shops closed their doors as their employees left to join the students. The police charged the crowd and beat up some of the demonstrators. A student who was killed was accompanied to his grave by a huge throng the next day amidst curses and imprecations. Lescot roused himself from his lethargy and issued a statement: "There are no presidential holidays. The Garde has received orders to act opportunely."

But the Garde, apparently out of deference to the sentiments of the U.S. embassy, refused to fire on the demonstrators. The very government offices began disgorging rebellious employees who joined the clamor for the release of political prisoners, elections, and the lifting of the state of siege. And then came something that must have sounded like the crack of doom to Lescot—Haitian employees of the Standard Fruit Company and other large U.S. firms joined the strike en masse. Chastened, he dismissed his cabinet. But despite the chronic political unemployment that afflicts Haiti, he was unable to organize another one.

On January 11 a Military Executive Committee announced that it had taken over the government and arrested Lescot. A few days later Lescot and his family were dispatched into Canadian exile.

No sooner had word of Lescot's detention got around than the
mob broke into a fury of pillaging. The homes and places of business
of prominent Lescot associates were wrecked or literally dismantled
and carried away brick by brick. The Bata Shoe store was sacked, not
so much for political reasons as because the poor blacks needed shoes.
The student organizations sent speakers to plead with the populace to
cease its disorders. But the ugly depths of Haiti's misery had been
stirred up and could not easily be settled again.

Civilian parties, which had sprung up by the score overnight,
protested against the army's seizure of power and ordered the strike
to continue. On the fourteenth Col. Frank Lavaud, president of the
Military Executive Committee, summoned one of the civilian strike
leaders and, in a state bordering on hysteria, told him that three U.S.
warships had been sighted off the island of Gonave. Unless the strike
and looting stopped, he pleaded, the North Americans would surely
land troops, and the occupation would begin anew. The awful news
coursed through the city, and had a stunning effect. It mattered not
that the U.S. radio later in the evening denied that U.S. forces would
be disembarked. So vivid were memories of the occupation that the
strike was called off and the disorders stopped as though by magic.
Armed intervention in the affairs of Latin American republics had
been forsworn by the U.S. government for thirteen years at least. But
Haiti, perhaps because of its complexion, tended to be a case apart.

With the strike suspended, the Military Executive Committee
stayed on, first for a mere matter of days, and then, pretexting the
inability of the civilian parties to reach an agreement, until the elections.

The Military Executive Committee released all political prisoners, froze Lescot's property, dissolved parliament, and corrected some
of the more glaring abuses of the previous administration. Elections
for the new Congress, which was to draw up a new constitution and
elect a president, were set for May 12. Opportunity unfolded itself
rosy and enticing to all the underfed lawyers and intellectuals of the
elite. Nine hundred candidates presented themselves for the fifty-
eight congressional seats; in the first flush of hopefulness it became
the mode for dignified, wordy gentlemen to have calling cards
printed with the words "Candidat à la Presidence de la République"
beneath their names. The elections occurred with considerable cor-
rectness; only in a few districts, where dear friends of his were running, did the strong man of the Military Executive Committee, Major
Paul E. Magloire, intervene to ensure that no mishap would befall
their candidacies.

The elite, indeed, seemed at first to have remained firmly in the
saddle. Even coal-black Magloire was from an old family of black
generals and had controlled the arsenal of automatic arms under the

presidential palace for Lescot. In the distant days before the United States occupation, revolutions would severely rattle Haiti's social hierarchy and bring to the top illiterate black warriors. But by establishing a military academy, the North Americans had converted soldiering into a liberal profession, like all other professions accessible only to the elite.

The war and the SHADA scandal had fanned the nationalist fires amongst the elite. In drawing up the new constitution the assembly restricted foreign land holdings to one hundred hectares. In reality this affected U.S. interests only in a minor way, since the large banana and sugar interests rented and sharecropped most of their lands. Another clause, limiting retail commerce to second-generation Haitians, was aimed largely at the Syrians who monopolised the retail textile trade. Still another of the banned monopolies was directed against Standard Fruit, which was alone empowered to export bananas from the entire national territory minus the southern peninsula. Unused to regulation in lands like Haiti, U.S. businessmen were needlessly disturbed. U.S. Ambassador Orme Wilson, speaking also for the British and French (most of the so-called "Syrians" were British and French subjects), called the government's attention to his opinion that these clauses violated the San Francisco treaties. Such ambassadorial conduct might be deemed anachronistic elsewhere in these Good-Neighborly days. Ambassador Wilson's resignation was shortly afterward accepted by the State Department.

I revisited Haiti for the election of the president by the new Congress, and was able to witness the hazardous methods by which the elite maintained its supremacy over the impoverished and primitive black masses. The following was sent to *Time* from Port-au-Prince:

"While debating ways of applying salt to the tail of the American eagle, the elite was set upon from behind. To poor blacks anti-imperialism is a remote issue. Daily they rub up against the parasitic elite and concentrate their resentment against it. Inflation and wartime speculation have ground the people down into issueless despair and left them receptive to the advent of a messiah. He came in the person of Daniel Fignolé, a twenty-eight-year-old former mathematics teacher, a black son of peasants. Slight, bashful, with embers for eyes and a rare magnetic timbre to his voice, Fignolé preached a racist war of the blacks against the mulatto elite. The faubourgs of Port-au-Prince were soon ablaze. Too young himself to run for president, Fignolé advanced the candidacy of Demosthenes Petrus Calixte, a humdrum black soldier risen from the ranks and named first Haitian commander of the Garde Nationale by the Americans in 1934. Fignolé was reported promising the blacks the houses, cars, and mistresses of the elite as soon as Calixte came to power. Poor Negroes took to insulting mulatto women and boasted that they would bed them once Calixte was elected. Yet at bottom it is a social rather than a racial problem. There is a creole adage: *"Mulat pov ce neg"* (A poor mulatto is a nigger). Most of the seven-odd presidential candidates who have remained in the running are indeed upper-class blacks, closely identified with the elite.

"There is little in Calixte's past or present on which to hang the millennium. He entered the National Guard as a private and took part in the suppression of the black Caco rebellions against the American occupation. In December 1937 President Vincent suppressed a conspiracy in the National Guard headed by its commander Calixte, and sent him abroad as inspector-general of the nonexistent consulates of the Mediterranean. In this conspiracy Calixte had lost his nerve at the last moment, because his mistress, a voodoo priestess, warned him that the fates were not propitious; but for this he might have became dictator, following the patterns of the commanders of the American-created National Guards in the Dominican Republic and Nicaragua. Instead he repudiated the conspiracy and signed the death warrants of several of his comrades. No sooner did Calixte arrive in Europe than Vincent cancelled his post and had a military court condemn him to death in his absence. In 1940 he took up residence in Ciudad Trujillo, sharing a house with two Haitians positively known to be in Trujillo's pay. Though Calixte denies it, there is every evidence that Trujillo is financing his election campaign.

"Calixte is inarticulate and without any church-founding qualities. When I pressed him for his program for ending poverty as he promises, he mumbled vaguely about education. Calixte's propaganda emphasizes that he stands well with the Americans and would be able to get a loan 'for productive purposes instead of road-building.' Calixte and Fignolé avoid all nationalist demands. Though uneasy about the prospects of anarchy, most American businessmen openly gloat over the discomfiture of the elite nationalists. If Calixte reaches the presidency, they feel that he can be induced to drop Fignole and serve once again as a reliable ex-soldier of the occupation.

"On Tuesday afternoon, along with George Leavens, a photographer on assignment for the magazine *Holiday*, I interviewed Fignolé. He suggested that we take a ride with him to see the popular reaction. As our car approached, the sordid huts, as far as the eye could see, disgorged their inmates. Boys sprang into the air, performing very fair *entrechats*. Men, women, children, in various stages of undress, clapped their hands, pressed about the car, climbed onto it, beat voodoo rhythms on its fenders, pawed us thoroughly. Frenzied eyeballs protruded from black heads. One woman shook her naked breast at us with both hands. Others fell onto their backs and kicked their legs. Our eardrums ached with the mighty roar: *"Vive Fignolé! Vive Calixte! A bas la misère!"* The sweet bouquet of Negro sweat became overpowering. Strangely mistaken for pale-faced arbiters of ebony destinies, we were beseeched to make Calixte president. It was mass hysteria with prominent religious and sexual elements.

"The whole downtown district simmered and surged. Shutters were closed. The Guard was called out to contain the storm that we had let loose. An hour later, when we had escaped to our hotel on the hill, we could still hear the roar of the people from afar.

"Haiti is still in the myth-creating age, and we learned that *telediol* (creole for 'rumor'—from 'tele' as in 'telegraph' and the French *geule;* in Haiti *telediol* is reported to travel faster than telegraph) had it that Leavens, who wears an impressive beard, was the new U.S. ambassador, and I his aide, who were riding with Fignolé as a gesture of support.

"To reestablish our neutrality, we began making the rounds of the other candidates the next day. When we tried visiting Calixte's most powerful opponent, Dumarsais Estimé, our chauffeur refused to take us. He pleaded that the Fignolé people had threatened to beat him up if we went there. I phoned Estimé and cancelled our appointment.

"The elite assembly is a frail islet in this angry ocean. Alarmed by these developments, the deputies on Monday agreed to postpone discussion of the constitution and elect the president at once. Unintimidated by the armored cars with mounted machine guns that guarded it, the Calixte people demonstrated before the assembly. Three were wounded by gunfire. The elite is engaged in withdrawing its money from the banks and preparing to leave Haiti in a hurry if necessary.

"In the Congress Fignolé's movement was denounced as the shock troops of fascism. But windy elite politicians, who include some Marxists, have no contact with the poor blacks. The whole range of political ideas from the right to communism is reflected by the elite, which is after all the nation's head, but Haiti's twitching body has repudiated its dim head. As I type this on Thursday night, voodoo drums can be heard beating feverishly in the Lower Town, punctuated by rifle shots. By latest reports twenty-five have been wounded by the Guard and two killed. The blacks are celebrating because *telediol* has spread word that Leavens and I, the two miraculous Americans, have arrested Major Magloire, the strong man of the Military Executive Committee and arch-foe of Calixte. Calixte's press describes the country as 'like Bethlehem the night before Jesus was born.' It remains to be seen what gifts the wise men will bring Haiti tomorrow.

"P.S., Friday. Today the assembly elected Dumarsais Estimé, a coal-black but elite politician, as president. There is raging despair in the poor black quarters. Men, women, and children walk the streets tearing their hair and cursing Estimé and the elite at the top of their voices. Armored cars, army transports, bristling with machine guns, patrol the Lower Town. The blacks have broken all the downtown street lamps. There is fear that they may set the whole city on fire tonight."

Port-au-Prince was not set on fire, and Estimé turned out a far better president than his background gave reason to expect. He had served as agricultural minister under Vincent, and had been a servile deputy under Lescot. Now he grasped how dangerous was the gulf that had opened between the black masses and the elite, and valiantly set about bridging it. He encouraged labor unions, and appointed blacks to public positions in great numbers. Fignolé himself became his education minister. At the same time he strengthened his position with the elite by doing something to reassert the sovereignty of the country.

A mission was sent to Washington to try to secure cancellation of the government's responsibility for the $5,000,000 debt of SHADA, reduction of the interest on the $6,700,000 still owed the National City Bank of New York from 6 percent to 2½ percent, and a new loan from the Export-Import Bank. The mission returned empty-handed: its first two requests had been turned down, and a new loan had been offered only on condition that all technicians in charge of the public works to be financed by it must be North Americans. Indignant, the little country reared itself to respond with a heroic gesture. North American fiscal supervisors had remained in the Haiti Ministry of Finance ever since the occupation to ensure that due moneys would be assigned to service the debt to the National City Bank of New York. Now the cry was raised that the debt had to be paid before the North American fiscal agents would go. Congressmen contributed a fifth of their salaries; waiters, chauffeurs, businessmen dug deep into their pockets. Schoolchildren threw in their pennies. The government treasury was scraped bare to bring the popular contributions to the requisite $6,700,000. But the debt was paid then and there, and the North American fiscal officers departed. Out of the depth of her poverty, Haiti had found a means of salvaging her dignity.

13

Land of Bolívar

IT WAS NOT ALTOGETHER A COINCIDENCE that Venezuela should have become the cradle of South American independence. Toward the end of the colonial period there was no more forward-looking region in Spanish America. For almost a century after the Dutch established themselves in Curaçao in 1634, Venezuela's trade had been mostly contraband with that island; to plug this leak in its revenues, the Spanish Crown in 1728 bestowed the monopoly of trade with Venezuela upon the Compañía Real de Guipúzcoa in return for its undertaking to suppress the smuggling. The Compañía achieved this end as much by cheaper prices and adequate supplies of goods from Spain as by police methods. The evils of the Spanish colonial system were thus relaxed, and the Venezuelan economy flourished. Between 1724 and 1760 the cocoa crop more than doubled, and the Guipúzcoa company promoted cotton culture and the export of hides and introduced indigo. Coffee was planted in Caracas Valley in 1784, and by 1808 ten million pounds were exported annually—almost a half-century before coffee cultivation got under way in Central America. Venezuela, so unsoundly dependent upon a single export commodity by the 1940s, had a balanced, many-faceted economy in the eighteenth century.

The Guipúzcoa's frequent boats brought to Venezuela the heady ideas of the French Encyclopedists, and at times even their books. It meant much to the colony to be linked with the Basque land, which had intimate ties with Britain and France and boasted one of the most alert mercantile populations in the peninsula. The haughty *criollo* aristocrats became the standard-bearers of independence from moldering Spain; but their power was fated not to hold up long under independence achieved.

With the mounting prosperity, class and caste relations had attained great complexity and tension. In Mexico and Central America the importation of black slaves had been early abandoned, for while

212

their arms were brawny, their backs were unbending, and they taught the Indians the ways of rebellion. In Venezuela, however, because of the importance of cacao on the torrid coast, Negroes continued to be brought in until there were fully 64,000 black slaves at the end of the eighteenth century. Others had fled to the semiwilderness of the *llanos* (plains) in the interior and contributed their share to the tough seminomad *llanero* race. To the *llaneros* and the *pardos* (brown-skinned) in general the villain was not Spain, but the Venezuelan *criollos,* who dominated the colony economically and developed such fancy notions of their own worth that they actually refused to inter-marry with Spaniards. When the Spanish Crown, hard-pressed for cash, began peddling titles to the richer *pardos,* it was assailed by the *godos* (local Spaniards) for undermining the foundations of civiliza-tion.

Once the struggle for independence began, these latent conflicts came to the surface, and plunged the country into a century of civil wars. In the first round the *pardos* naturally aligned themselves with the Spaniards against the *criollo* revolutionaries. Hard-riding cowboy bands from the *llanos* spread devastation throughout the country. More than a conflict of colonials against Spaniards, it was cruel civil war amongst Venezuelans. The aristocratic first republic succumbed, trampled under the hooves of the *llaneros'* horses.

Simón Bolívar, blue-blooded revolutionary chieftain, found ref-uge in black Haiti. There he was furnished not only with arms and money for a fresh attempt but with the example of colonial domina-tion swept away by the flood of slave revolt. On returning to Venezuela, Bolívar promised freedom for the slaves, and brought about his own financial ruin by liberating those on his own estates. He likewise pledged the republic to divide the haciendas of Royalists amongst the *llaneros.* The tactic was successful: promptly the *llaneros* switched sides, and rallied to the Republican cause under the leader-ship of a tough, resourceful peon, José Paez. Under new slogans they continued their old depredation: someone remarked that when they cried *"Viva la Libertad,"* they really meant *"Que mueran las vacas"* (Death to the cows). By the time the Spaniards were vanquished, the coun-try's livestock and cacao crop had dropped to half their former figures. Yet, whatever the price, independence was won.

Had the *criollos* fulfilled their promises of freedom to the slaves and land to the *llaneros,* the country might have settled down to peace and recuperation. But the complete emancipation of slaves was not achieved until 1854. Instead of land, the *llaneros* were given land bonds, which Paez and other *llanero* leaders bought up at five and ten per cent of their face value. When the royalist lands were eventually distributed, it was these generals of the independence who emerged as the new landowning class. Paez became a pillar of law and order, the darling of the *godos* and their tool against Bolívar. The harsh dictatorship that he established, prototype of many to follow, served to keep the bilked plebeian masses in their place.

Before that, however, another expedient was tried. The turbulent *llaneros* were packed off to Ecuador, Peru, and Bolivia, both to crush the Spaniards in their last redoubts in South America, and to get them out of Venezuela, where they were a menace. Such was the mechanism by which a continent was liberated. The one serious drawback was that when the shooting was over, Venezuela received more than her due share of returning liberators. A few managed to enter the new feudal group; the less successful provided an unfailing reservoir of rebel *caudillos* that kept the country in turmoil.

Though order was periodically restored by some strong-fisted savior, civil strife broke out again and again. The programs varied, but at bottom it was the cheated *pardo* masses groping for lands, and used by unscrupulous leaders as a stirrup for stepping into the *hacendado* (big landowner) class. The repetition of this pattern suffused a cynicism throughout every stratum of society—the famous Latin *viveza* that outsiders find it easier to condemn than to understand. The peon who stole his master's chickens, the government official who enriched himself with bribes, were applying the moral code that they observed in their superiors. With its recurrent revolutions, its barbarous tyrants who aped Parisian manners and occasionally managed to marry their daughters into European aristocracy, the country that had produced Bolívar came to amuse foreigners as one of the classic Latin American *opéra bouffe* lands. But beneath these bizarre externals lay deep tragedy: Venezuela was haunted by the ghost of a strangled revolution.

The unceasing strife had certain lasting effects. During the years of marching armies, plunder, and rape, the racial ingredients of the country—black, Indian, and white—became mixed as never before. The long line of *llanero* dictators, beginning with Paez, thought of wealth almost exclusively in the form of cattle, as the Mongols had in their invasion of Europe. As a result, much of the best land near the capital was turned from grain crops to pasture, and food became progressively scarcer.

Order seemed to have been brought into this chaos by Juan Vicente Gómez, the barely literate cattleman, who closed his grip on the presidency in 1908 and relaxed it only with his death in 1935. Under Gómez the *llanero caudillos* of the southern pampas who had dominated the governments since the war of independence were finally displaced by the clannish mountaineers from alongside the Colombian frontier, the Andinos. With Gómez's innumerable relatives to the fore, Andinos moved into all posts of the government and army, and even the diplomatic corps. Rude Andino troops garrisoned the restive capital; Andinos served as turnkeys in the dungeons where malcontents were loaded with irons and left to lie in their own excrement.

Under Gómez, as under the *llanero* rulers before him, political thought was obsessed by cattle. The best cattle ranches were acquired by him, his friends, and relatives; competitors were taxed out of existence. All meat sold in the capital had to pass through his slaughterhouse at Maracay. There was a touch of the symbolic when his cousin, Eustoquio Gómez, hanged rebels with meathooks stuck through their throats. The country's military and political organization was in large degree based on cattle ranches: the owners were trustworthy Andino generals, the administrators colonels, the foremen captains, and the peons in a pinch made up the troops. And since cowboys had always provided the mobile forces and herds of cattle the commissary of the revolutions that periodically assaulted power, there was no dearth of logic to Gómez's system.

At Maracay, some sixty-five miles west of Caracas, Gómez set up his Versailles. He distrusted the capital and rarely visited it. In Maracay he received delegations of deputies and diplomats; it was there that he established his industries—textiles, vegetable oil, dairies—and his slaughterhouse. There he had brought to him the young girls who mothered his hundred-odd children. For at least a hundred miles in all directions the fertile lands of the district were owned by his trusted henchmen; a special escape road was built from Maracay to the port of Turiama to provide the dictator with a quick getaway if the need arose. Paved roads were spooled out to link the Gómez properties. Progress it was, but progress tailored to the dictator's private convenience.

Peace was fastened upon the country like manacles. And the whole was lubricated by the black torrents of oil that had begun gushing from Venezuela's subsoil. In 1922 a decade of exploration had given way to a riotously booming oil production. By 1930 Gómez had paid off the country's foreign debt, and the treasury was brimming with oil royalties. Gómez bought friends and foes alike with oil concessions for resale to the foreign companies. He was constantly digging into pockets and drawers for fistfuls of bills and oil stocks to reward people: the French doctor who drained his bladder, compliant diplomats, visiting celebrities, poets and authors who sang his praise. He had an unlimited faith in the power of money, and there was nothing in his experience to shatter it. The thirst of the great powers for oil led them not only to deck him out with decorations, but to lend him a hand in hounding his opponents abroad. The foreign oil interests enjoyed low royalties and taxes and every consideration in the Venezuelan courts, and they did what they could to maintain the tyranny. Venezuelans have an earthy saying that summed up the role of the great powers: "It was like eating up the orphan's soup and breaking the plate on his head."

The ease with which Gómez, excellently forewarned by his espionage, suppressed the revolts against his regime earned him the title "Wizard of the Andes." But the wizard grew old: a dictator with prostate trouble is an invitation to revolution. Oil, moreover, had created an industrial proletariat and given rise to a new middle class in the rapidly growing capital. These were social forces that in the long run were called upon to challenge the old rustic *caudillo* for whom politics was but a grand version of cattle-rustling.

The year 1928 was memorable. During their carnival festivities the students of Caracas held a meeting where a suggestive poem to liberty was recited and a plaque with the dictator's name was stoned. Thirty-odd students were arrested; the rest sent the dictator a telegram bidding him arrest them, too, since they were equally responsible for what had occurred. Two hundred of those who signed were imprisoned, and released a fortnight later to be received by the capital like heroes. On April 7 a military revolt was crushed, and once again a couple of hundred students were arrested. They spent six months building roads.

Shortly afterward, a handful of Venezuelan exiles captured the fortress on the Dutch island of Curaçao by surprise and armed themselves with rifles and cartridges from its arsenal. Taking the Dutch governor as hostage, they forced the captain of a U.S. ship lying in Wilhelmstadt harbor to carry them to Venezuela. They landed near Coro, but the cartridges from Curaçao turned out to be largely blanks stored by the Dutch for ceremonial purposes. The revolutionaries withdrew, leaving many dead.

Expeditions and plots, one more harebrained than the other, followed in rapid succession. Exiles in Europe under the leadership of Román Delgado Chalbaud fitted out the good ship *Falke* in Danzig, and crossing the ocean landed at Cumana. Their antiaircraft guns ordered in France had been confiscated at the French border, and they were without means of defending themselves against Gómez's aviation. They were cut to pieces. An expedition from Mexico suffered the same fate.

Gómez weathered these successive storms, but their increasing frequency heralded a new epoch. A new generation of young revolutionaries was undergoing its apprenticeship. Its mentor was Rómulo Gallegos, one of the greatest of Latin American novelists.

Gallegos was a biggish man, with thinning black hair and a sensitive, shy manner. When you questioned him about his life he started by telling you that there was really nothing of interest, but soon the words came in ripples and his close-set eyes lit up mischievously. It was the novelist getting into stride on a subject of rich possibilities. He was born of poor parents in Caracas in 1884. At school he had no money for books and he would borrow his comrades' texts for a quick workout before each class. Yet his companions remembered that it was impossible to take a stroll with Rómulo without being treated to a lecture on philosophy. For a while he attended an agricultural school where all the ploughing was done on the blackboard. Then he enrolled in the law course at the university, but that, too, remained unfinished. He had vague ambitions of becoming a singer, and dabbled with painting. He entered a seminary to study for the priesthood, but one morning on leaving church he lost his faith in a flash "by divine inspiration." To eat, he abandoned his formal studies altogether and worked as a typesetter. Then he got a job selling tickets in a railway station. With unusual modesty Gallegos insisted that it was inevitable that he should end up as a novelist: he had simply tried his hand and failed at everything else.

It seemed, however, that there was some natural inclination. At fourteen he had completed the first paragraph of the first chapter of a Russian novel, but got no further because he could never decide why his characters were so sad. In time he was finishing plays and short stories, and in 1921 published his first novel, *Reinaldo Solar*. On the strength of it he was appointed director of the Caracas Liceo, devoid of degrees though he was. There he taught his pupils mathematics, philosophy, and a lot of things not on the curriculum. A whole generation of youngsters was formed to his touch. It was former Gallegos students who were the ringleaders of the students in the 1928 revolts—the "generation of 1928" that was largely responsible for Venezuela's transformation. And while Gallegos presided over the classroom, his wife Teotiste ran a boarding house and played mother to the pupils from out of town. The Gallegoses had no children of their own, but never wanted for filial affection.

There was little room for human dignity in Gómez's Venezuela. Several thousand Venezuelans went into exile; the culture that they absorbed accounted largely for Caracas's surprisingly cosmopolitan air in the 1940s. Gallegos stayed at home and his bitterness over his country's lot was deeper and more personal. In the novels that flowed from his pen with greater assurance, he portrayed as no one else had done the despair of his country, its soul smudged with black gold and its moral fibre wasted. The effect of his books was all the greater because he rarely resorted to the sharp angles of propaganda. Venezuela beheld its likeness, and it was not flattering. People soon found that tagging the name of a Gallegos character to a local despot got more off their chests than a rosary of obscenities. Their shame had been made articulate, and that was the first step toward removing its cause.

To his boys in prison in 1928 Gallegos was able to send a new novel of his, *Doña Bárbara*. He had written on practically every region of Venezuela, but it was when he turned to the *llanos* in *Doña Bárbara* that he really found himself. Spanish South America had won its independence when seminomad cowboys spilled over the continent from its two immense lowland plains—the Argentinian pampas and the Venezuelan *llanos*. Since then the pampas had prospered mightily, but the tropical *llanos*, where the cattle drowned one half the year and died of thirst for the rest, had become Venezuela's Tobacco Road. They had lost the flower of their manhood, first to endless wars and more recently to the oilfields. Gallegos sang tenderly their moods of blind rebellion, their throbbing solitudes, the crunch of the tyrant's heel, the humiliation of avenging cattle-rustler turned peon, the apathy of their disease-sapped folk, their pixies and ghosts, the hard-bitten characters that sprang from a cursed soil. The book had so authentic a ring that many readers were convinced that Gallegos had begun life as a *llanero* cowboy. Actually, he had visited the *llanos* but once for a single week, and found it very difficult to stay on a horse.

Someone told Gómez that *Doña Bárbara* was an attack upon his regime, and he had his secretary read it to him. So delighted was the cattle-happy dictator with the cowboy setting that he decided to name Gallegos senator. Gallegos declined. Enraged, Gómez thundered: "That man will go to the senate or to jail." Instead, Gallegos slipped out of the country and stayed away until the senate had been installed. The following five years Gallegos spent abroad, mostly in Spain. For a while he lived on the trickle of royalties from *Doña Bárbara*, and a couple of his former students who shared his exile twitted him about living off a woman, to wit, *Doña Bárbara*. There came a day when the iron entered his soul and he declared that he would be a kept man no longer. He got a job instructing salesmen for the National Cash Register Company. Few mechanical cash boxes were sold that year, but Gallegos eked out a living on his performance till Hollywood came to his rescue and purchased the film rights to his novel *Cantaclaro*.

On December 19, 1935, Gómez died at Maracay. For the people it was release from a grim epoch that stretched as far back as most adult memories. No sooner had the news reached the capital than crowds surged onto the Plaza Bolívar and were fired upon by the troops. The houses of prominent Gomecistas were sacked; La Rotunda penitentiary was assaulted and its political prisoners released. Gómez had neglected to designate a successor, and his presumptive heirs were

given little peace in which to dispute his throne. His relative Eustoquio Gómez arrived at the Palacio de Gobernación to claim the presidency, but was arrested and killed. Outside, the mob burned the cars
that his party had arrived in, and were not satisfied that he was dead
until his clothes and shoes were thrown to them from the balcony.
With the popular furies thus appeased for the moment, the
Gomecista Congress was able to meet and choose Eleazar López Contreras, the dictator's gangling and verbose war minister, as president.
But the cavalry was kept busy charging the crowds that thronged the
squares throughout the city. Improvised opposition organizations
sprang up, and Bolívar's statue became a tribunal for popular orators,
who called for the liquidation of Gomecismo and the election of a
constituent assembly to reorganize the country's political structure
from the roots up. López suspended constitutional guarantees, never
very effective, and clamped censorship onto the press; oppositionists
began peopling La Rotunda once more.

But the nation which had matured through suffering during the
long years of dictatorship was no longer to be contained in the old
straitjacket. On February 14 a general strike was declared by the new
unions. Though the troops fired on the public, López was finally
compelled to dismiss his minister of the interior. He promised a
parade of 60,000 people who marched in somber discipline that he
would restore constitutional guarantees and gradually eliminate the
Gomecistas from power.

To lend plausibility to his regime López cabled Gallegos in Spain
to return to investigate the educational system, and shortly afterward
named him education minister. In June 1936, however, when leftists
and the trade unions declared a general strike demanding reform of
the constitution along democratic lines, the government suppressed
them. He did throw a sop to the left by confiscating Gómez's properties, but his Congress amended the constitution after its own tastes:
"Communists and anarchists" were declared traitors to the fatherland, and the president was empowered to expel them from
Venezuela. The clause was intended against all popular movements,
and Gallegos resigned from the cabinet in protest.

The people were showing no respect for the holiest of holies: in
December 1936 the oil fields were shut down by a strike that lasted for
six weeks and won the workers substantial wage increases. Shortly
afterward came López's riposte: all parties were dissolved and forty-
six leftist leaders, both Communist and non-Communist, were ordered expelled from the country. Throughout López's regime no
political parties existed. Ephemeral electoral groups (behind some of
which loomed the leftist parties, as visible as the full harvest moon)
were tolerated. In 1937 and again in 1939, for example, the joint

leftist slate won nineteen of the twenty-two seats on the Caracas council.

Presidential elections remained an elaborate conspiracy for cheating the popular will. Municipal councils and state assemblies were elected by popular vote and these in turn elected the national Congress. The president of the Republic was chosen by the Congress. The government employed a rather unsubtle technique for keeping the carefully screened national congressmen in line. Deputies and senators were given lucrative administrative jobs to ensure their allegiance. The foresight of the constitution in banning such a practice was gracefully sidestepped by having the legislators resign their other jobs while Congress was in session.

With such a setup it caused no great surprise when López, in 1941, managed to elect his man Isaias Medina Angarita to succeed him in the presidency against Rómulo Gallegos. For a while López had toyed with the idea of remaining in power for another term, but he seemed to run little risk with Medina there. When Colombian President Eduardo Santos asked López whether he felt confident in handing the post over to Medina, López replied: "He used to pack my bags for me in the barracks." About the only thing that there was to commend Medina, a pudgy, hearty colonel who loved his bottle, was that he had not grown rich while serving as López's war minister. That, indeed, was no small distinction, but he soon set about making up for lost time.

Under Medina parties became legal, and the left soon split into two well-defined camps, the Communist Unión Popular Venezolana and the non-Communist Acción Democrática. Throughout Latin America the Communists had acquired a new flexibility of principles, and the most corrupt and antidemocratic politicians were finding an alliance with the Communists some sort of protection against popular wrath. What happened in Cuba, Costa Rica, Nicaragua, Peru, and the Dominican Republic was paralleled in Venezuela, where the Communists presented joint slates with Medina's Partido Democrático Venezolano. Medina did undertake a patchy program of social reform to go with this new friendship. The labor code was revised to provide the distribution of ten percent of all companies' earnings among their workers. Agrarian reform came in for considerable discussion. In their new role as social reformers the old Gomecista bureaucrats were about as ungainly as circus elephants dancing a minuet.

Elsewhere the alliance of Communists with corrupt politicians opened up brilliant strategic opportunities for the extreme right, which lumped together the official profiteering and its attempts at social betterment and mobilized a considerable sector of public opinion against both. The Venezuelan conservatives, particularly those traditionally associated with foreign oil interests and grouped around the Caracas newspaper *La Esfera,* tried doing the same. But the existence of an independent left in Venezuela, Acción Democrática, spoiled their game.

The outstanding leader of Acción Democrática was a former pupil of Gallegos, Rómulo Betancourt. Of humble origin, Betancourt belonged to the "generation of 1928" and like many of its members underwent a schooling of hardship and indoctrination comparable in its intensity and consistency only to that of the old Russian socialists. Still in his teens, he worked on roads in a convict's uniform. When the *Falke* expedition took place in 1929, he set out in a little nutshell of a boat from Puerto Rico to join it at Cumana but arrived after it had been defeated. There followed long years of exile in several Latin American countries, unceasing study, and the harrowing struggle to earn a living. In Barranquilla he ran a fruit store with other refugees. Like many of Gallego's pupils he passed through a brief Communist period, and was one of the organizers of the Communist party of Costa Rica. He abandoned communism while still in his early twenties, but carried away from that experience an organizational skill that few democratic politicians ever possess. It was to enable him to outorganize the Venezuelan Communists in the trade unions and on the political field. On abandoning communism he came under the influence of the Peruvian APRA, with many of whose leaders he formed an intimate friendship in Chile. He adopted their view that European socialist ideas could not be mechanically implanted in Latin America, and that instead of a working-class party, a party of workers, peasants, and progressive businessmen was required to uproot feudalism and combat imperialism. The mystic trappings of APRA, however, he left aside.

After Gómez's death Betancourt returned to Venezuela. From 1936 when the López government ordered him expelled, he spent three years in hiding in Caracas. These were active years, with the police ever on his track and no lack of dramatic episodes. On one occasion he had been summoned to the hospital where his little girl was gravely ill, and the police seized the opportunity to try to arrest him. Betancourt, quick-witted and lithe as a cat, shot it out with them and made his escape. But the same man, slight, *simpatiquísimo,* was a profound student of economic problems. The collection of his journalistic articles on economic themes, entirely devoid of the empty rhetoric that is the curse of so many Latin politicians, constitutes one of the best sources on the subject.

The ten year interregnum between the death of Gómez and the final liquidation of his heritage permitted Acción Democrática to lay by a rich store of political experience and perfect a farflung well-weathered organization. It matured into the most competent independent leftist party in Latin America. When the moment came for it to assume power, there was nothing improvised or amateurish about it.

Venezuela's oil made it one of Latin America's most strategically important countries for the United States. It might have followed that Washington would have viewed with gratitude the existence of a non-Communist party of the left, able to defeat the Communists at their own game and with no other axe to grind than the betterment of conditions for the Venezuelan masses and the defense of national interests against the old abuses of the oil companies. Yet on the very eve of the 1945 revolution the U.S. embassy in Caracas, reflecting the views of the least enlightened oil people, regarded Acción Democrática as a dangerously red organization, and shunned all contact with it. Undoubtedly there were U.S. State Department officials who would take a dim view of Santa Claus coming down their chimney because of the color of his coat.

The pressure of Acción Democrática on its left served to push Medina into some brave progressive steps. Foremost amongst these was his oil law of 1943.

The greatest oil boom in Latin American history had enveloped Venezuela. Production, which had been confined to the Lake Maracaibo region during the twenties, now spread over the land. The accents of Oklahoma and Texas were heard in the east and throughout the *llanos* as exploration parties opened new wells in the wilderness; pipelines were built from the interior to the sea, and there was scarcely a region of the country that did not bristle with derricks. By the end of 1945 a million barrels were gushing forth from the subsoil each day, and production was still in rapid ascent.

Under Gómez, operations in Venezuela had been much the same uncomplicated pastime for the foreign oil companies as growing bananas in Honduras for the United Fruit Company. At most there were the dictator and his friends to pay off. On one of the chief concessions the royalties were as low as five percent of the product, and the 1922 petroleum law fixed them at ten percent for future concessions. Medina's 1943 law provided for a minimum 16⅔ percent royalty, and made provision for competitive bidding amongst the companies which in the case of one concession (Phillips) had permitted the government to drive the royalty up to 33⅓ percent. In other instances the companies agreed to build roads and undertake other public works as "special advantages" for Venezuela. The companies' exemption from import duties on materials and equipment brought into the country was done away with altogether.

But that was not the most important part of the story. Previous oil laws had applied only to future concessions. In 1943 the Medina government accomplished a brilliant bit of bargaining that could bear serious study by other Latin American republics. Many of the old concessions, resplendent with low royalties though they were, had been acquired in dubious ways. In some instances the companies had for years exploited areas far larger than those to which they had legal claim. The law courts were clogged with government suits against oil companies for tax evasion and other irregularities. Once the 1943 oil law was adopted, the government proposed to the companies that they surrender their old concessions on the understanding that they would be granted new concessions under the terms of the 1943 law for exactly the same areas and in turn agreed to drop all suits against them for past irregularities. The companies had the good sense to snap up the offer. The head of Standard of New Jersey's Venezuelan company, Creole, resigned his post rather than have any part in this arrangement. But the responsible heads of the oil industry realized that a new era had dawned and that they were operating in a land determined to assert its sovereignty.

What helped them arrive at this realization was the Mexican oil expropriation of 1938. Venezuela had had a baleful effect on Mexico's oil tangle: the stubborn attitude of the oil companies in their negotiations with the Mexican state had been due largely to their determination not to set a precedent that might be followed in Venezuela, where the holdings of the U.S. companies were far more important than in Mexico. But Mexico's expropriation, no matter how questionable its results for her own oil industry, was a blessing for Venezuela and many another Latin American land. Cárdenas's nationalization of the oil fields had taught the companies a painful lesson, and throughout their discussions with the Caracas government they were the very soul of tact. Thus no bones were broken, and by the 1940s even though paying swollen royalties they still managed to show brilliant earnings.

In labor policy, housing, and educational facilities the oil companies were equally ready to heed the urgings of trade unions and the government, until Venezuelan oil fields began taking on an entirely novel aspect. Instead of bedraggled peons housed in shacks, there were self-respecting citizens.

Under Gómez, Shell had established its refineries for the processing of Venezuelan oil on Curaçao, and Standard on Aruba. They chose the adjacent Dutch islands primarily because they feared exposing such considerable capital investments to the unrest that they foresaw after Gómez's fall. The 1943 oil law required a minimum of 10 percent of the oil to be refined within the country, and the companies began constructing refineries there.

The dickcissel is a black-throated finch with strange habits. In the autumn the bird leaves the Midwestern United States and migrates to Peru and Bolivia, in flocks of thousands upon thousands. By the time they reach Venezuela they have put an edge on their appetite, and they descend en masse on the rice fields of Yaracuy, Carabobo, and Zulia and do a dreadful amount of damage. On the other hand, when they return north and come to the Mississippi Valley, they scatter for mating, and needing a lot of fat for reproducing, they concentrate on worms and harmful grubs. The dickcissel is thus a blight to Venezuela and a boon to the United States. Because of that, evil-tongued Venezuelans used to compare the oil companies to the dickcissel. But after the 1943 oil law there were many Venezuelans who were convinced that with a little effort the dickcissels themselves could be taught better table manners.

As the dark torrent of oil poured out, the dollars poured in. Government oil revenues shot up from 56,068,000 bolivars in 1935 to 242,355,266 in 1944, and continued mounting at an ever dizzier pace. The state coffers bulged; Venezuela's foreign debt had been paid off entirely in 1930. The bolivar jumped from 7.75 to the dollar in 1932 to 3.35 a couple of years later. Medina's 400,000,000-bolivar public works program helped transform Caracas into one of the most gorgeously deceptive window displays in the hemisphere. Where the red light district once stood, a magnificent housing project, El Silencio, was erected, comprising 1,100 apartments. A 60,000,000-bolivar university city was begun. Speculators and middlemen became millionaires overnight, almost as a matter of routine, and elegant residential suburbs came into existence by the acre to accommodate them. Yet, barring the capital, the rich torrent of oil flowed past Venezuela, and contributed little to it other than erosion: 57 percent of the population remained illiterate; 34 percent of the school-age children had no schools to attend; 60 percent of the nation was housed in dirt-floored huts of straw; only 28 percent of Venezuelan homes had running water.

Chronically starved for dollars, other Latin American countries might find it hard to understand why Venezuelans shuddered when their thoughts turned to the future of their republic.

While Caracas bloomed for the benefit of visitors, agriculture languished and decayed. Not only had the oil fields syphoned off laborers from the farms, but the government itself was a serious culprit and used its increased revenues to increase the federal bureaucracy from 7,000 to 35,000 in the single decade before 1945. The flood of oil dollars engulfed the land, and even before the war Venezuelan inflation became a byword throughout the hemisphere. In 1939 the Caracas price of wheat flour was 268 percent that of the U.S. price, of lard 447 percent, of soap 620 percent, of butter 324 percent. This fantastically inflated price level choked off exports: excluding petroleum, Venezuela's exports between 1913 and 1939 fell from 149,800,000 bolivars to 58,000,000. Though the majority of the population was still on the land, 40 percent of the country's food supply had to be brought in from abroad. Venezuelans were haunted by visions of having nothing but holes in the ground left to them, when their oil wealth would eventually become exhausted. It was a Midas-like quandary, and for a decade there had been anxious talk of "sowing our oil," of translating the ephemeral oil riches into expanded productive capacity that would save the country from beggary when the oil gave out.

A subsidy was introduced for agricultural exports in the form of special exchange rates. While the general public received 3.35 bolivars for its dollars, and the oil companies a mere 3.09, coffee and cacao exporters were given 3.75 for theirs. But that was at best a pitiful crutch that could prop up the country's wasted agriculture, but restore little life to it.

Since there was no lack of money on hand, foreign experts were brought in to study the source of the evil and make recommendations. Venezuela achieved the distinction of being the country with the greatest number of foreign experts' reports per capita of population: there were reports on the tariff, on the cattle industry, on soil erosion. But nothing very much was ever done toward putting the experts' recommendations into practice.

Little was done toward reducing the fabulously high customs tariff, which was a key factor in the high cost of living. The exaggerated duties dated from a distant period before the oil boom, when a bankrupt government was sorely in need of income; that it should have been retained when petroleum had filled the state treasury to overflowing was one of the paradoxes of Gómez's Venezuela. To keep the formidable Andino peasants happy a 252 percent tariff was imposed on wheat flour, though wheat cultivation was rapidly bringing on the disastrous erosion of the Andean countryside.

Soaring food prices in Caracas had no effect in stimulating greater production in the countryside. Part of the reason was wretched communications. While Medina spent hundreds of millions to build marble halls in Caracas, road construction was sadly neglected. Apart from a few roads built by Gómez to link his properties, and a few constructed by the oil companies, Venezuela still stuck to the old maxim that "the best road engineers are the sun and the mules' hooves."

Everything that Medina constructed betrayed a folly of grandeur. Tourists in Caracas gasped over the new, elegant university and luxurious secondary schools, but in the provinces children often had to go to school with soapboxes on their heads so that they would have something to sit on. The provinces were woefully short of hospitals, but when Medina finally got around to building one at Barquisimeto, it was five times bigger than the region required.

Feckless toward the country's pressing problems, Medina and his clique were alert to grasp every opening for private enrichment. Toward the end of his regime, Medina's antechamber was so cluttered with people come to see him on private business—usually contractors or traders in black-market or rationed products—that anyone who came merely on an official matter found it difficult to get an appointment.

Medina's alliance with the Communists and his dabbling with social reform had put the propertied classes in an ugly mood. As his term drew to a close, the conservative forces undertook a feverish campaign to bring back López Contreras to "save the country from communism." López, who had always rather fancied himself as the man of providence, was convinced that he heard the call of destiny. He could flatter himself on unusually cordial relations with the oil companies, native business circles, and the U.S. embassy. A rift had developed between Medina and López. Medina had become enamored with the comforts of office and was reluctant to surrender them to his former protector. Because of its Gomecista implications, the left, both Acción Democrática and the Communists, were alarmed by the López boom. For a while they reached an agreement with Medina to support jointly the candidacy of Diógenes Escalante, the Venezuelan ambassador in Washington.

But Medina, pretexting Escalante's ill health, discarded the plan. On behalf of Acción Democrática, Rómulo Gallegos visited Medina and, as a way out of the crisis that loomed before the country, proposed a "national candidate" agreeable to all parties who would be elected to office only provisionally for one year, to permit constitutional reform allowing direct presidential elections. Direct presidential elections had been the goal of the democratic forces since Gómez's death, and Medina promised to reply to Acción Democrática within four days. But he did not bother replying. Instead, he launched the candidacy of his agriculture minister, Angel Biaggini, an Andino wheel horse who was such a preposterous nonentity that it became clear that Medina intended to continue running the show from behind the scenes. Two of the three groups into which the Venezuelan Communists were split at once proclaimed their backing of Biaggini.

Biaggini's candidacy widened the breach between López and Medina, and the atmosphere began reeking of gunpowder. In accepting the nomination of a rightist convention, López minced no words: "I keep my campaign uniform hung in a preferred place at home, and not as a historical relic, but as a symbol of the physical force at the service of the fatherland." The rightist press had ridiculed as a "pacifist coup" Acción Democrática's formula of a "national candidate" to reform the constitution. Clearly their hero López had no such pacifist intentions. But he omitted to reckon with the profound evolution the country had undergone since the days of his master Gómez.

In the course of this book we have had abundant proof of the pernicious effects of Washington's military program in Latin America. Yet no wind is so ill but that it blows some good. Many younger Venezuelan army officers, who had been sent to the United States, Mexico, and Colombia for training, had absorbed democratic ideas along with their technical knowledge. Though in their overwhelming majority Andinos, these academy graduates resented the old rustic generals—*chopos de piedra* (flintlocks) is the Venezuelan expression—who continued running the army in spite of their total ignorance of modern military science. Medina had stored the entire U.S. lend-lease armament, with the exception of the coastal batteries, in Maracay under lock and key. For he distrusted the young technically trained officers, and the *chopos de piedra* had not the vaguest idea of how to use these outlandish modern weapons. It was only in May 1945, when a U.S. military mission arrived in Venezuela to enquire into what happened to the lend-lease armament, that Medina hastily organized an armored regiment.

In June, when Medina promoted two illiterate colonels to the rank of general, serious plotting began amongst the younger officers. They had been outraged in their professional pride as soldiers, and as citizens they resented Medina's crude efforts to perpetuate himself in power. The original committee of seventeen was headed by Major Carlos Delgado Chalbaud and Captain Mario Vargas, and it early contacted Acción Democrática. When Acción Democrática's proposal of a national candidate and constitutional reform was spurned by Medina, the date for the revolution was set for November 11. But the oath sworn by the military conspirators obliged them to strike immediately if there was evidence of the plot having been denounced.

On the night of October 17 Rómulo Betancourt warned a mass meeting in Caracas: "The regime has split into two sectors headed by generals, and Venezuelan history proves that generals do not settle their disputes by civilized means, by written or spoken words. It had been our purpose to promote a pacific solution to a situation that can lead to violent civil war." Betancourt at the time was unaware that the plot had been denounced to the government that very night.

The following morning officers came to the military school to arrest Delgado Chalbaud, the chief of studies there, but the cadets prevented that. True to their oath, Delgado and his comrades at once proclaimed the revolution. They communicated by telephone with their friends in Maracay and the various barracks of Caracas. Major Miguel Nucete Paoli with seven other officers took the gaudy presidential palace of Miraflores in Medina's absence without a fight, and immediately shut the doors. Medina arrived in an alcoholic stupor and was refused entry. He went off to the police barracks, where he could count on a loyal force of fourteen hundred men, and from there proceeded to Ambrosio Plaza fortress below the military school, from where he directed the resistence. López Contreras presented himself at Miraflores to offer his services to the regime. Under Gómez, he had once quelled an army revolt by his mere imposing presence. This time he was allowed into the palace and arrested. Incredulous, he tried browbeating the young lieutenant who led him away as a *niño*, scoffing at the entire revolution as a "boy's escapade." It did not occur to the old fossil that the youth had inherited Venezuela.

Throughout the following night the police attacked the military school in force with rifles and machine guns. But they overlooked cutting its telephone connections, and from the inside Delgado Chalbaud and Vargas were able to direct revolutionary operations throughout the country. In Maracay the newly organized tank unit quelled government resistance and captured the airfield. The air force was with the revolution almost to a man. San Carlos fortress at the entrance of Lake Maracaibo declared for the revolution. The military school began bombarding Ambrosio Plaza with mortars. By the morning of the nineteenth revolutionary planes from Maracay were dropping ten-kilo bombs on the government barracks and threatening to follow up with fifty-kilo bombs. The government troops fled in panic from San Carlos fortress, and the mob rushed in and armed itself. When the aviation began its attack on Ambrosio Plaza, Medina surrendered. There were antiaircraft guns in the barracks, but neither Medina nor his officers had the remotest idea how to use them.

Because the revolution had broken out in so impromptu a fashion, Acción Democrática was in doubt during the first few hours of the fighting whether the revolt was headed by López Contreras or by its own army friends. Once they found out the facts, they went on the air and broadcast continuous appeals to the civilians. Men, women, and children besieged the revolutionary barracks for arms—and were given them. Six hundred of the fifteen hundred students who offered themselves obtained revolvers and rifles captured from the police. They gathered in the arms seized by the irresponsible mob that had meanwhile gone about looting houses of well-known Gomecistas; they brought food for the soldiers. Schoolchildren directed traffic, while the police were confined to their barracks.

The Communists had broadcast from the police radio denouncing the revolution as fascist and "Peronista." They were amongst the last to lay down their arms in defense of the Medina regime.

By the night of the nineteenth the fighting was over. Tanks from Maracay rumbled through the streets. Workers and soldiers could be seen arm in arm, jubilant over their victory. The streets were crowded with happy people; civilians and soldiers shared their pride over a task well done. Ten years before old Gómez had died; now he had finally been buried. "The stone age," one of the young revolutionary officers remarked to me, "is over at last."

On the night of the nineteenth a revolutionary junta headed by Rómulo Betanourt was formed, consisting of five civilians and two military men. It was a rare type of army officer that had made the revolution. They had no other political ambition than to implant a civilian democracy that would set their country abreast of the century. The new state governors named by the junta were in their entirety civilians. Venezuela had served a hard ten years of apprenticeship in the ways of democracy: but it was not necessary, as in Guatemala, where the ferocious Ubico dictatorship had blacked out all political life for fourteen years, to improvise everything on the morrow of the revolution. But as competent a force as Acción Democrática was, the prospects of a democratic revolution would have been highly problematical in the age of lend-lease armament, were it not for the democrats in military uniform. In their majority the young revolutionary officers, like Captain Mario Vargas, "the soul of the revolution," were Andinos: for it had been practically impossible for non-Andinos to obtain entrance into the military school. But the new ideals had made inroads into the privileged Andino states. "Now we Andinos will cease being a hated caste in Venezuela," one of these Andino officers remarked to me. "We made the revolution to restore to Caracas its constitutional role as capital of the republic."

Major Carlos Delgado Chalbaud, the defense minister in the junta, was the son of Román Delgado, who, after spending fourteen years in Gómez's dungeons, had organized the ill-fated *Falke* expedition in Gdynia and brought it to Venezuela. Carlos, a mere lad of nineteen, had gone along. When his father landed with the first party and was killed by Gómez's air force, he had tried putting the armament ashore elsewhere for a new attempt. But his German sailors mutinied and brought the ship back to Europe. During his years in France he studied at Saint-Cyr.

The junta lost no time in getting down to business. The auditing of the accounts of the previous regimes was undertaken, and the property of over one hundred functionaries frozen pending the results of that operation. Publication of the secret articles seven and twenty of the budget revealed a shameful list of journalists, generals, deputies, Communists, and plain "honest intellectuals" who had been in Medina's pay. With some malice aforethought López and Medina were confined in the same room. And as though that were not enough, Caracas wits attributed to the junta an even further finesse of torture: Medina was supposed to have been given an empty whiskey bottle for solace, and the grandiloquent López a dead microphone. The intention of the junta was to hold them until they had accounted to the tribunal for their prosperity, but considerable unofficial pressure was brought to bear by the U.S. embassy, particularly on behalf of López. On November 29 Medina, López, and fourteen other former high officials were placed on a Miami-bound plane.

When the tribunal concluded its investigations months later, López was ordered to pay back to the treasury 13,352,876 bolivars, and his property in Venezuela worth Bs. 863,000 was confiscated. Medina's Bs. 2,725,335 of property was likewise confiscated, and he was declared in debt to the government for an additional 11,879,566 bolivars—for illegal remittances made to him by the treasury via third persons and other such items. When in power he had taken special pride not only in the seven magnificent blocks of the El Silencio housing project, but in his own new mansion, which the public, guessing that the materials had come from the El Silencio construction, at once nicknamed Block 8. After the revolution the auditors' researches confirmed the suspicion.

Lesser figures in the previous regimes were sentenced to make similar restitutions. It was neither a play for the gallery nor sadism toward the vanquished on the junta's part. By establishing such precedents—which could naturally be used against them if they ever gave the slightest occasion for it—the members of the junta showed a grim determination to restore morality in public affairs. The president's salary and expenses were reduced from 10,250 bolivars monthly to 4,000, and all public officials were required to declare their property on assuming and leaving office.

Boldly, the revolutionary government attacked the country's root problems that its predecessors had sidestepped. To alleviate the transportation situation, it removed most of the tax on gasoline and persuaded the companies to cut the retail price in Caracas by half; air transport rates were reduced thirty percent. The import duty on wheat flour was scaled down. Bs. 50,000,000 were allotted to the Banco Obrero to build four thousand workers' houses—only one thousand of which were to be in the capital—for sale on easy terms; special credit facilities were extended by the Banco Obero for middle-class homes. The simplification of customs red tape—a serious factor in the high cost of living—was undertaken, and work was begun on a new customs law. A beginning was made on parceling out the huge Gómez estates among small peasants, with credit facilities extended for their exploitation. Ceilings were imposed on rents for new buildings, and on interest rates.

Under Gómez, López, and Medina, the swollen oil revenues had served for little more than to pay off the debt, multiply the government bureaucracy, and accumulate a treasury surplus, of which the rulers boasted as the last proof of statesmanship. Apart from a few display pieces in Caracas, the government had followed a routinist policy. In two years the revolutionary government almost tripled the national budget to the undreamt-of figure of Bs. 1,290,000,000. A surplus income tax introduced *retroactively* at the end of 1945 brought an additional 57,000,000 from the largest oil company, Creole Petroleum. State revenues from oil were raised to something approximating the companies' net profits—the original idea when the 1943 oil law was being planned. And these huge amounts of dollars were neither hoarded nor allowed to lie about sluggishly and inflate prices. They were actively thrown into the breach to open up new productive sources.

The Corporación Venezolana de Fomento was created with a capital of 200,000,000 bolivars to lend money to private enterprises or to take a direct hand in creating new industries of an urgently needed character. Credits went to increase sugar, beans, milk, and livestock production. Electrification of the countryside was undertaken to make life on the farms more attractive and reduce the exodus to the towns. The paving of 482 kilometers of roads was begun and others were completed. The country's chief ports were modernized and new ones constructed. Bs. 9,000,000 were earmarked for irrigation in 1946–47 as compared with 4,000,000 spent for the purpose during the previous decade. At Cenizo in Trujillo state 4,000 peasants were settled on 40,000 virgin hectares. A new water system was put in for Caracas, enough to take care of the capital's growing needs until the year 2000. Bs. 10,000,000 annually were invested in a DDT campaign destined to eliminate malaria from the country.

"Children's kitchens" were increased to provide meals for 22,000 children where 1,500 had been served before. Food was obtained by shrewd barter with Argentina and other countries of petroleum received by the Venezuelan government as royalties in kind; it was sold at a loss to help the struggle against inflation. Free markets were built to eliminate profiteering middlemen and establish a direct link between producer and consumer. The number of primary schoolchildren jumped from 280,000 to 400,000 and the teaching personnel increased by 50 percent in two years. More money was spent in the same period on school materials than during the previous forty-five years. Secondary students increased from 7,500 to 12,000, and a new stress was placed on technical training.

A national merchant marine was created for coastal trade, and the Gran Colombian Fleet set up with Colombia and Ecuador for international transport. The latter reduced rates by 25 percent in defiance of the powerful Caribbean Conference. The Corporación Venezolana de Fomento reached agreement with the Corporación de Económica Básica of Nelson Rockefeller to produce and market foods and other products with a maximum turnover and a minimum profit per unit. Though there was a great outcry of middlemen and Communists against the scheme as a new imperialist encroachment, there was provision for the Rockefeller outfit to sell its holdings to Venezuelans within ten years. It undertook to set up refrigeration and storage facilities to permit the economical provisioning of the large cities without the intervention of too many rapacious middlemen, to organize milk supply in the large cities, and to develop fishing along modern lines.

Instead of having cattle driven on foot from the distant *llanos* to the capital—a costly trek during which they lost much of their weight—the government built slaughterhouses at strategic points in the *llanos* and had the meat flown in by plane. The doors were thrown open to European peasant immigrants as never before; 15,000 arrived in a single year. These were settled in mixed colonies with Veneuzelan peasants and furnished with credit facilities.

The government set itself the goal of promoting agriculture as a means of combatting labor shortage and high prices. Tractors and other farm machinery were imported on an unprecedented scale, and when insufficient machinery was forthcoming from the United States, Betancourt sounded a powerful bargaining note. He announced that no further oil concessions would be granted until Venezuela had the assurance that the resulting dollars could be transformed into needed machinery, and would not serve only to inflate the country's economy still more.

The revolutionary government had avoided the error of returning to a constitutional regime before it had enough time to prune away the dead growth of Gomecismo. Yet nothing was farther from its mind than to perpetuate itself in power. When the constituent assembly finally terminated its labors and gave the country a new fundamental law, presidential elections were held in December 1947. The electoral law had given the vote to all citizens from eighteen years up, and guaranteed the fairness of the vote with elaborate precautions. The old Gómez crew, who with the help of Dominican dictator Trujillo had repeatedly tried to intervene with a series of harebrained expeditions, were given a shattering reply. In December Rómulo Gallegos was elected to the presidency against the rightist and Communist candidates by a landslide vote. A long painful era had reached its close. Gallego's novels would live on, but the tragic Venezuela they described was being transformed. From the fatherland of Gómez, Venezuela had once more become the fatherland of Bolívar.

Epilogue, 1948

SINCE THE MAIN PORTION of the preceding chapters was written, the wave of popular revolution that had swept over Latin America has visibly begun to ebb. The dictatorships have been breathing more freely again since the Bogotá Pan-American Conference. In Venezuela the military has snuffed out the young democratic regime, shortly after similar happenings in distant Peru. The average reader of such news items in the North American press is likely to shrug his shoulders and reflect that Latin America is returning to normality, and that democracy is a tender shrub that cannot thrive in an extravagant tropical setting.

But he would be very wrong. The current defeat of democracy in several Latin American lands is due to a large degree to a grave defect in the democratic system of the United States itself.

The Washington officialdom that molds the destinies of Latin America is to a great extent irresponsible; the U.S. electorate is both too little interested and too poorly informed to exercise the slightest control over it. Thus there has been no one to challenge effectively the right of the United States government to ship modern armament into Latin America, despite the warnings of democrats of the entire continent that such a course would have a pernicious effect. It has cut across Latin America's social evolution: just as Latin America was growing out of its old-style *caudillo* militarism, a new sort of militarism has been imposed upon it.

The old *caudillo* militarism had very definite social roots. Republicanism had come to Latin America at the time of independence as a faddish aping of the United States and France, but the social setup continued feudal. For stability and inner logic, feudalism requires the crowning edifice of a monarchy; nowhere else in the nineteenth century was the attempt made to run it on a republican basis. The hallowing veil of tradition was thus torn, and the essence of things laid as bare as an ugly snarl. It was inevitable that new adventurers should

234

arise periodically to assault political power as a means of elbowing their way into the landowning class. Masses of ignorant peons with no stake in the status quo provided ready insurrectionary bands. Wretched communications palsied the hand of the central regime in the provinces and permitted revolutionary forces to gather. What emerged from so much strife was the cult of the *caudillo*, the political and military leader who could integrate the appetites of his followers and rouse them to fight for a place at the trough and occasionally for the glimmer of an idea. Now and then a crafty dictator managed to bring a heavy-handed peace to this anarchy; civil liberties fared badly, but such regimes afforded the countries periods of recuperation and development. As unpleasant as was this state of affairs, democracy in such a setting was a Utopia; the social forces to make it possible simply did not exist, and trying to establish it was, in Bolívar's words, like "ploughing the sea."

But all this has changed notably in recent decades. Industrialization has led to an increasing urban population. Modern communications make stable government feasible without brutal repression. The advance of literacy has brought into existence a civic conscience. The Guatemalan civilians who braved Ubico's gunfire voted for democracy at least as eloquently as the people of the United States do in their quieter elections.

With modern arms, however, unscrupulous army officers are able to defy this grandiose awakening, and defeat and occupy their countries much as the Germans in the last war did Norway or Denmark. And no one in his mind would cite the German occupation of these countries as proof of their incapacity for democracy. The root of the trouble is that the armament that is being pumped into these republics is creating a neo-militarism which has not even that flimsy justification that the nineteenth-century *caudillos* had. When President José Figueres of Costa Rica recently "abolished" the Costa Rican army by transforming it into a police force, he was not only returning to Costa Rica's happy nonmilitarist tradition. He was also giving voice to Latin America's deep alarm at the new militarism that Washington has been imposing upon it at a time when it has been growing out of the old.

Not that it is a question of abolishing armies everywhere. There are plenty of conscientious democrats in military uniform in Latin America, notably the young officers at the head of the Guatemalan army. But the accumulation of the latest armament is a luxury that no Latin American country can really afford; and it places a cruel temptation in the way of the military group.

Washington has tried to justify its arming of Latin America on grounds of hemispherical defense. It is an argument that will bear little scrutiny. Tanks and planes rapidly become antiquated, and meanwhile do incalculable harm to the internal life of the republics. On the other hand, the economic development of these countries would not only increase their production of strategic raw materials and foodstuffs, but would result in the training of mechanics and technicians. In an international emergency modern armies can be improvised more readily from technically trained populations than in backward lands tyrannized by militarists. Economic development, too, would strengthen the social forces upon which democracy rests. Yet the very United States government that has been flooding Latin America with armament in the name of continental defense, turned a deaf ear to the plea of the Latin American republics at the Bogotá conference for adequate loans to permit their economic development.

It is not enough for Latin America to have a Good Neighbor. She needs a *wise* Good Neighbor. Or if that is asking too much, a Good Neighbor with a sufficiently good sense of hearing to take heed of the anguished plea of a continent. Latin America needs not tanks but tractors.

Index

American Affairs, 19, 21, 46, 97
Oil, in Costa Rica, 131–32; in
Venezuela, 215–16, 222–25, 231
Orellana, José María, 32, 33, 34, 35
Operation Success, 55n., 60n.
Pacific Railway (Costa Rica), 132
Padilla, Ezequiel, 75
Páez, José, 213–14
Panama, 160–68
Panama Canal, 103, 157, 160, 161,
165, 168
Panama Canal Zone, *see* Canal Zone
Pan-American Airways, 3, 26–27,
91, 114, 116
Pan-American Conference, 18, 234
Pan-American Congress (1826), 197
Pan-American Highway, 121, 134
Partido de Unión Democrática
(Guatemala), 63, 64
Partido Democrático Venezolano,
220
Partido Nacional (Guatemala), 60
Pasos, Carlos, 119, 122, 123, 125
Paz Barahona, Miguel, 85
Pérez, Sixto, 30
Pérez Damara, Genoveno, 194
Perón, Juan D., 50n., 55, 75n., 192
Peynado, Jacinto, 172, 178, 179
Phillips Petroleum, 222
Picado Michalsky, Teodoro, 136,
137, 138–39, 145
Pina Chevalier, Teodolo, 174–75
Pinto, Jorge, 17
Platt Amendment, 104
Ponce, Federico, 49, 50, 51, 52, 55,
56, 66, 69, 100–101

Railway building: in Honduras, 81,
82–83, 84, 87; in Costa Rica, 131
Readaptaciones y cambios, 94
Reagan, Ronald, 166n.
Real Sandino, The, 111
Recinos, Adrián, 51
Reinaldo Solar, 217
Republic of Central America, 146
Rerum Novarum, 141, 142, 143, 144
Reyes, José, 33
Rice, in Dominican Republic, 179,
180
Rochac, Alfonso, 11, 13, 67, 181
Rockefeller, Nelson, 19, 191, 192,
232

Rockefeller Office, 19, 21, 97
Román y Reyes, Victor, 125n.
Romerismo, 63–67, 71–73, 77, 155
Romero, Arturo, 13, 14, 15, 16, 18,
63, 64, 70, 71, 72, 73, 74
Romero Bosque, Pío, 6, 155n.
Roosevelt, Franklin D., 12, 19, 25,
44, 75, 135, 153n., 166n., 173n.,
176n., 205
Rosario Mining Company, 80
Royal Dutch Shell, 132n.
Rubber Reserve Corporation, 115
Ruche, La (Haiti), 206
Russel, H., 176

Sacasa, Juan Batista, 105, 107, 109,
110, 111, 122
Sáenz, Vicente, 65n.
Salazar, Carlos, 44
Salomon, Louis, 198
Salvatierra, Sofonías, 110n.
Sam, Vilbrun Giullaume, 198
San José Conference (1942), 154–55
Sanabria, Carlos, 91
Sanabria, Victor, 139–41, 144
Sánchez Lustrino, Gilberto, 171
Sandino, Augusto C., 7, 106, 107,
108, 109, 110
Sandino, Sócrates, 110n.
Santos, Eduardo, 220
Savinón Trujillo, Julieta, 186
Savinón Lluberes, Ramón, 186
Schlesinger, Alfredo, 85
Schlesinger, Stephen, 55n.
Selser, Gregorio, 55n.
Selva, Salomón de la, 106n., 122
Sevilla, Nicolosa, 123
Sevilla, Ramón, 117
Sevilla Sacasa, Guillermo, 117
Sevilla Somoza, Guillermo, 118
Shell Oil Company, 223
Simmons, John S., 68
Sisal, in Haiti, 156, 203–4
Société Haitienne-Americaine de
Développement Agricole
(SHADA), 203–5, 206, 208, 211
Somoza, José, 113
Somoza Debayle, Anastacio, 117n.
Somoza García, Anastacio, 17n., 65,
153n., 169, 176n.; appointed head
of National Guard, 42n., 108; and
Aguirre, 76; background, 108–9;